SHORTCAKE CAKE

STORY AND ART BY

suu Morishita

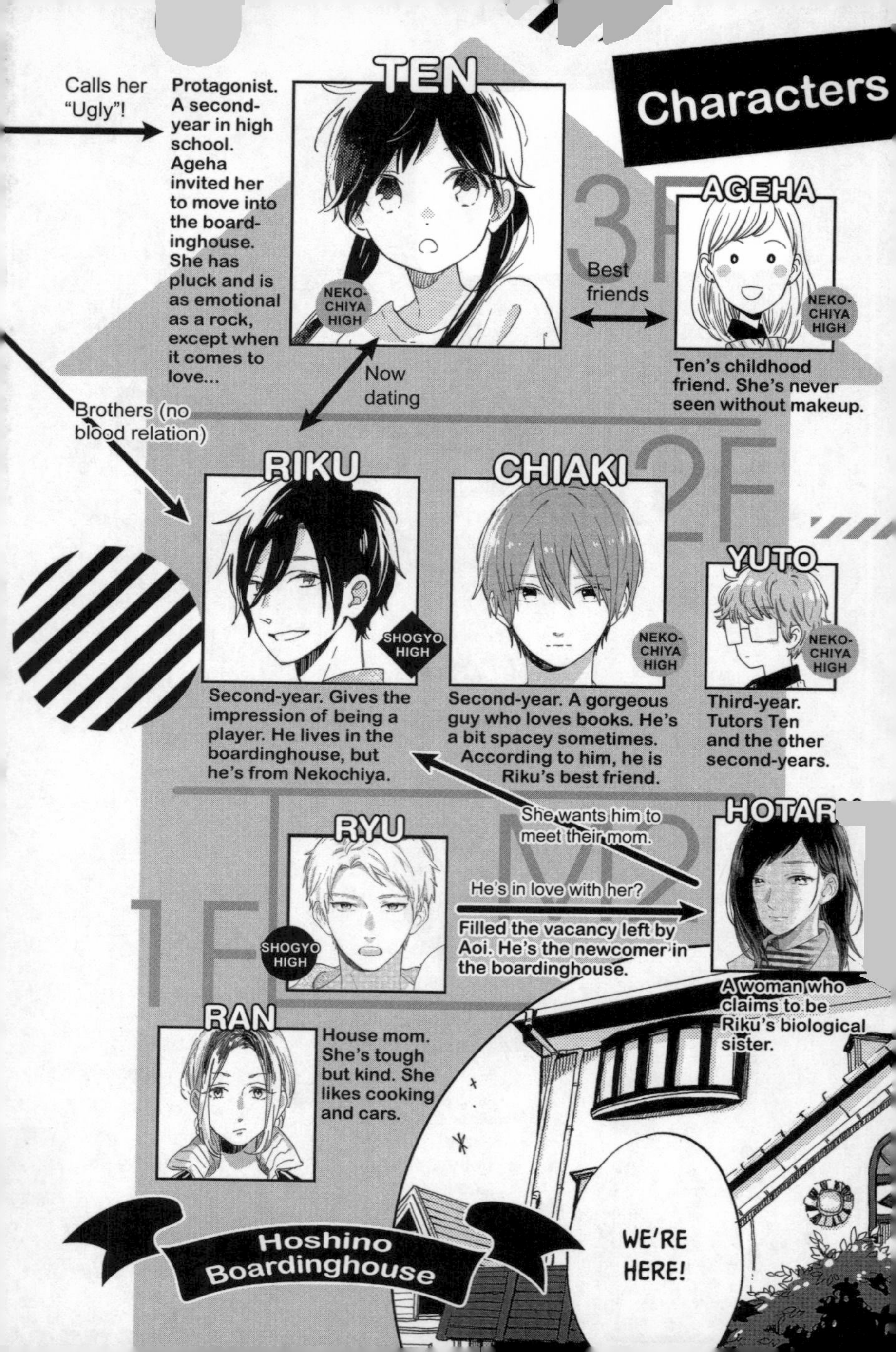
Characters
TEN
Protagonist. A second-year in high school. Ageha invited her to move into the boardinghouse. She has pluck and is as emotional as a rock, except when it comes to love...
NEKO-CHIYA HIGH
Calls her "Ugly"!
AGEHA
NEKO-CHIYA HIGH
Best friends
Ten's childhood friend. She's never seen without makeup.
Now dating
Brothers (no blood relation)
3F
RIKU
SHOGYO HIGH
Second-year. Gives the impression of being a player. He lives in the boardinghouse, but he's from Nekochiya.
CHIAKI
NEKO-CHIYA HIGH
Second-year. A gorgeous guy who loves books. He's a bit spacey sometimes. According to him, he is Riku's best friend.
YUTO
NEKO-CHIYA HIGH
Third-year. Tutors Ten and the other second-years.
2F
HOTAR
She wants him to meet their mom.
A woman who claims to be Riku's biological sister.
RYU
SHOGYO HIGH
He's in love with her?
Filled the vacancy left by Aoi. He's the newcomer in the boardinghouse.
M2
1F
RAN
House mom. She's tough but kind. She likes cooking and cars.
Hoshino Boardinghouse
WE'RE HERE!

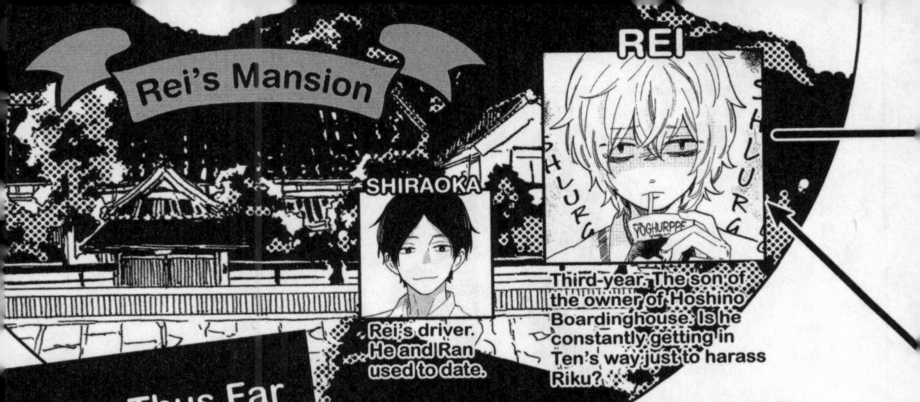
REI
Rei's Mansion
SHLURG
SHLURG
YOGHURPPE
SHIRAOKA
Third-year. The son of the owner of Hoshino Boardinghouse. Is he constantly getting in Ten's way just to harass Riku?
Rei's driver. He and Ran used to date.

Story Thus Far

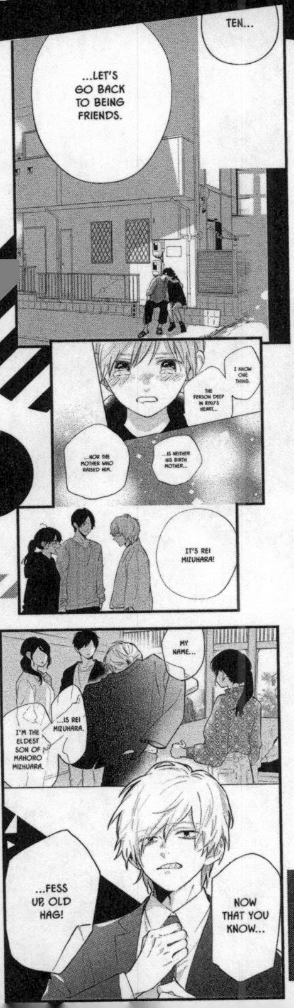
TEN...
...LET'S GO BACK TO BEING FRIENDS.
I KNOW ONE THING.
THE PERSON DEEP IN RIKU'S HEART...
...IS NEITHER HIS BIRTH MOTHER...
...NOR THE MOTHER WHO RAISED HIM.
IT'S REI MIZUHARA!
MY NAME...
...IS REI MIZUHARA.
I'M THE ELDEST SON OF MAHORO MIZUHARA.
NOW THAT YOU KNOW...
...FESS UP, OLD HAG!

Ten commuted two-hours to school by bus, until her friend Ageha invited her to move into the Hoshino Boardinghouse. The place is full of characters, and it's there that she meets Riku and Chiaki, and soon starts going out with Riku.

Ten is determined to learn more about the past that Riku refuses to talk about. She and Chiaki reach out to Shiraoka to find out more.

They learn from Shiraoka that Riku never knew his biological parents, and that he was raised by Rei's parents. Riku was eventually kicked out of the Mizuhara household by Rei after their parents died. After Shiraoka relates the crushing family history, he asks Ten and Chiaki to please put an end to the ongoing sibling feud.

Ryu moves into the boardinghouse in April and is accompanied by a woman who is Riku's older sister, Hotaru. She asks Riku to meet their biological mother.

Ten wants to help Riku, but when he finds out that she knows all about his past, he tells her he wants to start fresh. He asks her go back to being just friends until he's ready.

Through tears, Ten tells Riku that she won't just wait. True to her word, she goes straight to the person who lies deepest within Riku's heart: the perverse spirit Rei. Ten discovers how Rei truly feels.

Thanks to Chiaki's meddling, Riku decides to meet his biological mother. And just when they finally meet, Rei comes barging in!

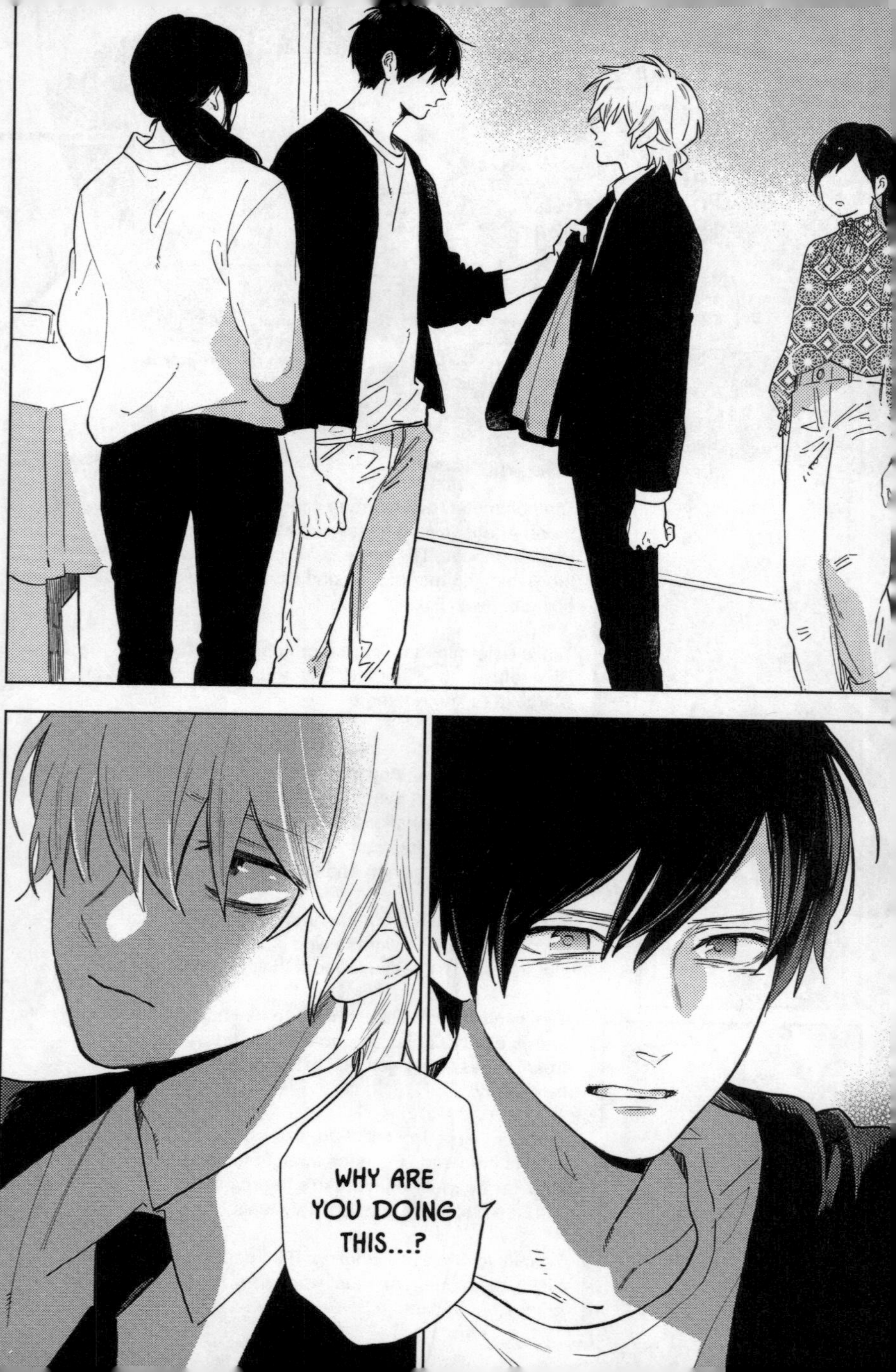
WHY ARE YOU DOING THIS...?

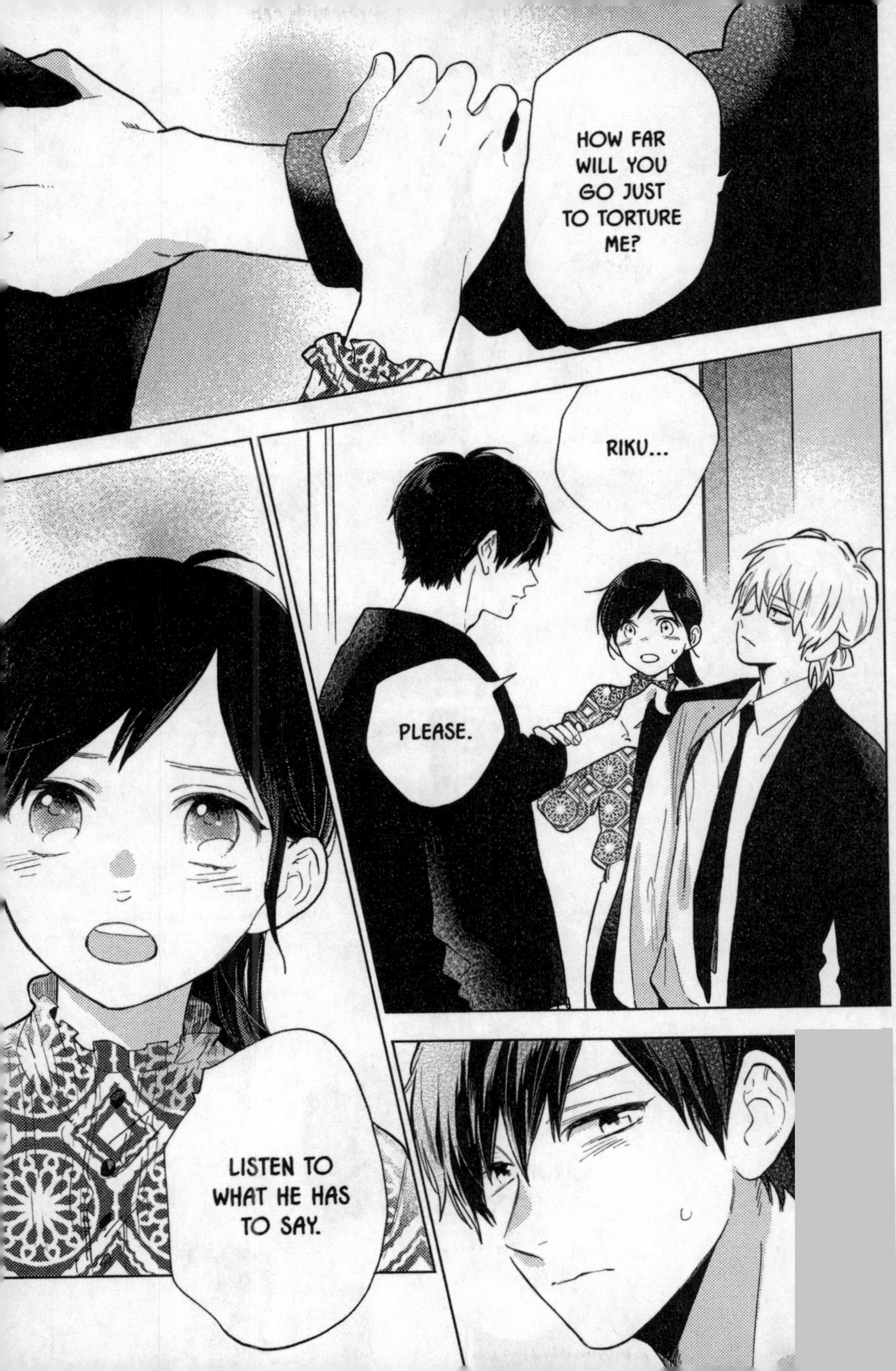
HOW FAR WILL YOU GO JUST TO TORTURE ME?
RIKU...
PLEASE.
LISTEN TO WHAT HE HAS TO SAY.

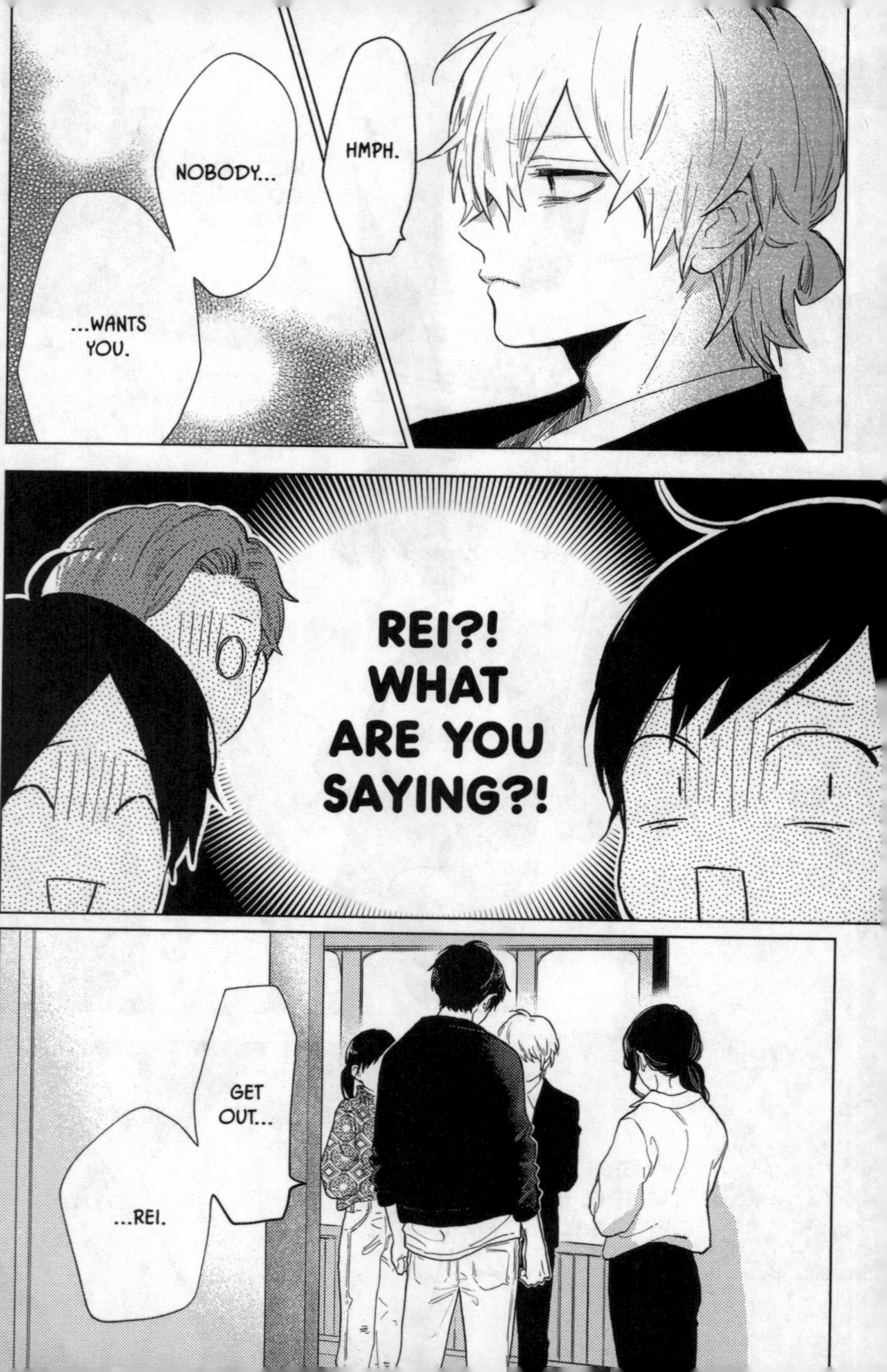
HMPH.
NOBODY...
...WANTS YOU.
REI?! WHAT ARE YOU SAYING?!
GET OUT...
...REI.

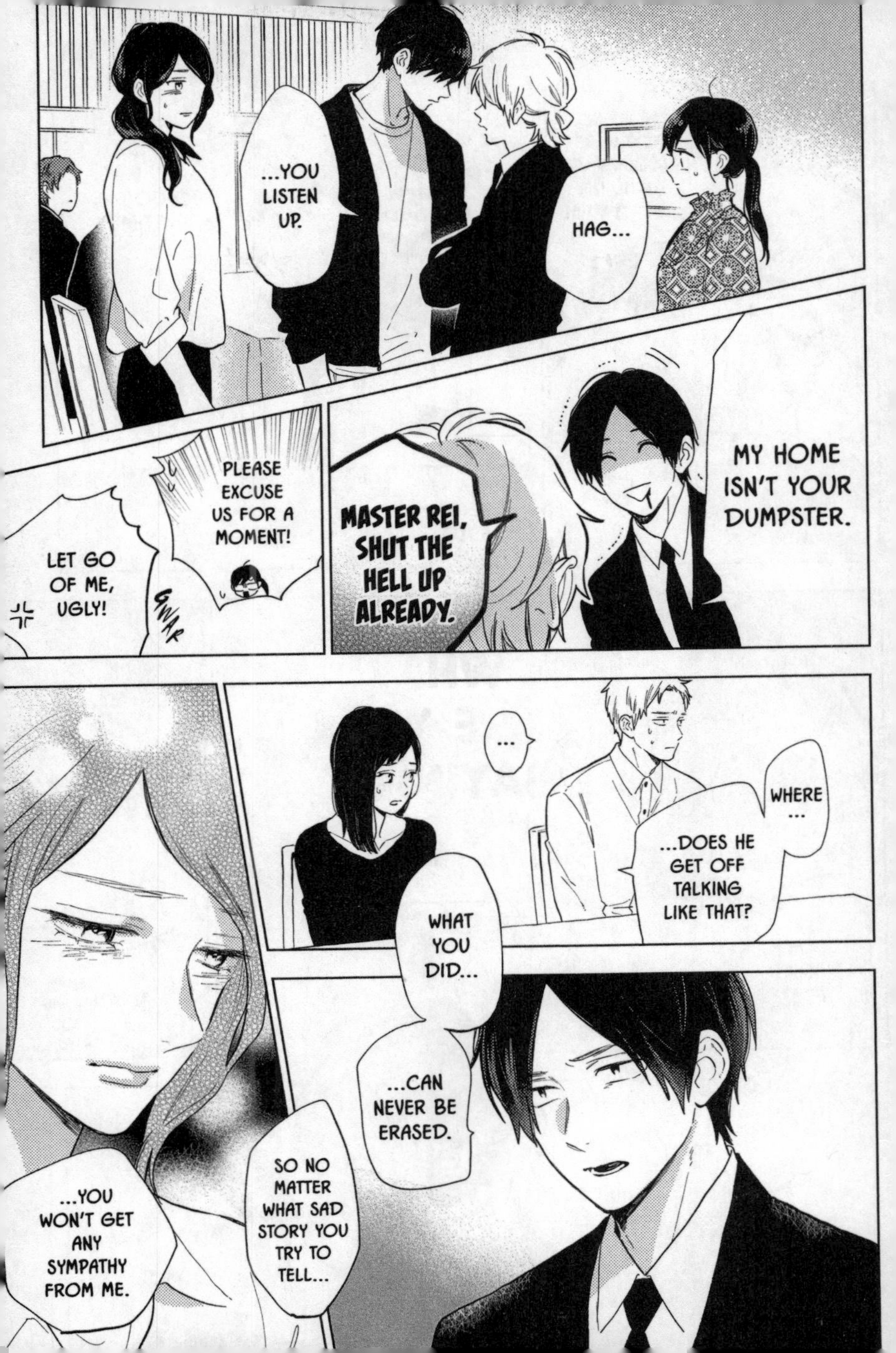
HAG...
...YOU LISTEN UP.
MY HOME ISN'T YOUR DUMPSTER.
MASTER REI, SHUT THE HELL UP ALREADY.
PLEASE EXCUSE US FOR A MOMENT!
LET GO OF ME, UGLY!
GWAR
WHERE ...
...DOES HE GET OFF TALKING LIKE THAT?
...
WHAT YOU DID...
...CAN NEVER BE ERASED.
SO NO MATTER WHAT SAD STORY YOU TRY TO TELL...
...YOU WON'T GET ANY SYMPATHY FROM ME.

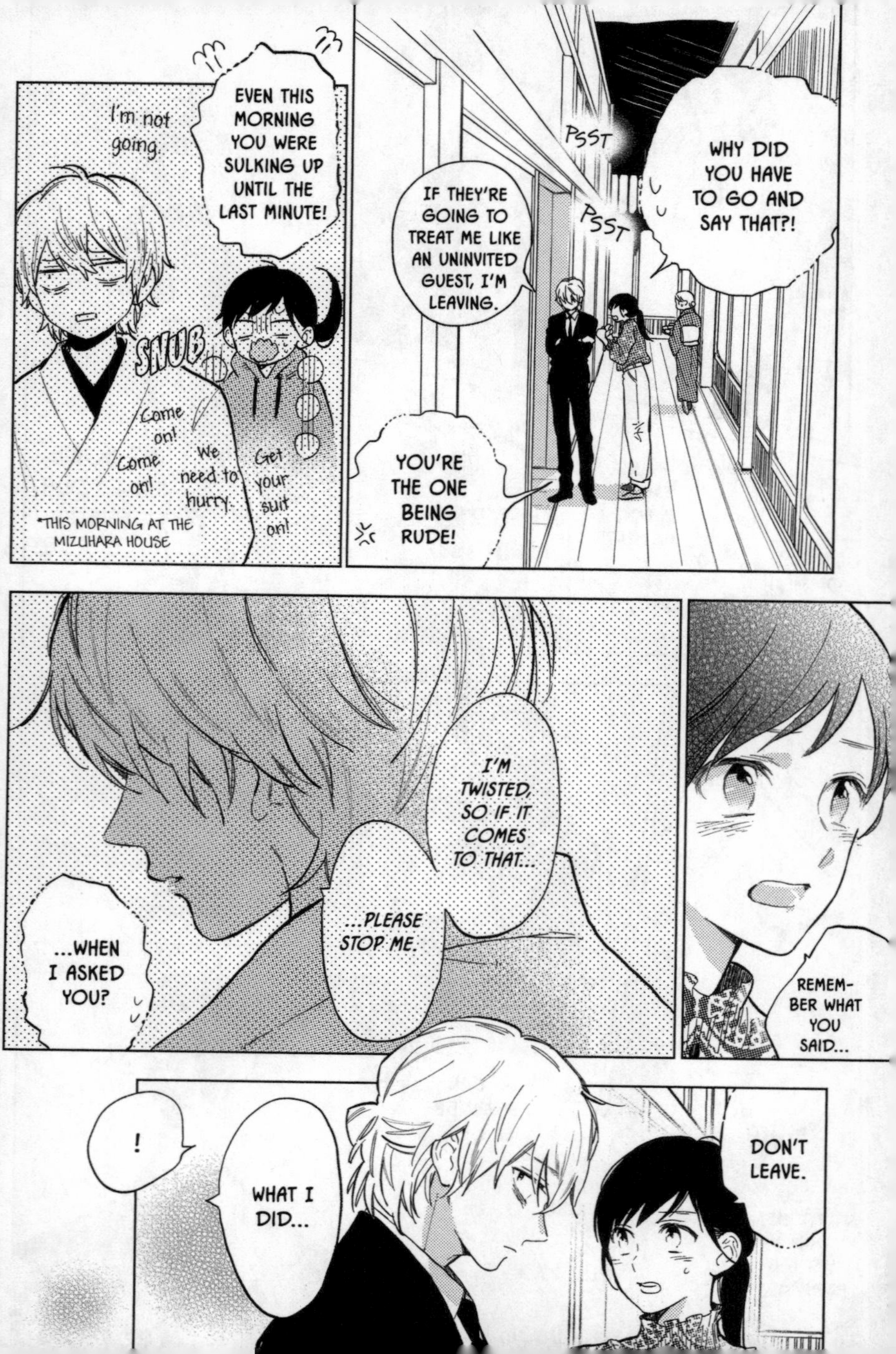
WHY DID YOU HAVE TO GO AND SAY THAT?!
PSST
PSST
IF THEY'RE GOING TO TREAT ME LIKE AN UNINVITED GUEST, I'M LEAVING.
YOU'RE THE ONE BEING RUDE!
EVEN THIS MORNING YOU WERE SULKING UP UNTIL THE LAST MINUTE!
I'm not going.
SNUB
Come on!
Come on!
We need to hurry.
Get your suit on!
*THIS MORNING AT THE MIZUHARA HOUSE
REMEMBER WHAT YOU SAID...
I'M TWISTED, SO IF IT COMES TO THAT...
...PLEASE STOP ME.
...WHEN I ASKED YOU?
DON'T LEAVE.
WHAT I DID...
!

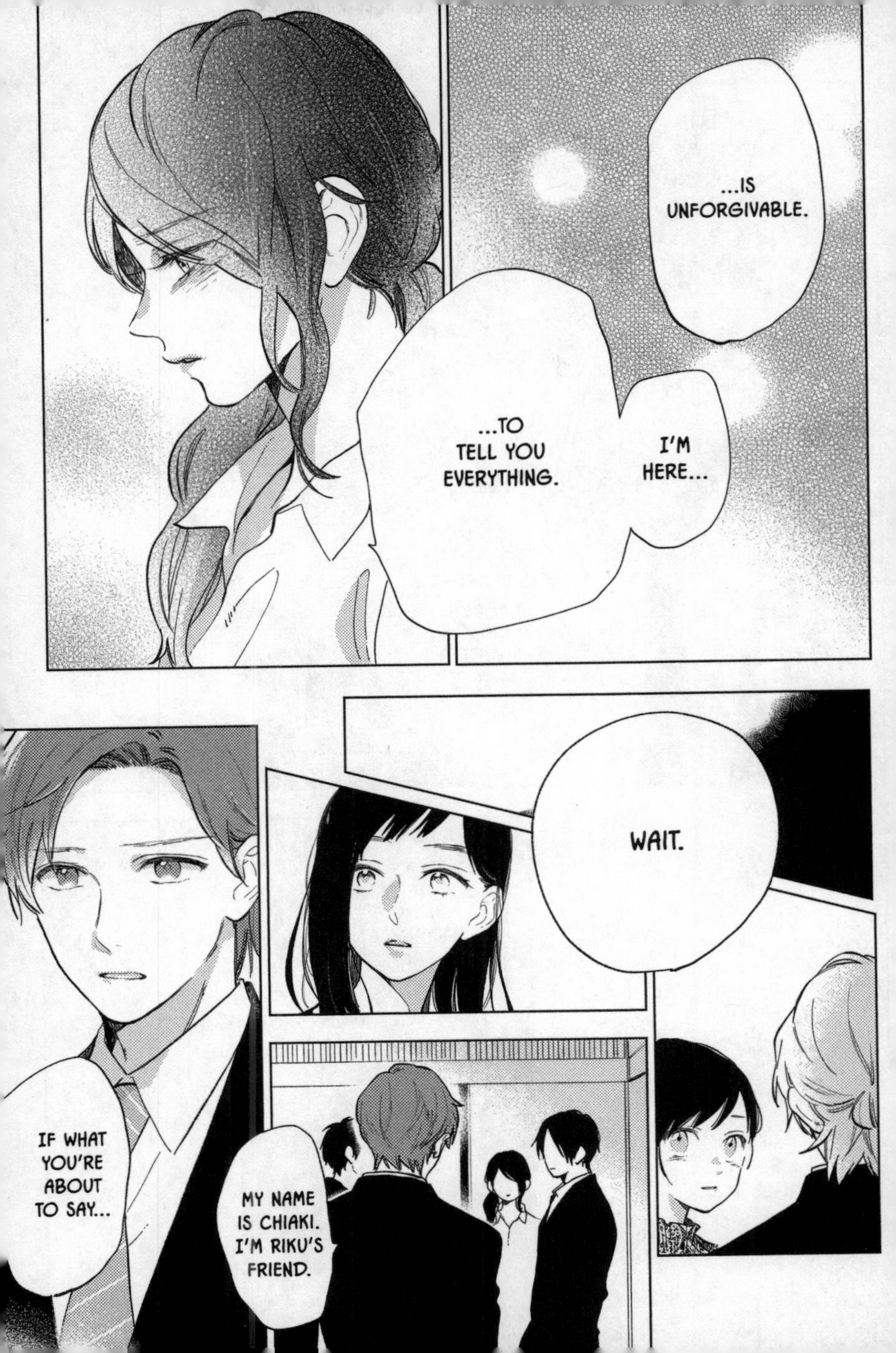
...IS UNFORGIVABLE.
I'M HERE...
...TO TELL YOU EVERYTHING.
WAIT.
MY NAME IS CHIAKI. I'M RIKU'S FRIEND.
IF WHAT YOU'RE ABOUT TO SAY...

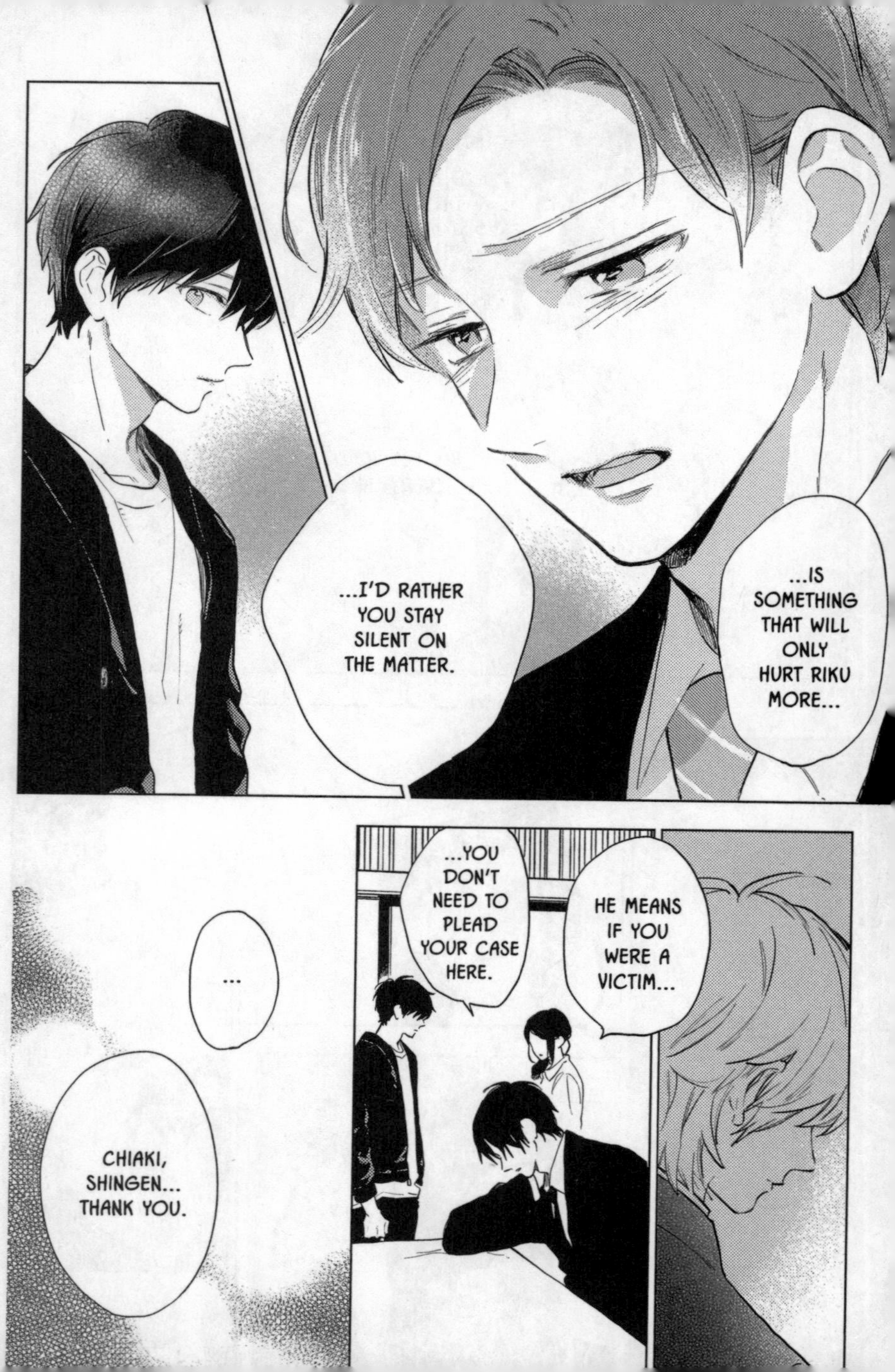
...IS SOMETHING THAT WILL ONLY HURT RIKU MORE...
...I'D RATHER YOU STAY SILENT ON THE MATTER.
HE MEANS IF YOU WERE A VICTIM...
...YOU DON'T NEED TO PLEAD YOUR CASE HERE.
...
CHIAKI, SHINGEN... THANK YOU.

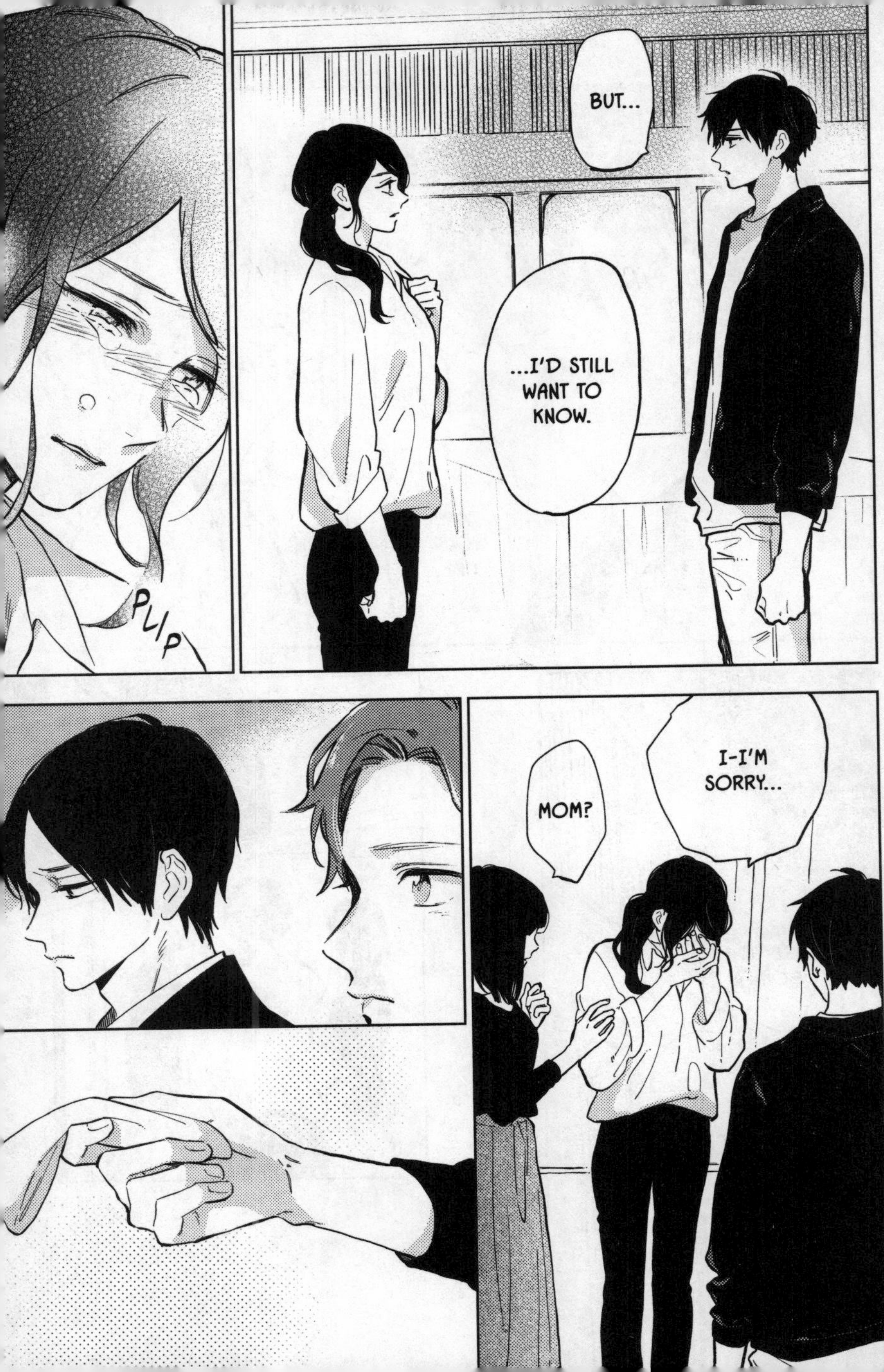
BUT...
...I'D STILL WANT TO KNOW.
PLIP
I-I'M SORRY...
MOM?

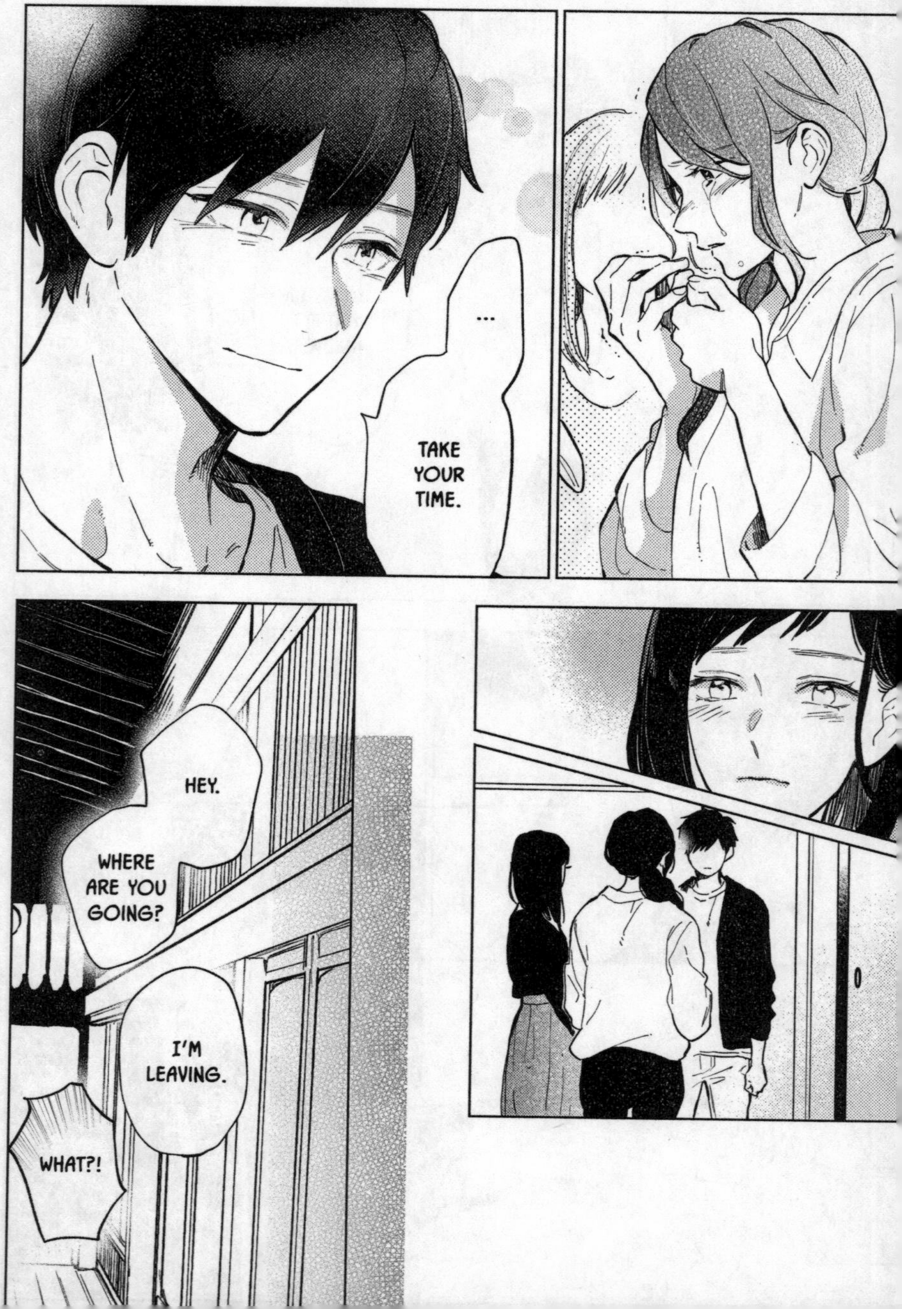
...
TAKE YOUR TIME.
HEY.
WHERE ARE YOU GOING?
I'M LEAVING.
WHAT?!

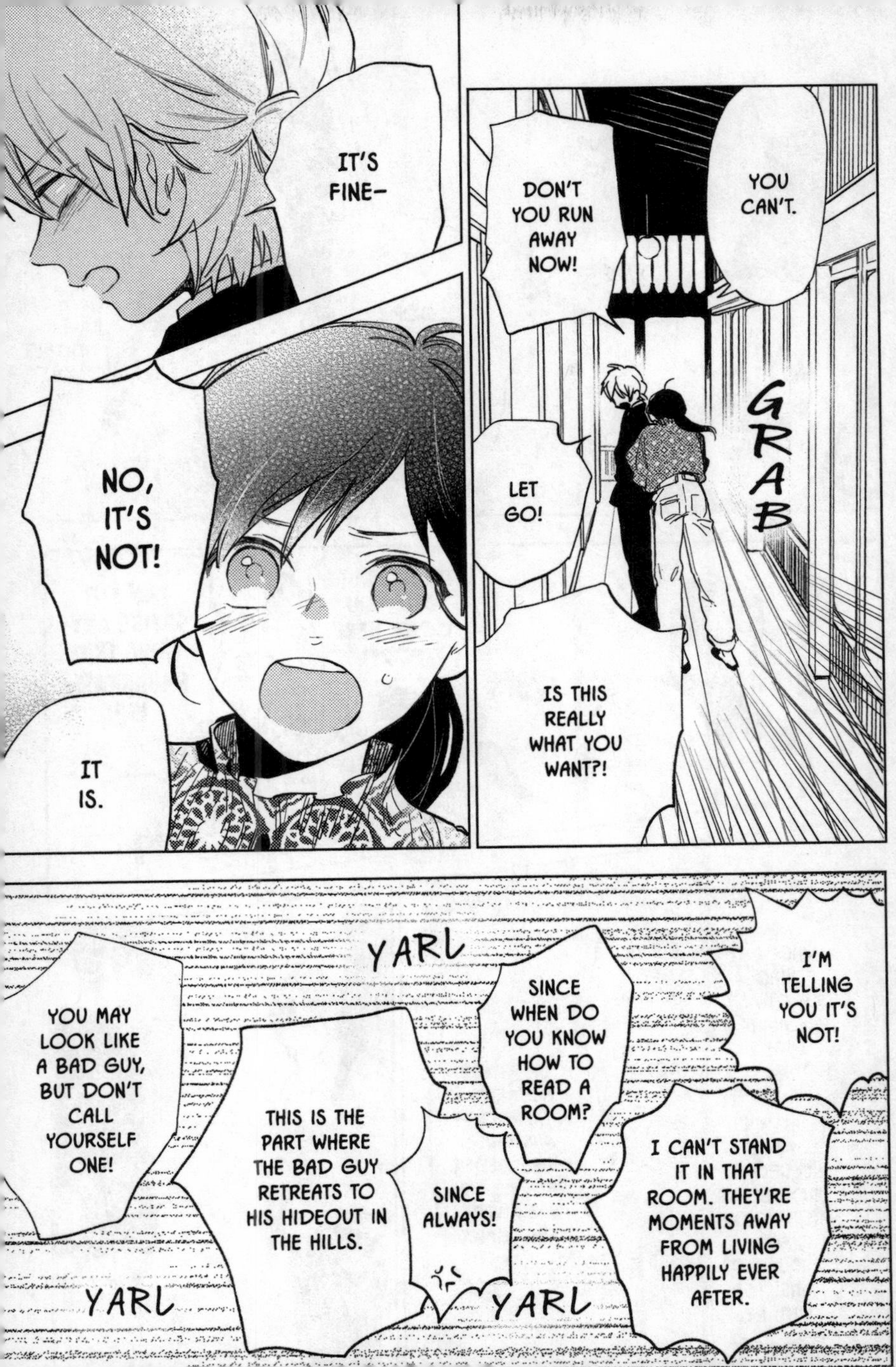

YOU CAN'T.
DON'T YOU RUN AWAY NOW!
GRAB
LET GO!
IS THIS REALLY WHAT YOU WANT?!
IT'S FINE–
NO, IT'S NOT!
IT IS.
I'M TELLING YOU IT'S NOT!
I CAN'T STAND IT IN THAT ROOM. THEY'RE MOMENTS AWAY FROM LIVING HAPPILY EVER AFTER.
SINCE WHEN DO YOU KNOW HOW TO READ A ROOM?
SINCE ALWAYS!
YARL
YARL
THIS IS THE PART WHERE THE BAD GUY RETREATS TO HIS HIDEOUT IN THE HILLS.
YOU MAY LOOK LIKE A BAD GUY, BUT DON'T CALL YOURSELF ONE!
YARL

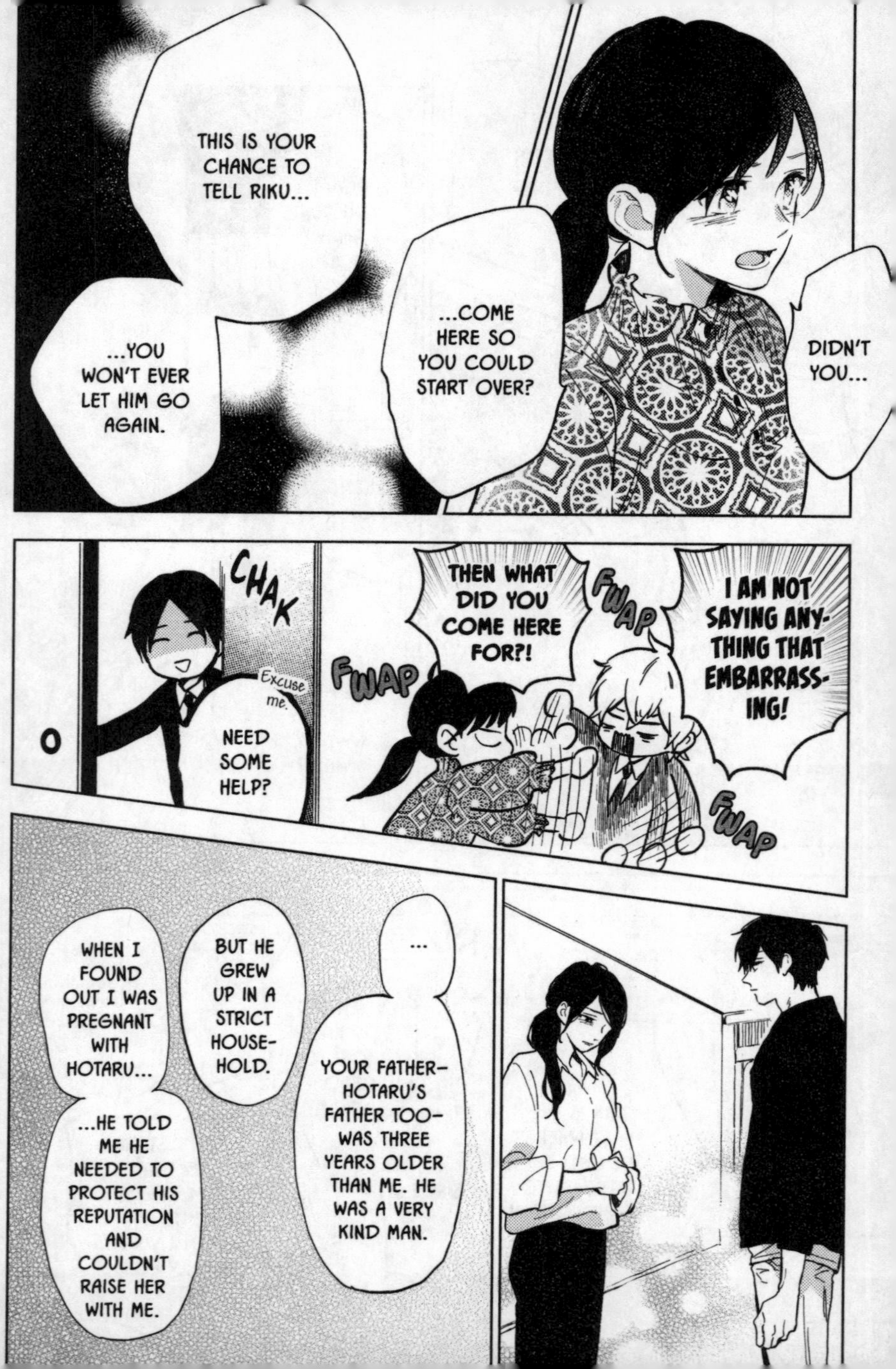
DIDN'T YOU...
...COME HERE SO YOU COULD START OVER?
THIS IS YOUR CHANCE TO TELL RIKU...
...YOU WON'T EVER LET HIM GO AGAIN.
I AM NOT SAYING ANYTHING THAT EMBARRASSING!
FWAP
THEN WHAT DID YOU COME HERE FOR?!
FWAP
FWAP
CHAK
Excuse me.
NEED SOME HELP?
...
YOUR FATHER—HOTARU'S FATHER TOO—WAS THREE YEARS OLDER THAN ME. HE WAS A VERY KIND MAN.
BUT HE GREW UP IN A STRICT HOUSEHOLD.
WHEN I FOUND OUT I WAS PREGNANT WITH HOTARU...
...HE TOLD ME HE NEEDED TO PROTECT HIS REPUTATION AND COULDN'T RAISE HER WITH ME.

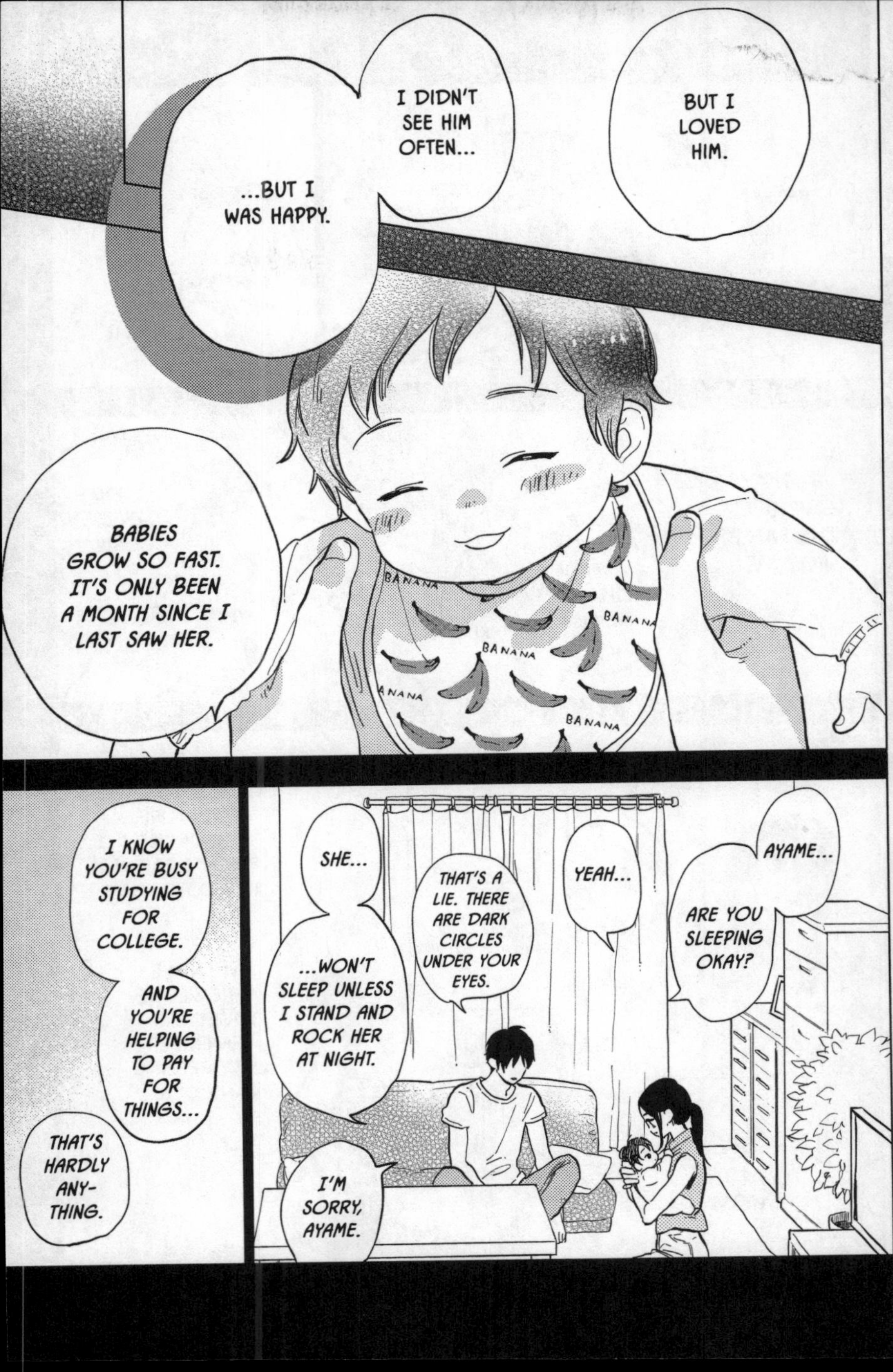
BUT I LOVED HIM.
I DIDN'T SEE HIM OFTEN...
...BUT I WAS HAPPY.
BABIES GROW SO FAST. IT'S ONLY BEEN A MONTH SINCE I LAST SAW HER.
AYAME...
ARE YOU SLEEPING OKAY?
YEAH...
THAT'S A LIE. THERE ARE DARK CIRCLES UNDER YOUR EYES.
SHE...
...WON'T SLEEP UNLESS I STAND AND ROCK HER AT NIGHT.
I'M SORRY, AYAME.
I KNOW YOU'RE BUSY STUDYING FOR COLLEGE.
AND YOU'RE HELPING TO PAY FOR THINGS...
THAT'S HARDLY ANY-THING.

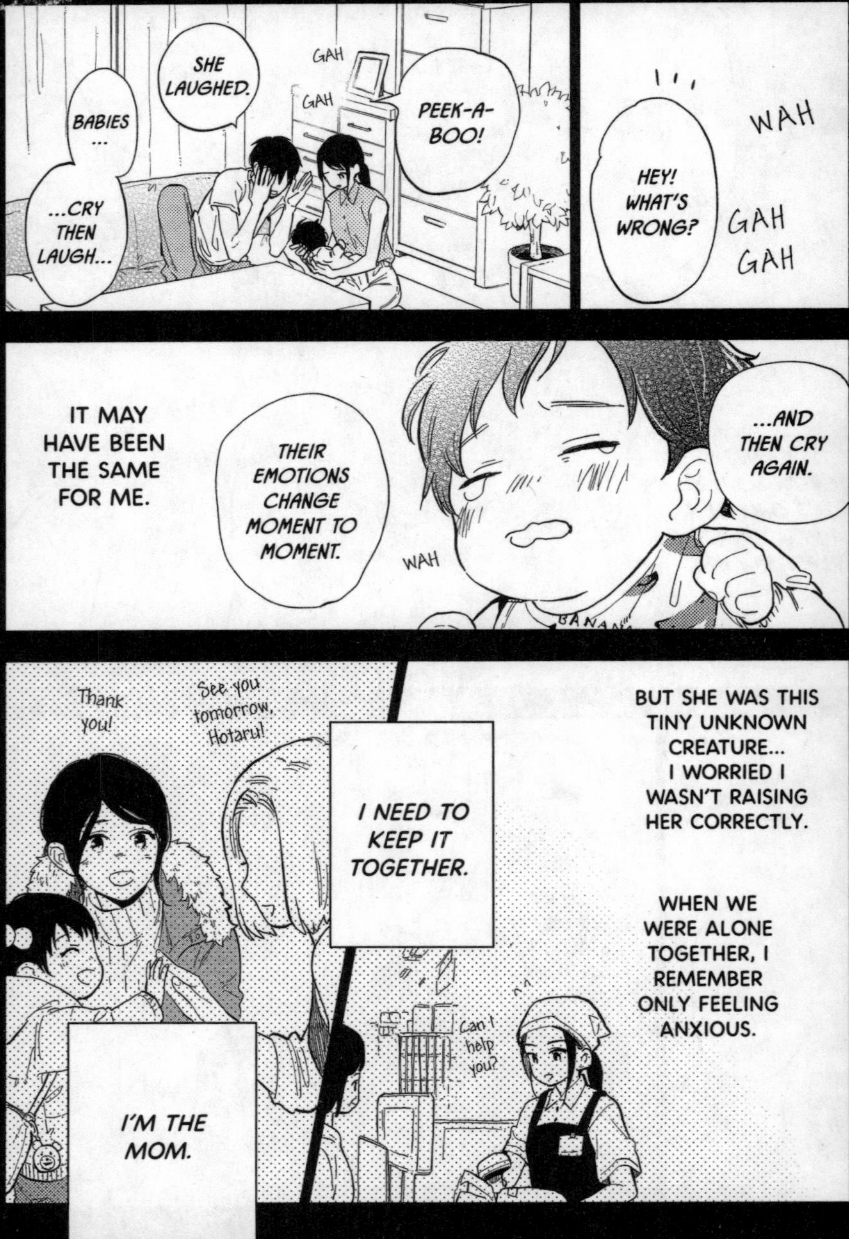
HEY! WHAT'S WRONG?
WAH
GAH GAH
PEEK-A-BOO!
GAH
GAH
SHE LAUGHED.
BABIES ...
...CRY THEN LAUGH...
...AND THEN CRY AGAIN.
WAH
THEIR EMOTIONS CHANGE MOMENT TO MOMENT.
IT MAY HAVE BEEN THE SAME FOR ME.
BUT SHE WAS THIS TINY UNKNOWN CREATURE... I WORRIED I WASN'T RAISING HER CORRECTLY.
WHEN WE WERE ALONE TOGETHER, I REMEMBER ONLY FEELING ANXIOUS.
Can I help you?
I NEED TO KEEP IT TOGETHER.
See you tomorrow, Hotaru!
Thank you!
I'M THE MOM.

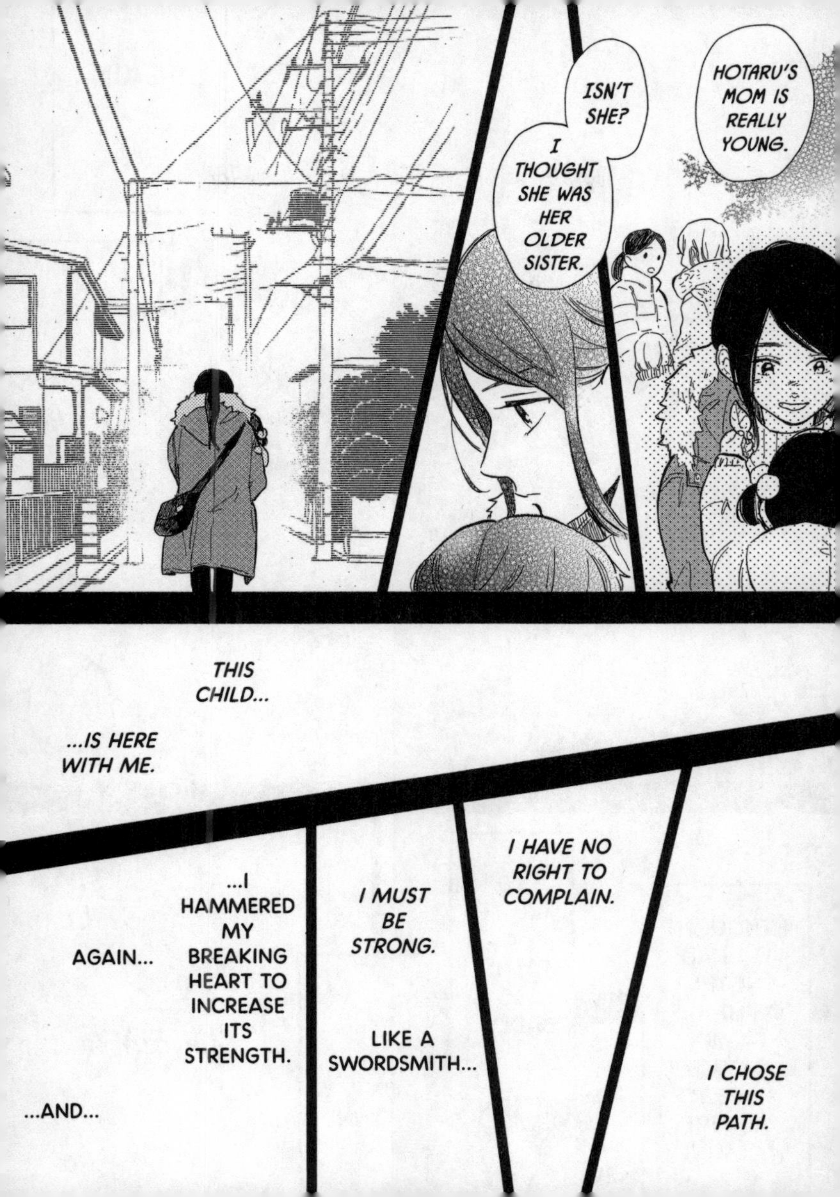
HOTARU'S MOM IS REALLY YOUNG.
ISN'T SHE?
I THOUGHT SHE WAS HER OLDER SISTER.
THIS CHILD...
...IS HERE WITH ME.
I CHOSE THIS PATH.
I HAVE NO RIGHT TO COMPLAIN.
I MUST BE STRONG.
LIKE A SWORDSMITH...
...I HAMMERED MY BREAKING HEART TO INCREASE ITS STRENGTH.
AGAIN...
...AND...

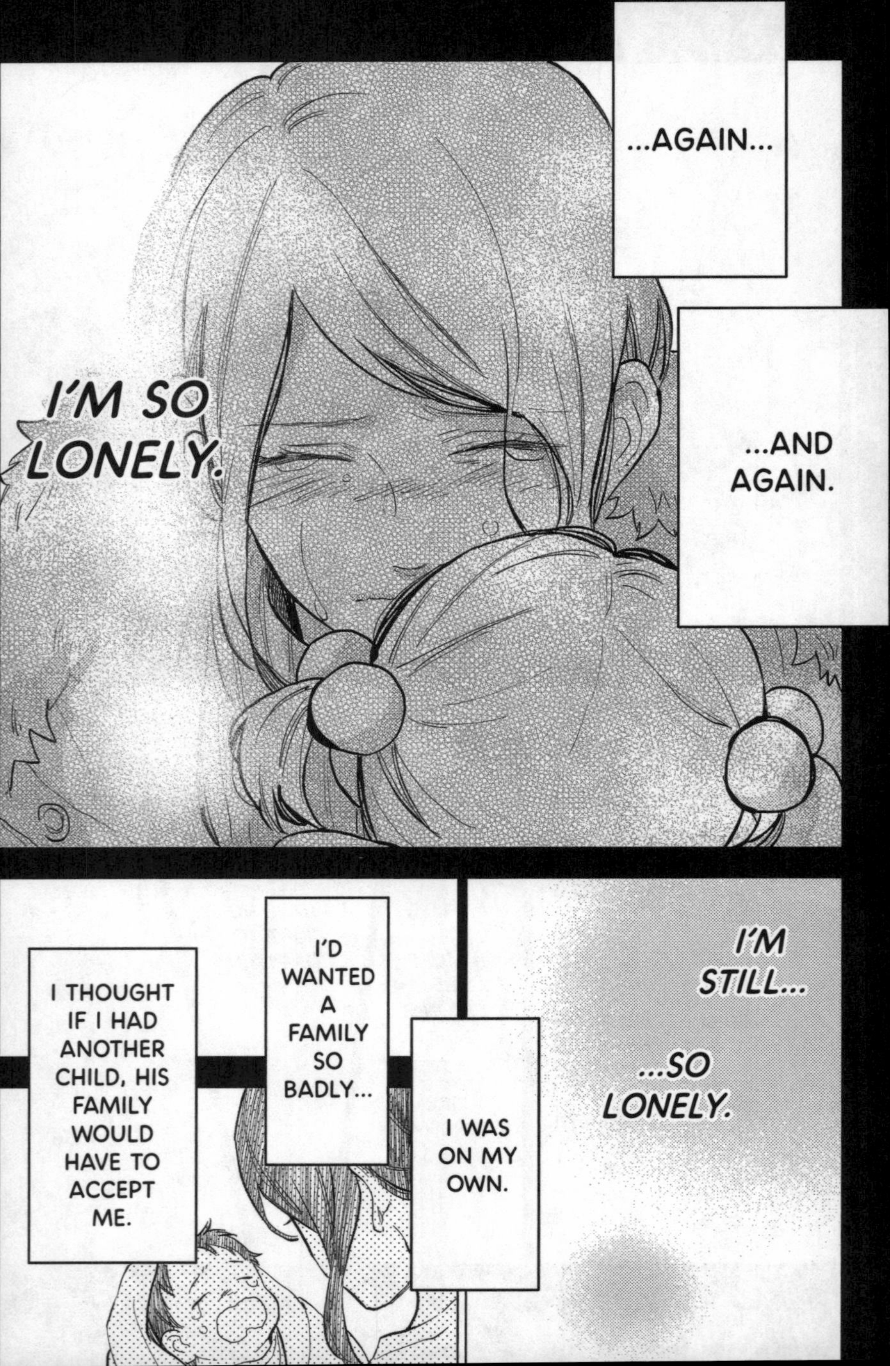
...AGAIN...
...AND AGAIN.
I'M SO LONELY.
I'M STILL...
...SO LONELY.
I'D WANTED A FAMILY SO BADLY...
I WAS ON MY OWN.
I THOUGHT IF I HAD ANOTHER CHILD, HIS FAMILY WOULD HAVE TO ACCEPT ME.

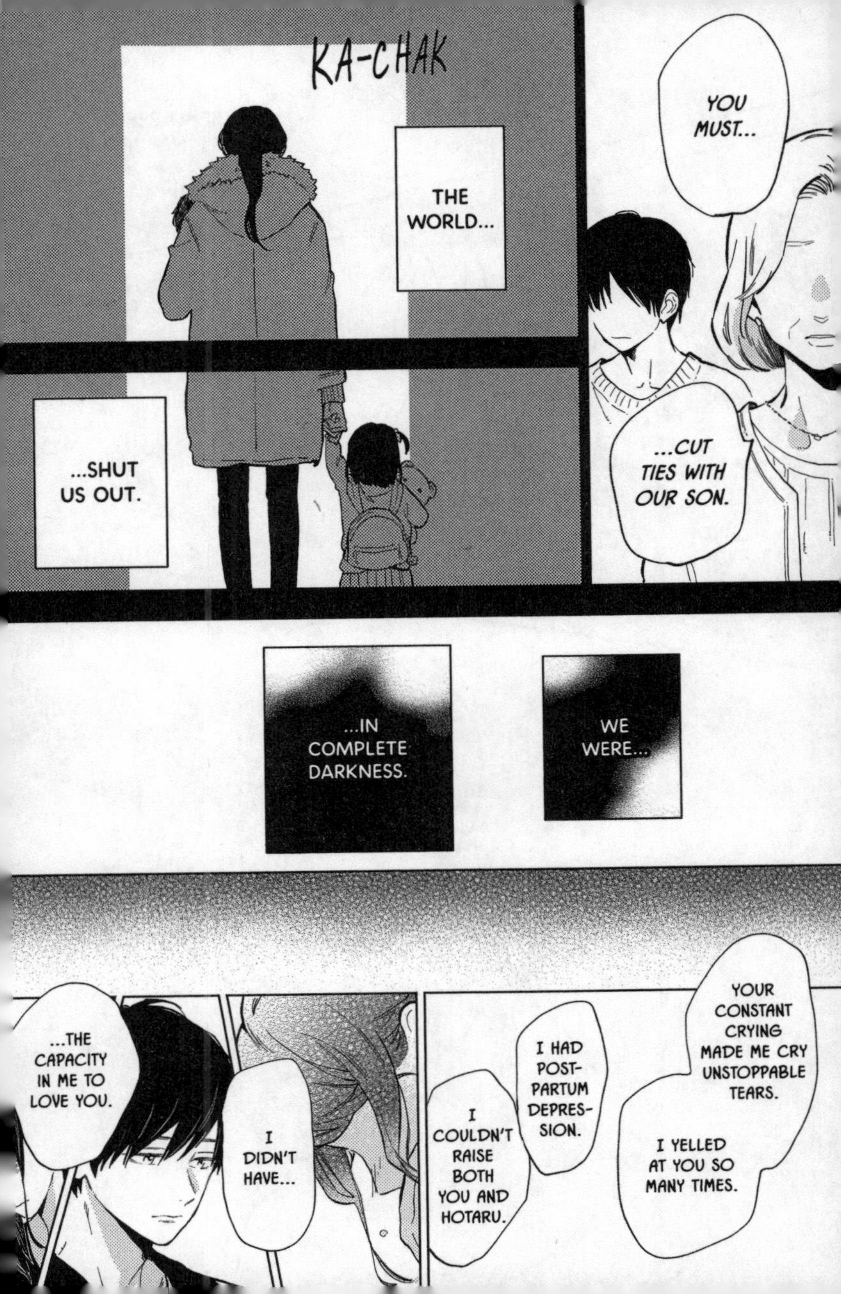
YOU MUST...
...CUT TIES WITH OUR SON.
KA-CHAK
THE WORLD...
...SHUT US OUT.
WE WERE...
...IN COMPLETE DARKNESS.
YOUR CONSTANT CRYING MADE ME CRY UNSTOPPABLE TEARS.
I YELLED AT YOU SO MANY TIMES.
I HAD POST-PARTUM DEPRES-SION.
I COULDN'T RAISE BOTH YOU AND HOTARU.
I DIDN'T HAVE...
...THE CAPACITY IN ME TO LOVE YOU.

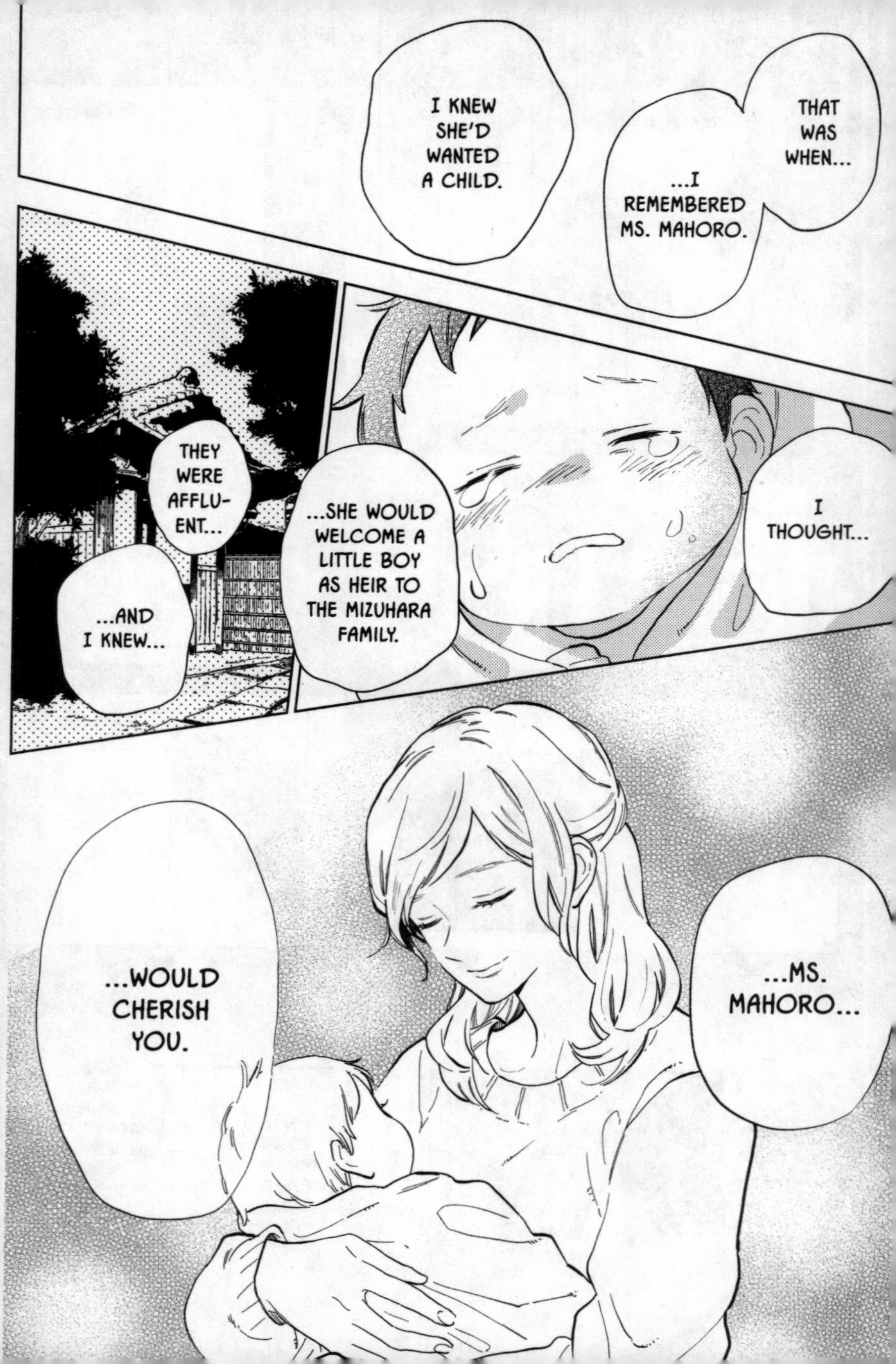
THAT WAS WHEN...
...I REMEMBERED MS. MAHORO.
I KNEW SHE'D WANTED A CHILD.
I THOUGHT...
...SHE WOULD WELCOME A LITTLE BOY AS HEIR TO THE MIZUHARA FAMILY.
THEY WERE AFFLU- ENT...
...AND I KNEW...
...MS. MAHORO...
...WOULD CHERISH YOU.

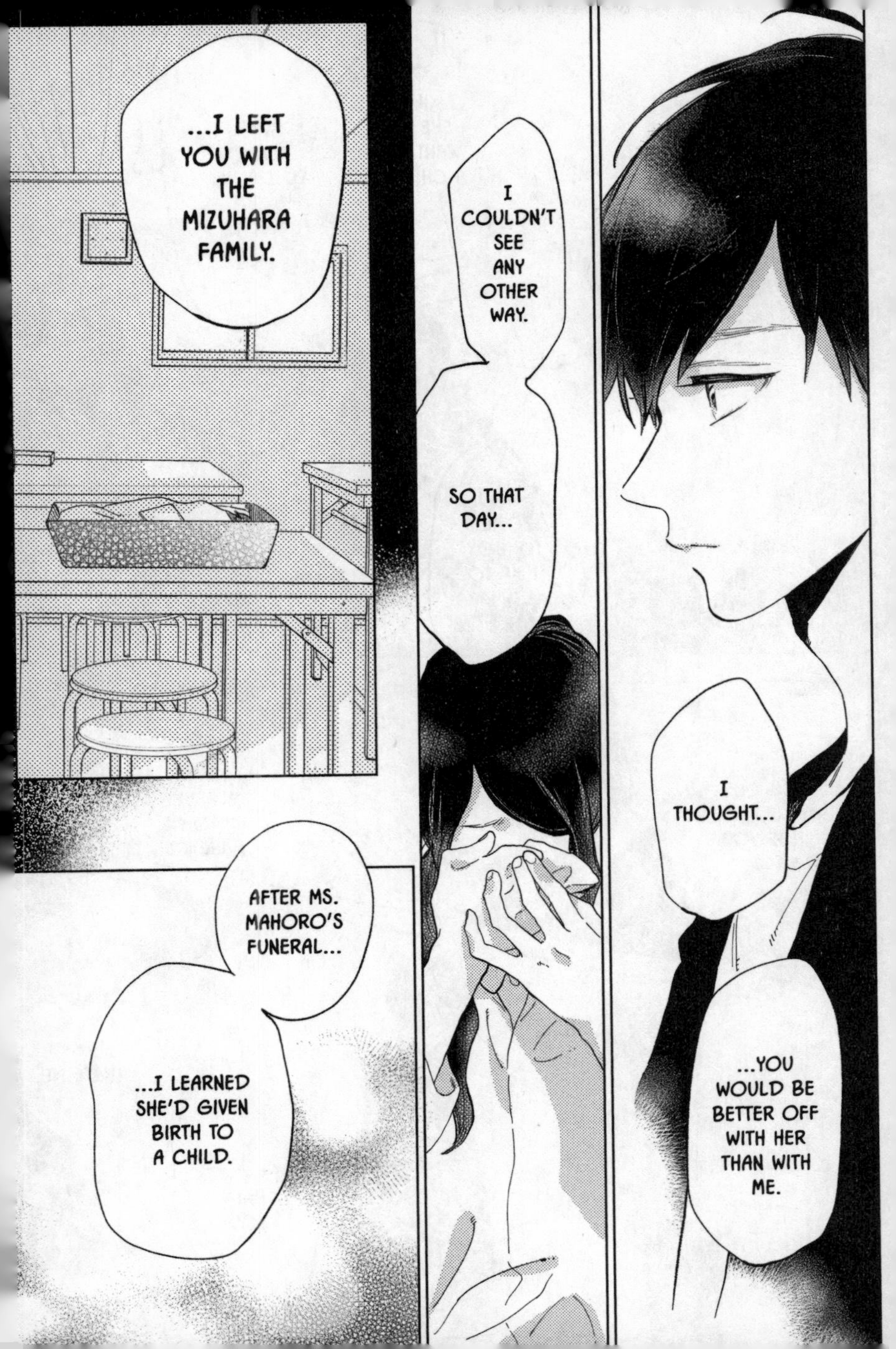
I THOUGHT...
...YOU WOULD BE BETTER OFF WITH HER THAN WITH ME.
I COULDN'T SEE ANY OTHER WAY.
SO THAT DAY...
...I LEFT YOU WITH THE MIZUHARA FAMILY.
AFTER MS. MAHORO'S FUNERAL...
...I LEARNED SHE'D GIVEN BIRTH TO A CHILD.

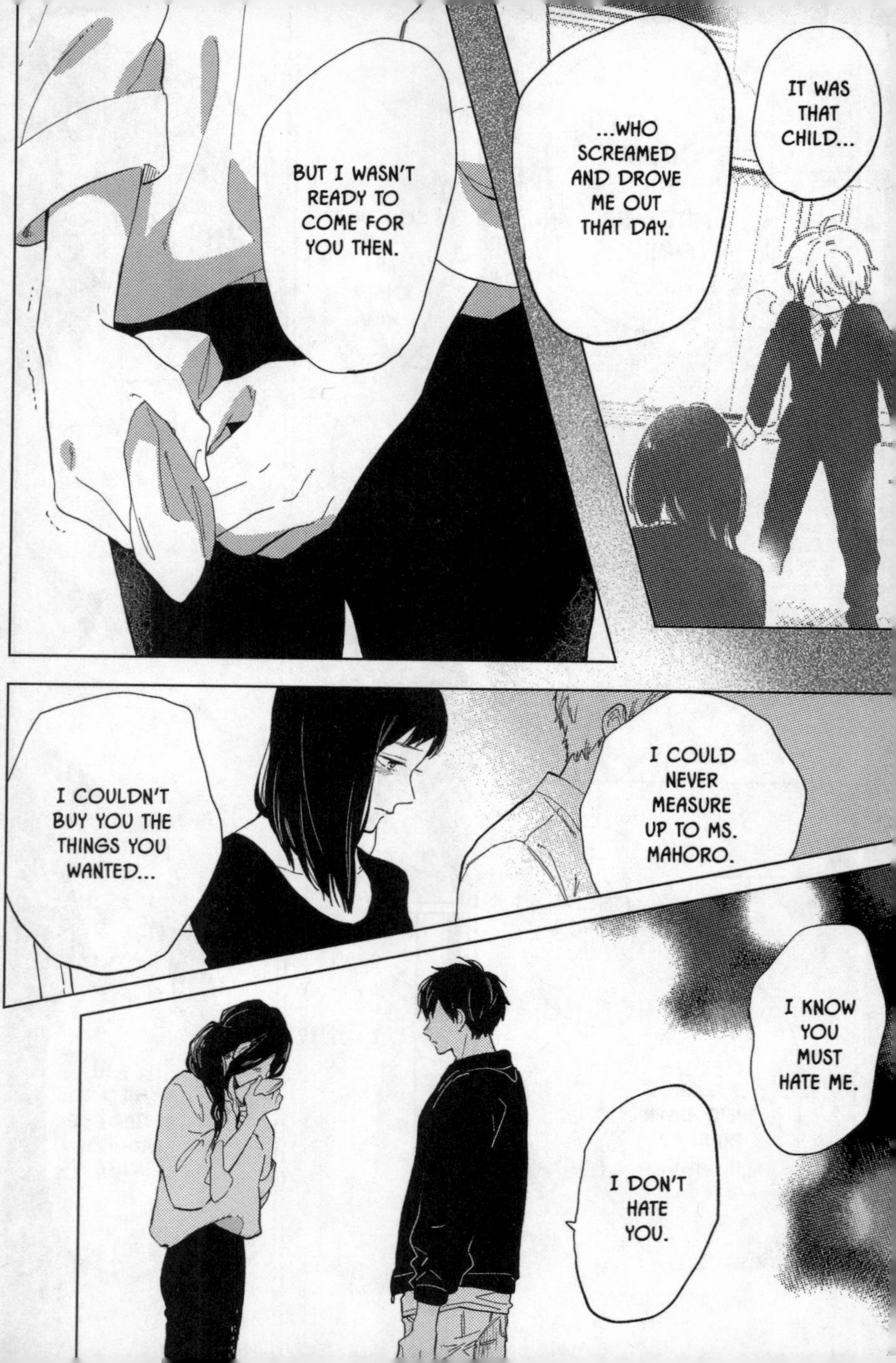
IT WAS THAT CHILD...
...WHO SCREAMED AND DROVE ME OUT THAT DAY.
BUT I WASN'T READY TO COME FOR YOU THEN.
I COULD NEVER MEASURE UP TO MS. MAHORO.
I COULDN'T BUY YOU THE THINGS YOU WANTED...
I KNOW YOU MUST HATE ME.
I DON'T HATE YOU.

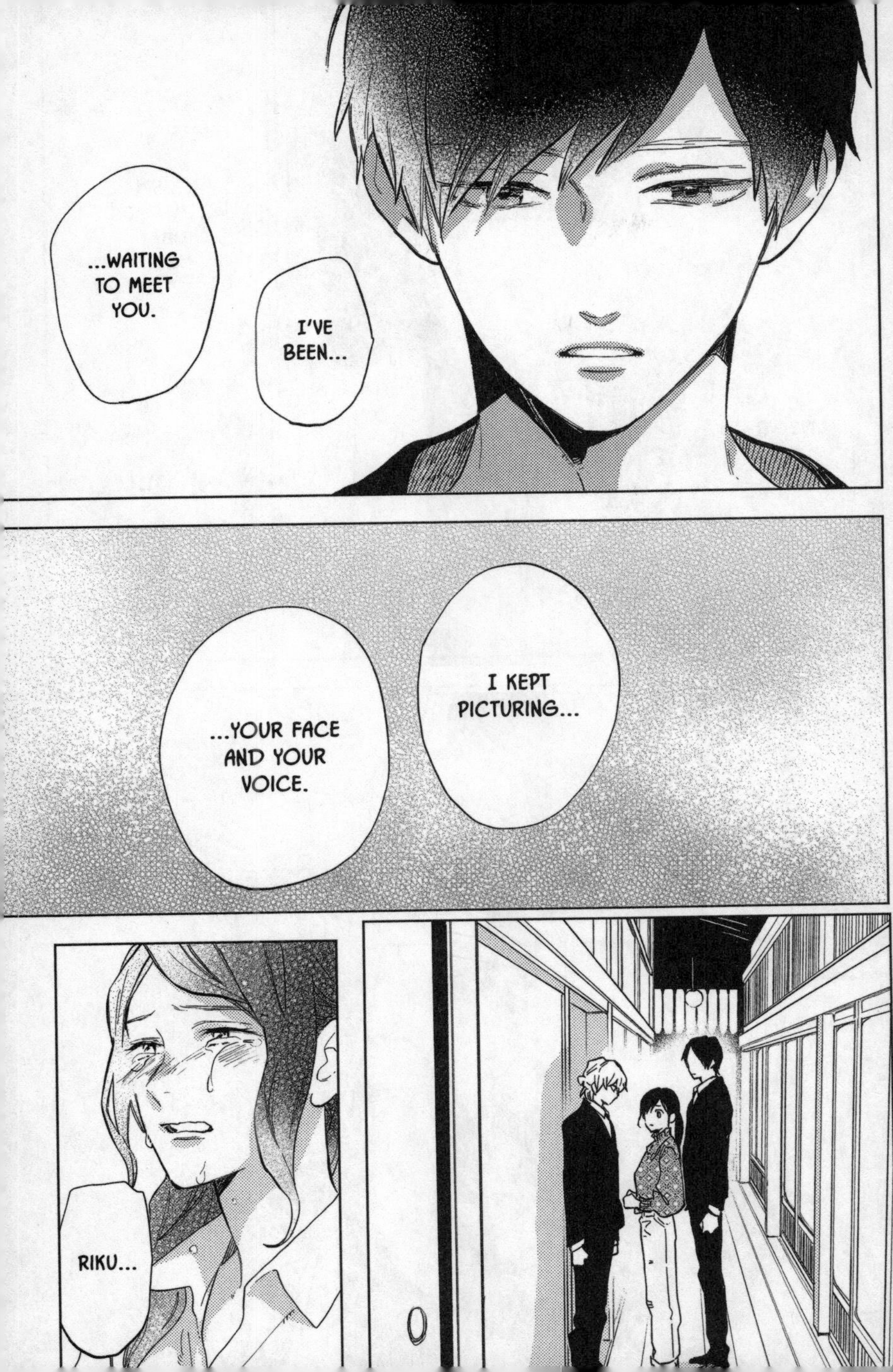
I'VE BEEN...
...WAITING TO MEET YOU.
I KEPT PICTURING...
...YOUR FACE AND YOUR VOICE.
RIKU...

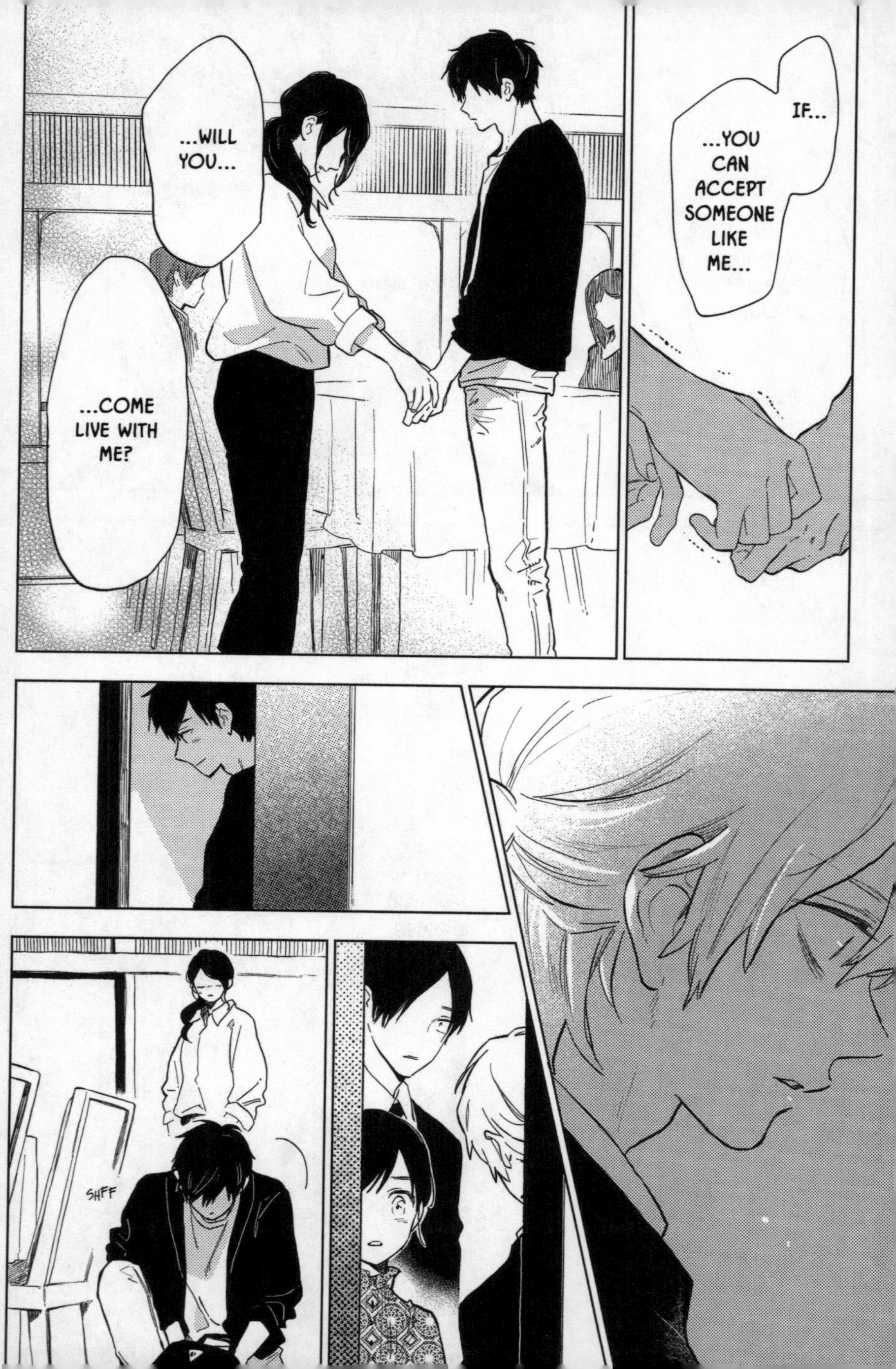
IF...
...YOU CAN ACCEPT SOMEONE LIKE ME...
...WILL YOU...
...COME LIVE WITH ME?
SHFF

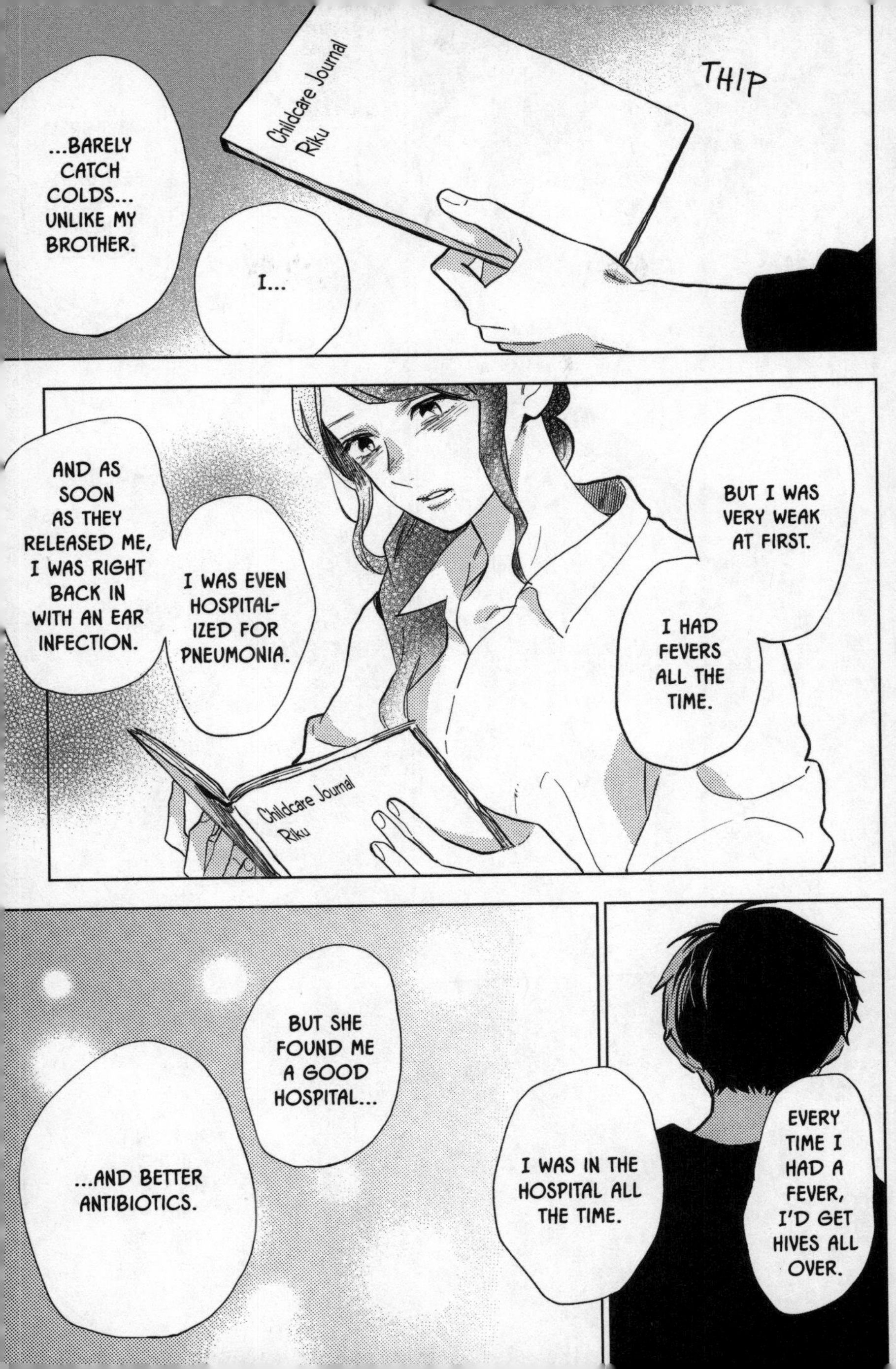
THIP
Childcare Journal Riku
I...
...BARELY CATCH COLDS... UNLIKE MY BROTHER.
BUT I WAS VERY WEAK AT FIRST.
I HAD FEVERS ALL THE TIME.
I WAS EVEN HOSPITAL-IZED FOR PNEUMONIA.
AND AS SOON AS THEY RELEASED ME, I WAS RIGHT BACK IN WITH AN EAR INFECTION.
Childcare Journal Riku
EVERY TIME I HAD A FEVER, I'D GET HIVES ALL OVER.
I WAS IN THE HOSPITAL ALL THE TIME.
BUT SHE FOUND ME A GOOD HOSPITAL...
...AND BETTER ANTIBIOTICS.

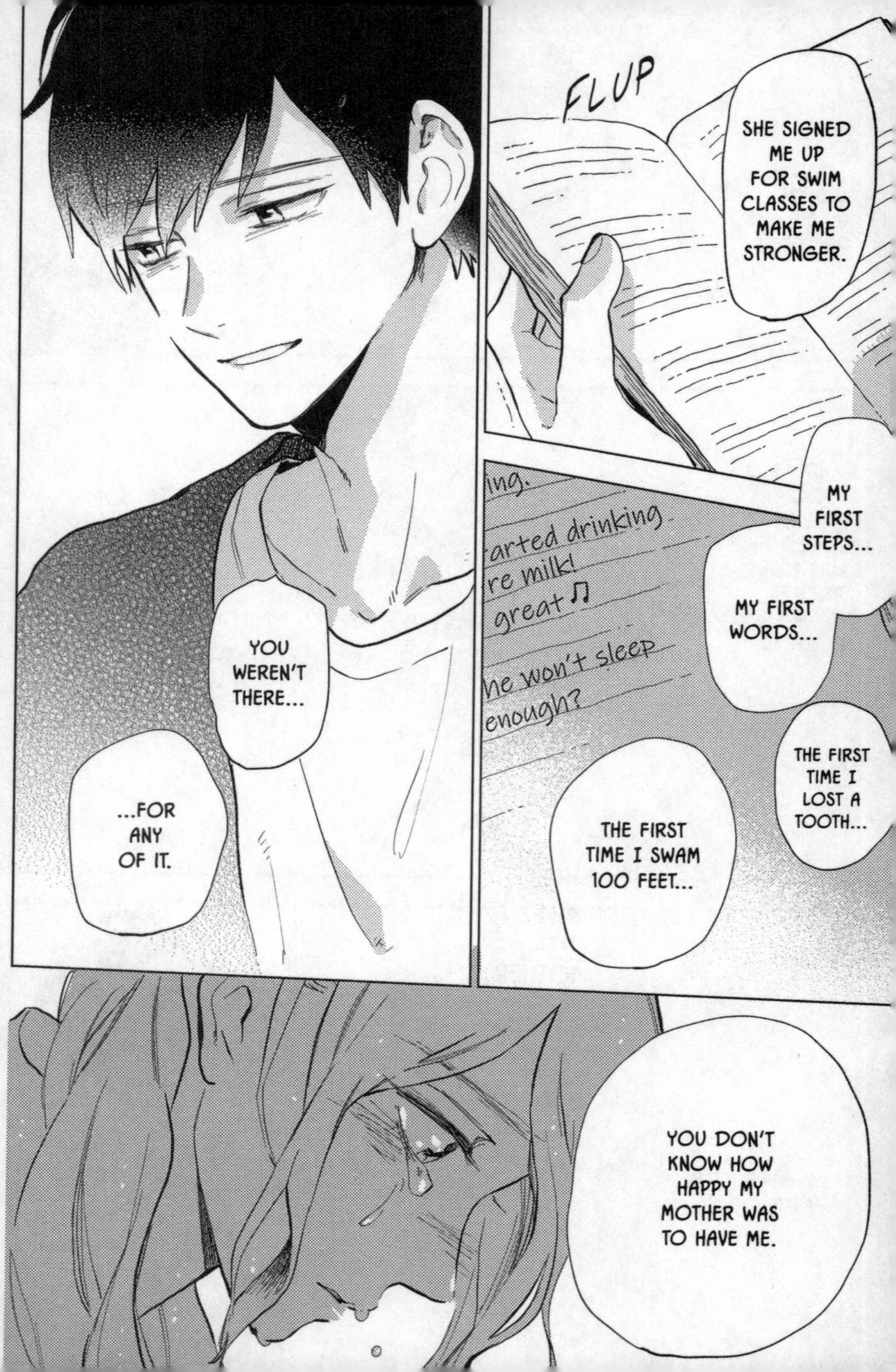
FLUP
SHE SIGNED ME UP FOR SWIM CLASSES TO MAKE ME STRONGER.
ing.
arted drinking
re milk!
great♫
he won't sleep
enough?
MY FIRST STEPS...
MY FIRST WORDS...
THE FIRST TIME I LOST A TOOTH...
THE FIRST TIME I SWAM 100 FEET...
YOU WEREN'T THERE...
...FOR ANY OF IT.
YOU DON'T KNOW HOW HAPPY MY MOTHER WAS TO HAVE ME.

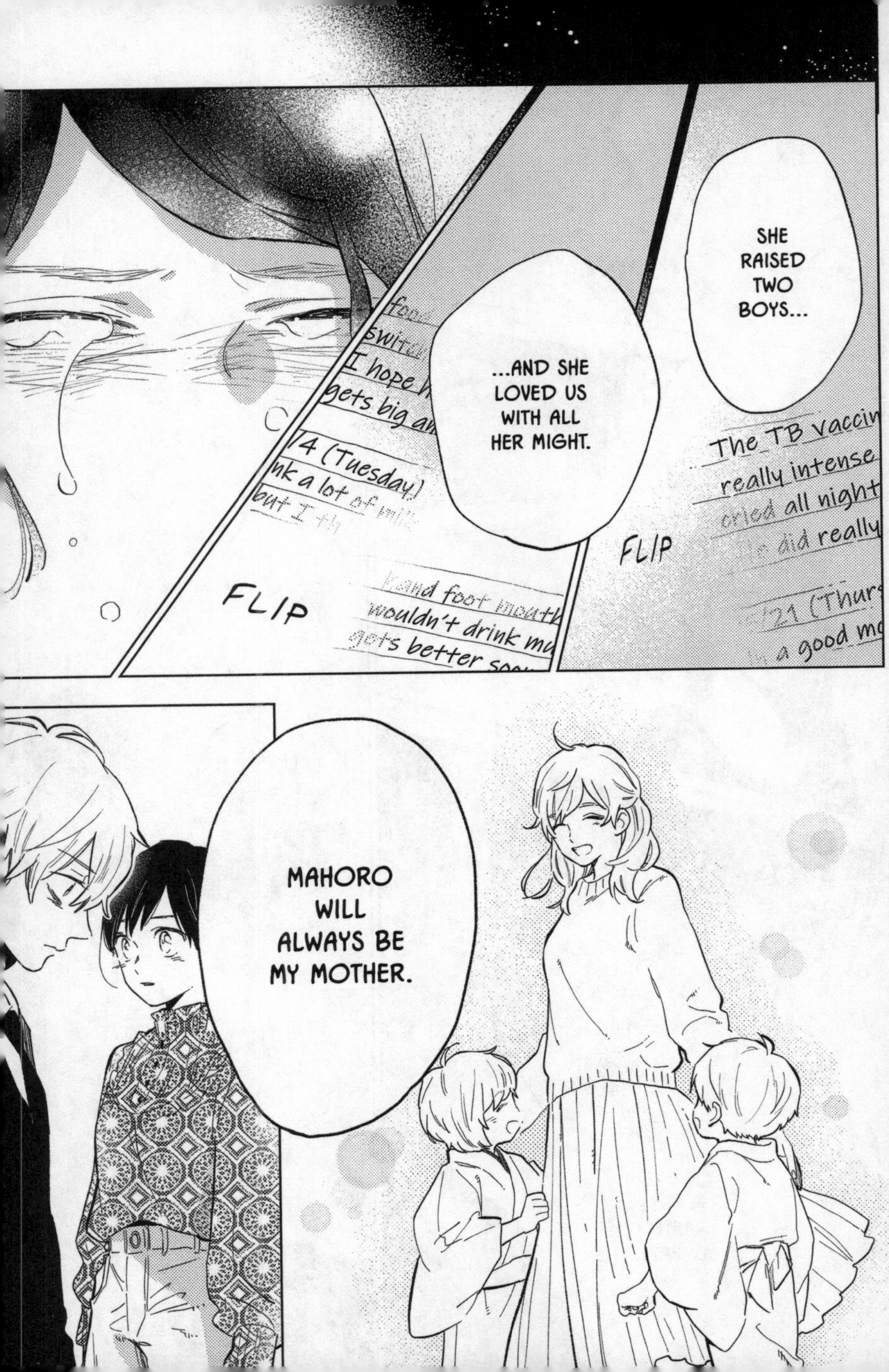
SHE RAISED TWO BOYS...
The TB vaccin
really intense
cried all night
did really
'21 (Thurs
a good mo
FLIP
...AND SHE LOVED US WITH ALL HER MIGHT.
I hope h
gets big a
4 (Tuesday)
nk a lot of mil
but I th
hand foot mouth
wouldn't drink m
gets better soo
FLIP
MAHORO WILL ALWAYS BE MY MOTHER.

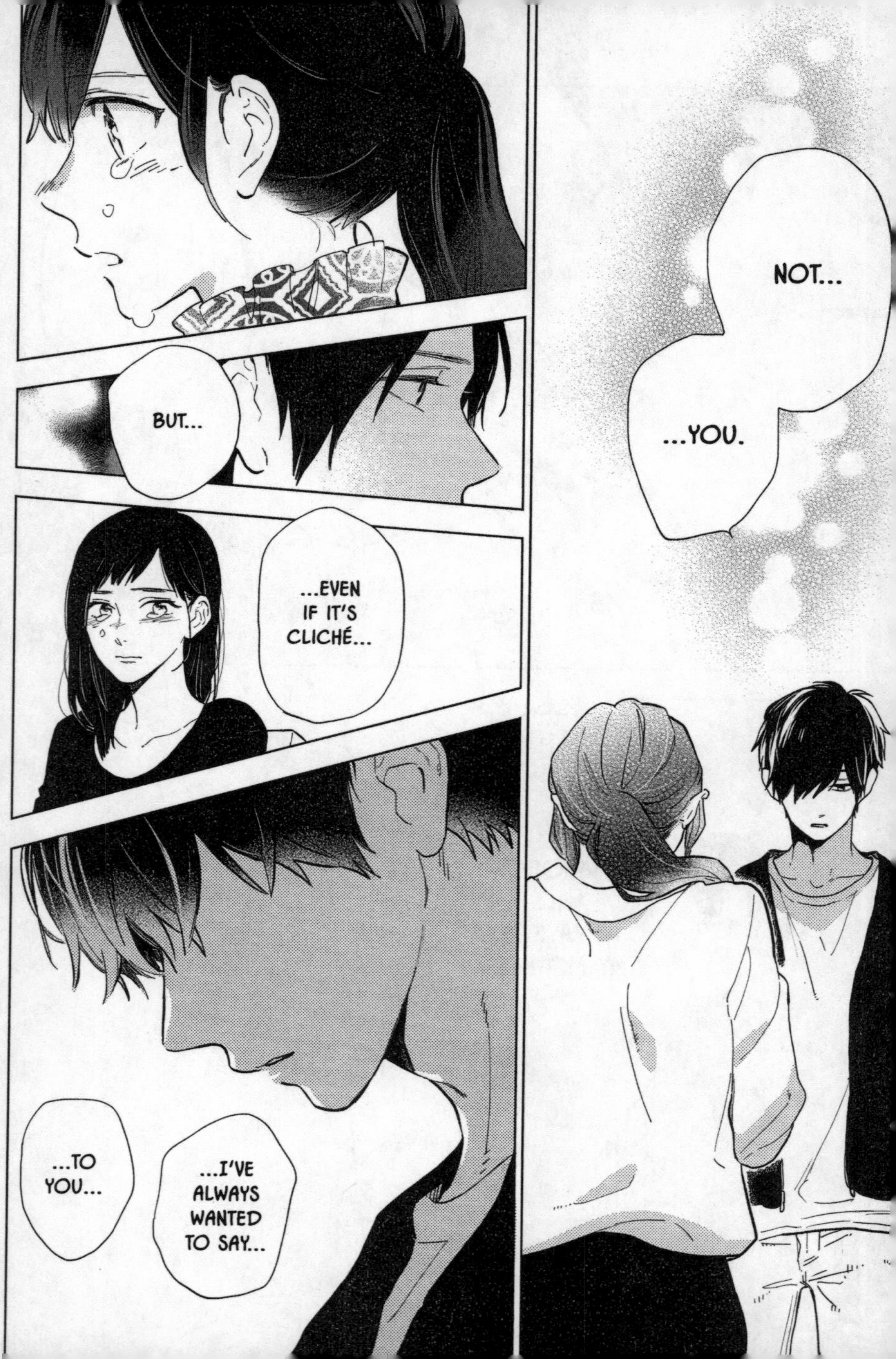
NOT...
...YOU.
BUT...
...EVEN IF IT'S CLICHÉ...
...I'VE ALWAYS WANTED TO SAY...
...TO YOU...

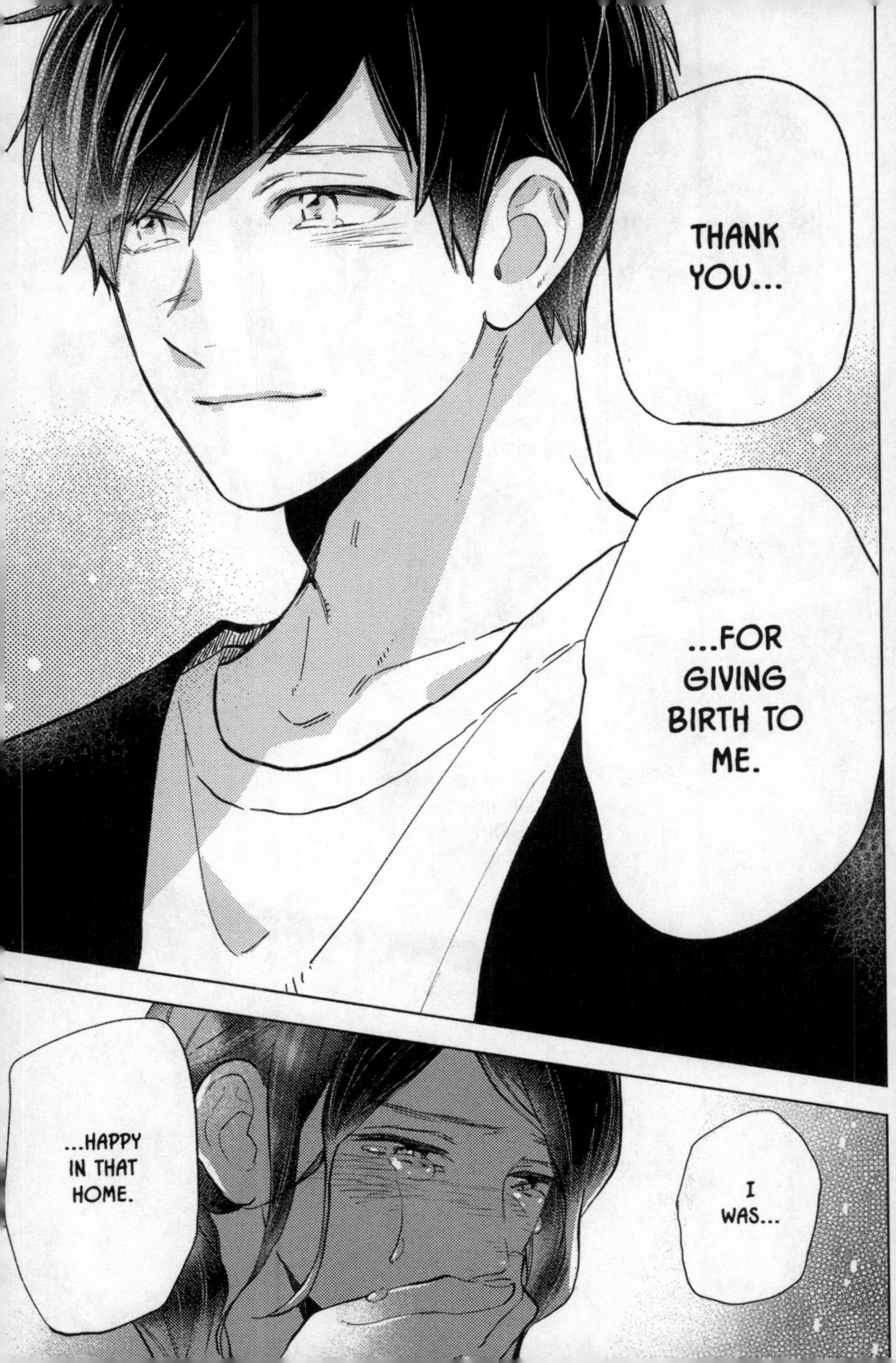
THANK YOU...
...FOR GIVING BIRTH TO ME.
I WAS...
...HAPPY IN THAT HOME.

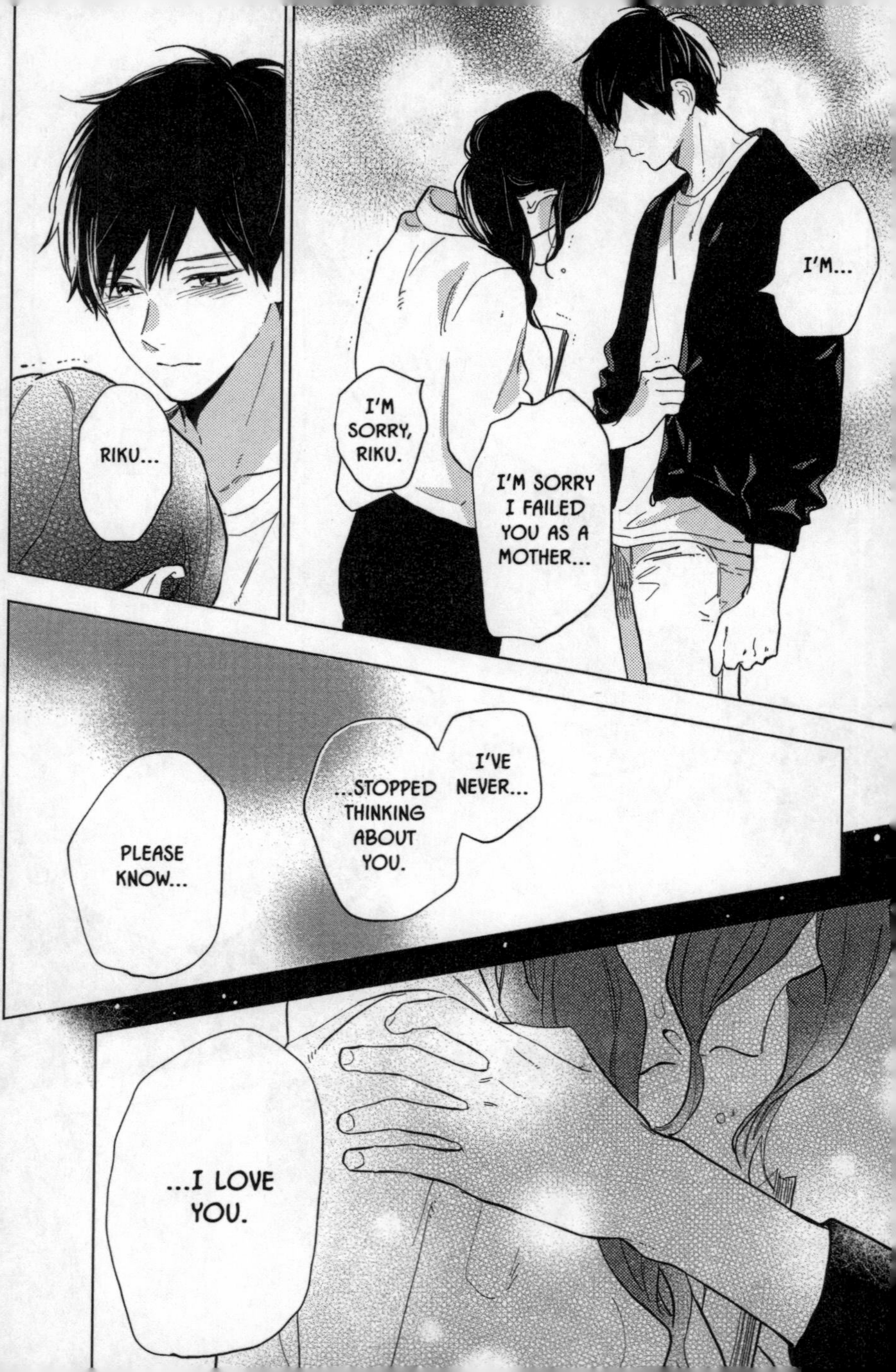
I'M...
I'M SORRY, RIKU.
I'M SORRY I FAILED YOU AS A MOTHER...
RIKU...
I'VE NEVER...
...STOPPED THINKING ABOUT YOU.
PLEASE KNOW...
...I LOVE YOU.

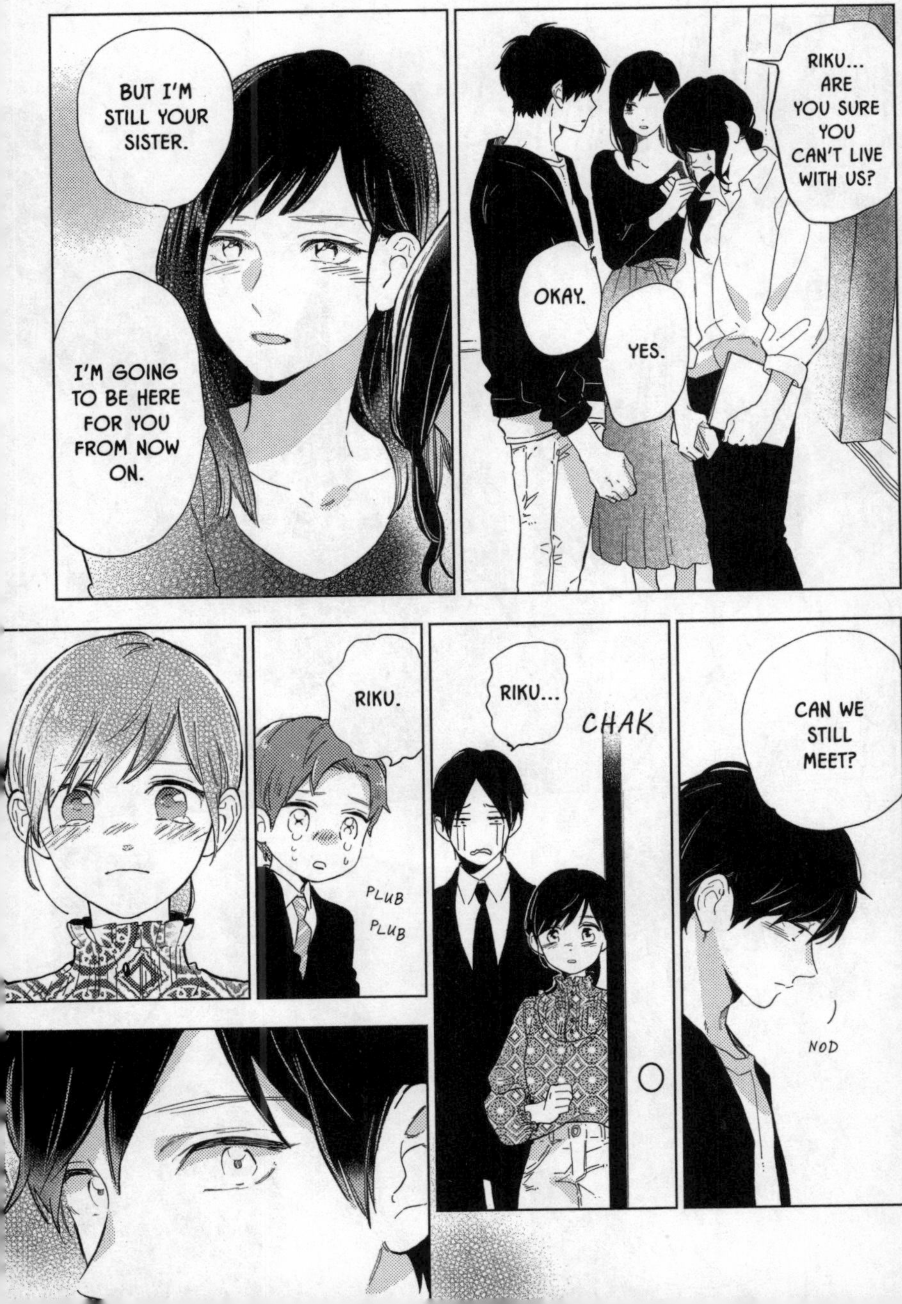
RIKU... ARE YOU SURE YOU CAN'T LIVE WITH US?
YES.
OKAY.
BUT I'M STILL YOUR SISTER.
I'M GOING TO BE HERE FOR YOU FROM NOW ON.
CAN WE STILL MEET?
NOD
RIKU...
CHAK
RIKU.
PLUB
PLUB

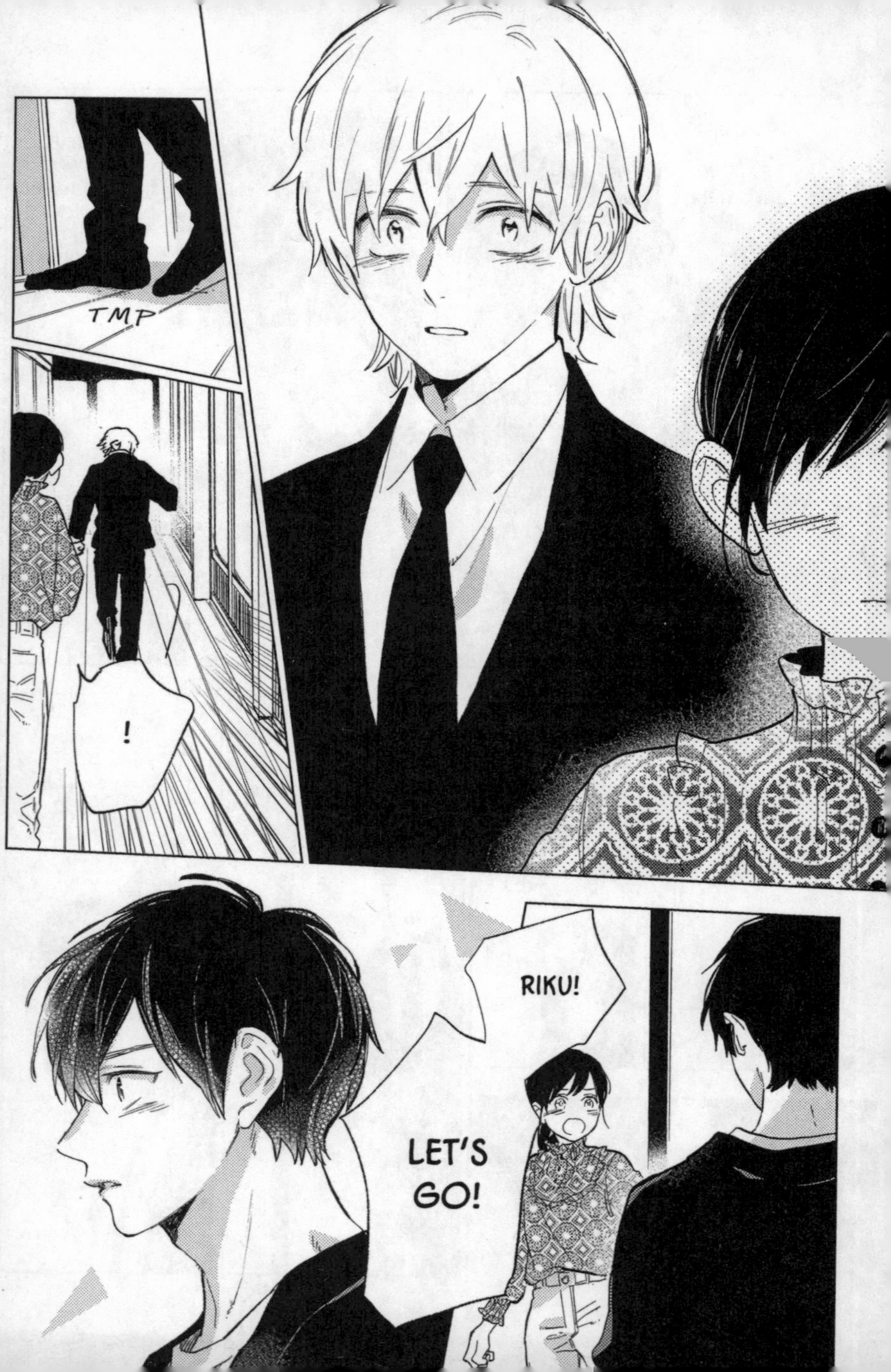
TMP
!
RIKU!
LET'S GO!

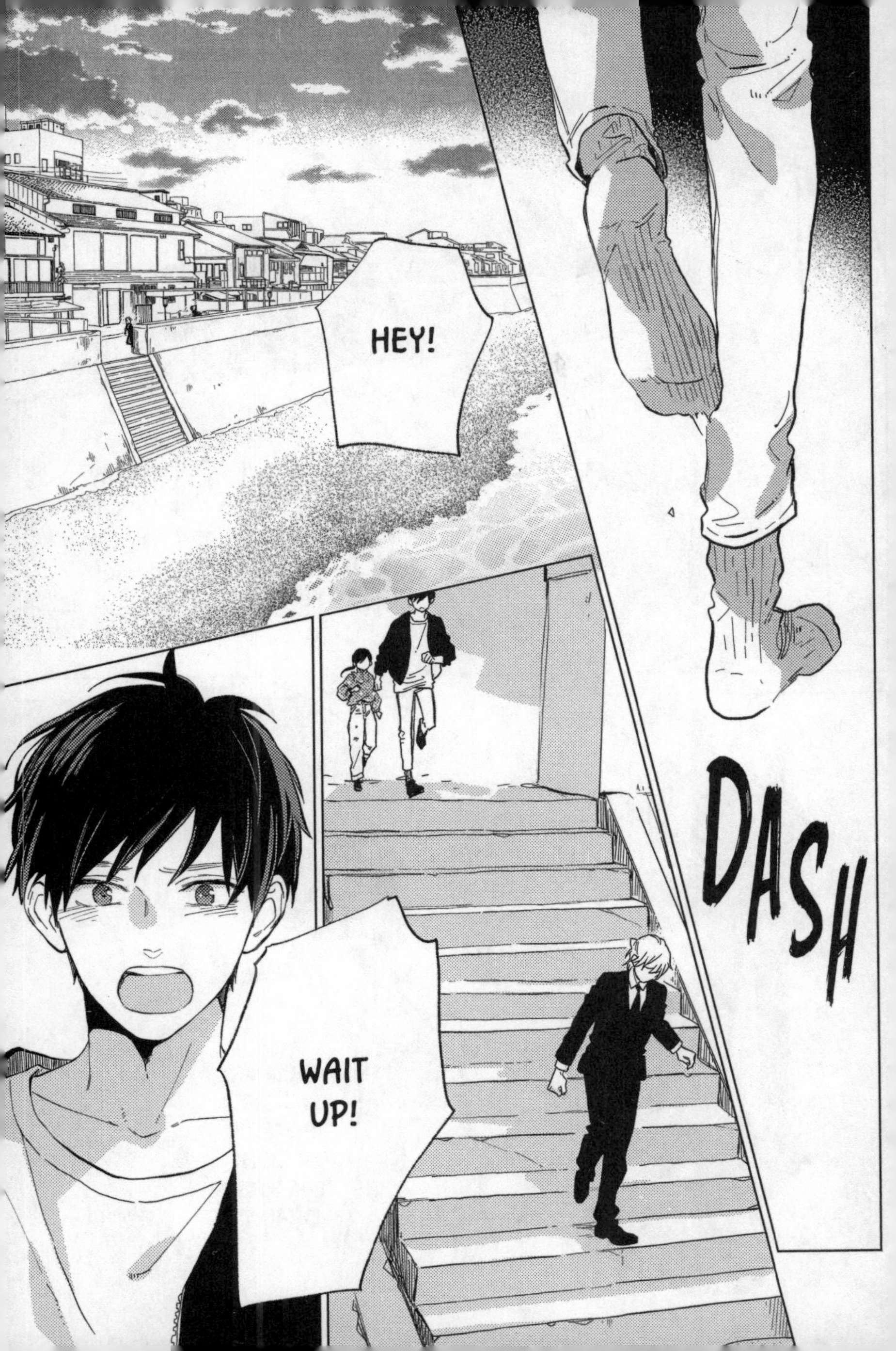
DASH
HEY!
WAIT UP!

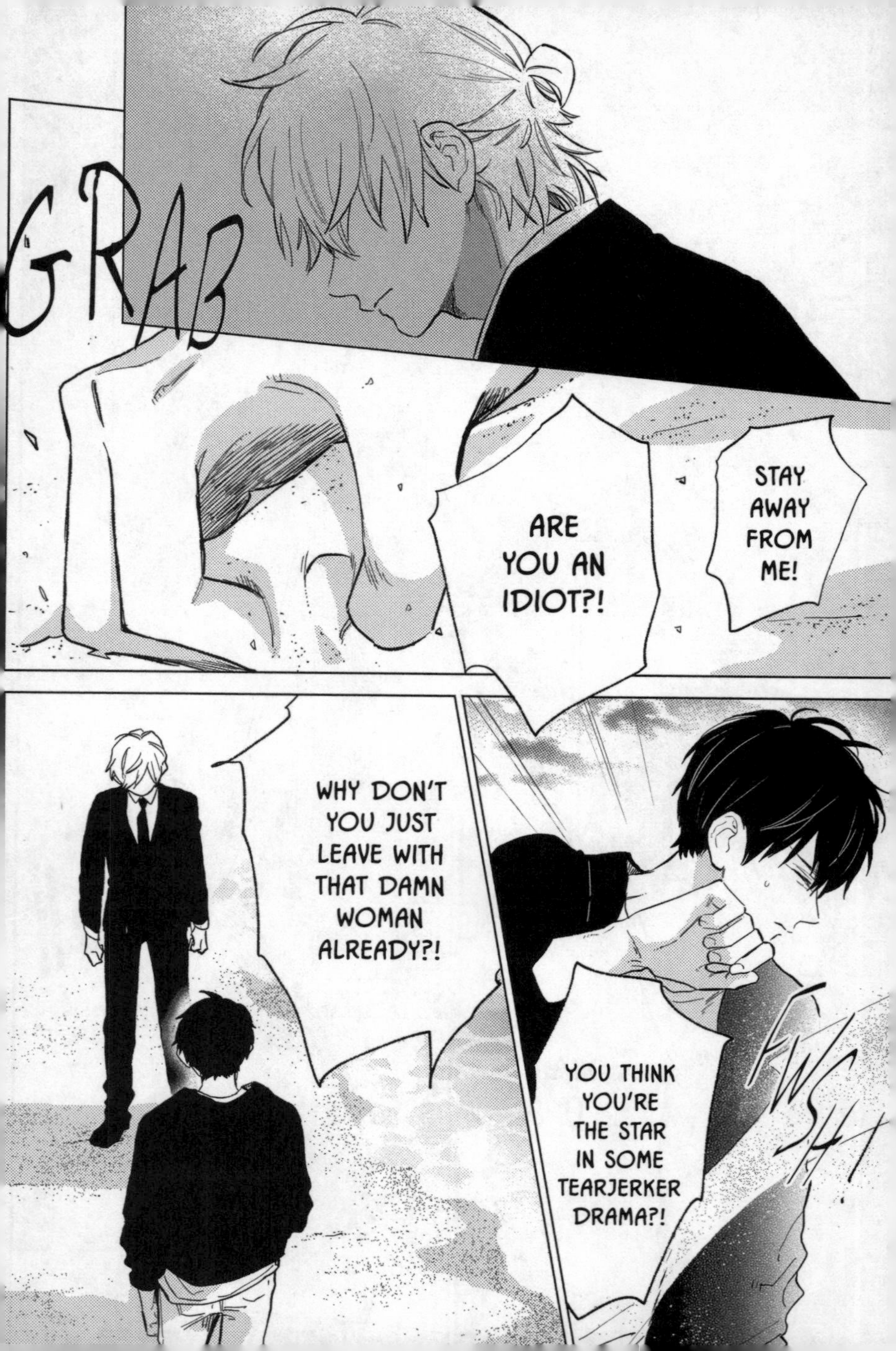
GRAB
STAY AWAY FROM ME!
ARE YOU AN IDIOT?!
FWSH!
YOU THINK YOU'RE THE STAR IN SOME TEARJERKER DRAMA?!
WHY DON'T YOU JUST LEAVE WITH THAT DAMN WOMAN ALREADY?!

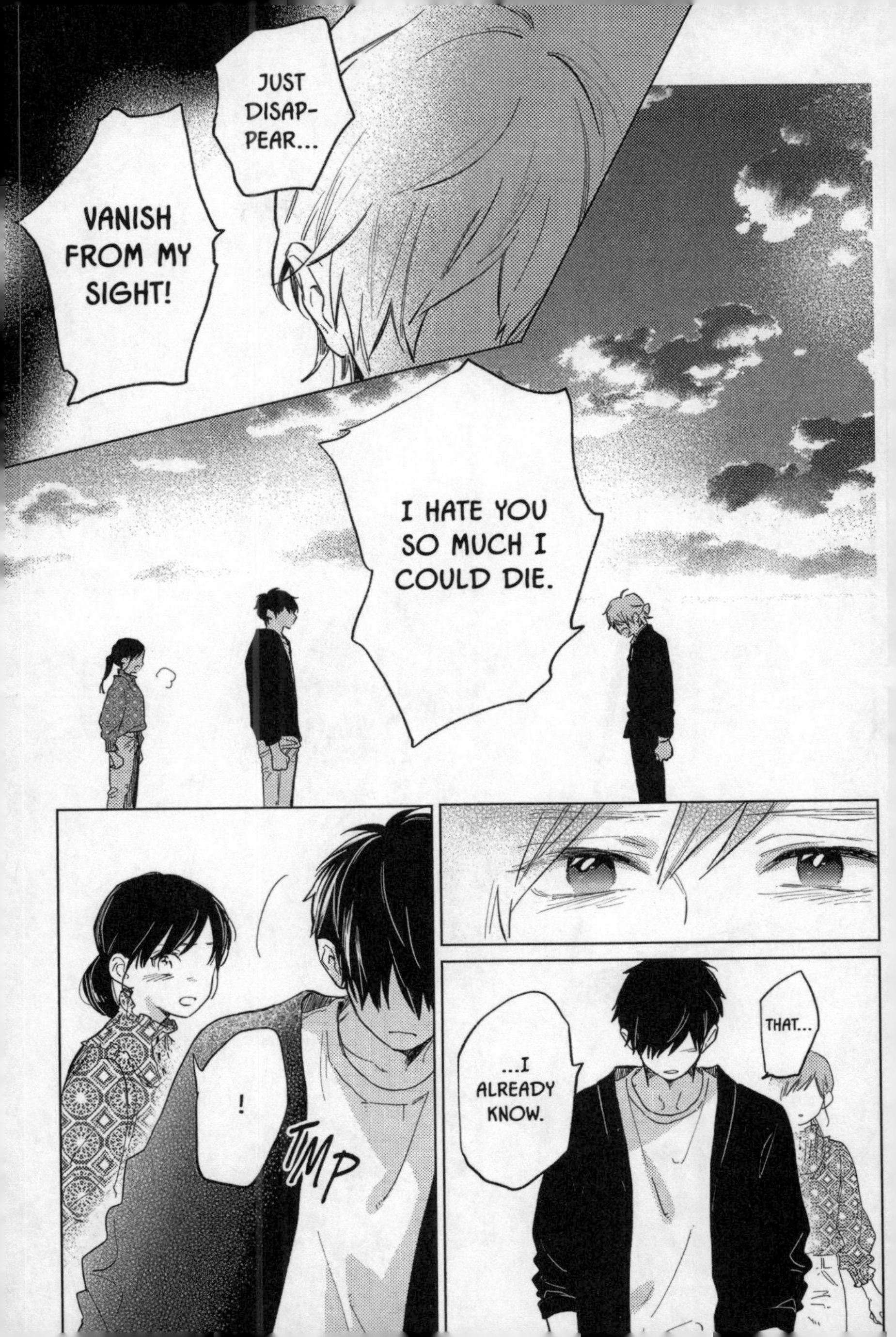
JUST DISAP-PEAR...
VANISH FROM MY SIGHT!
I HATE YOU SO MUCH I COULD DIE.
THAT...
...I ALREADY KNOW.
!
TMP

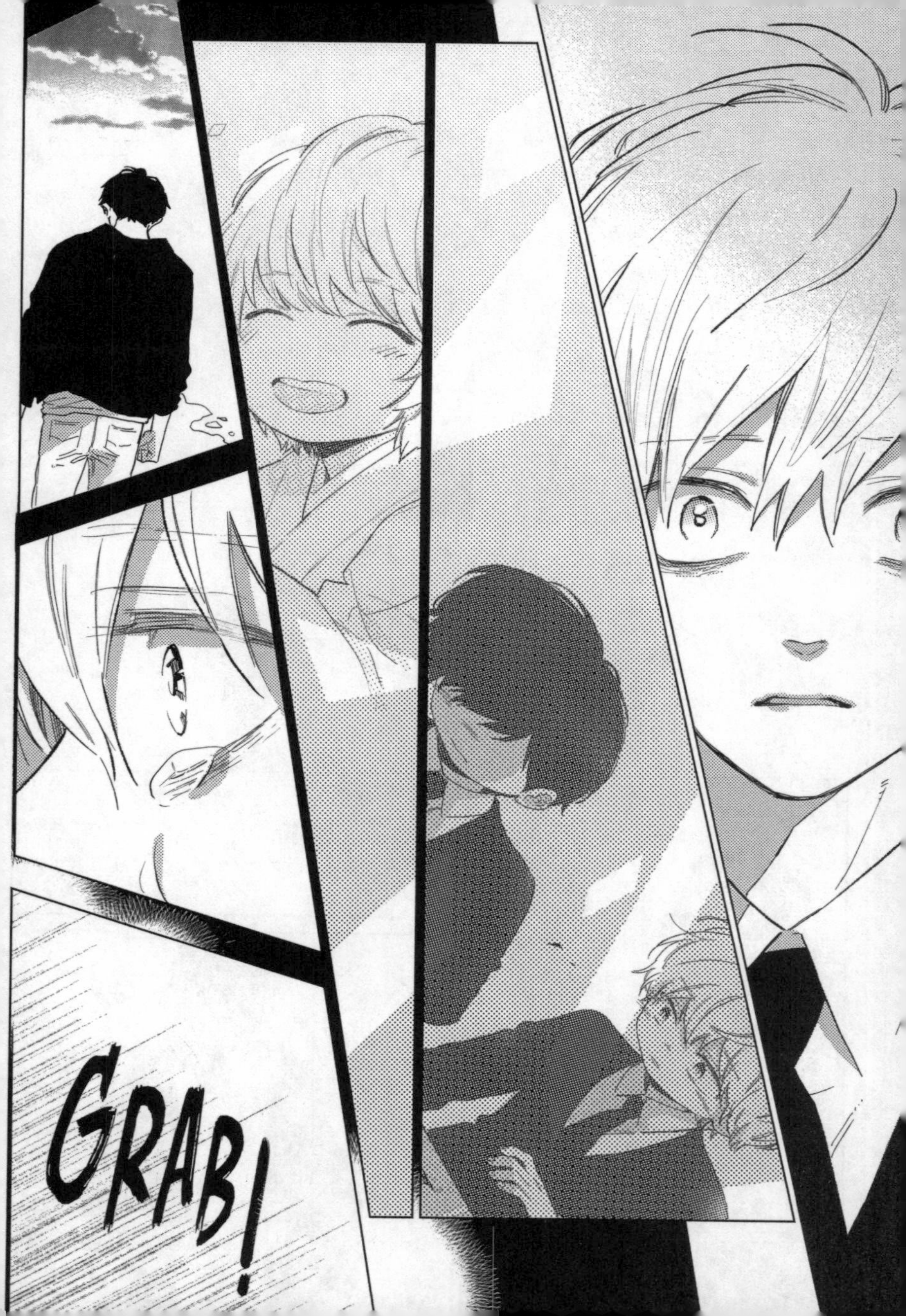
GRAB!

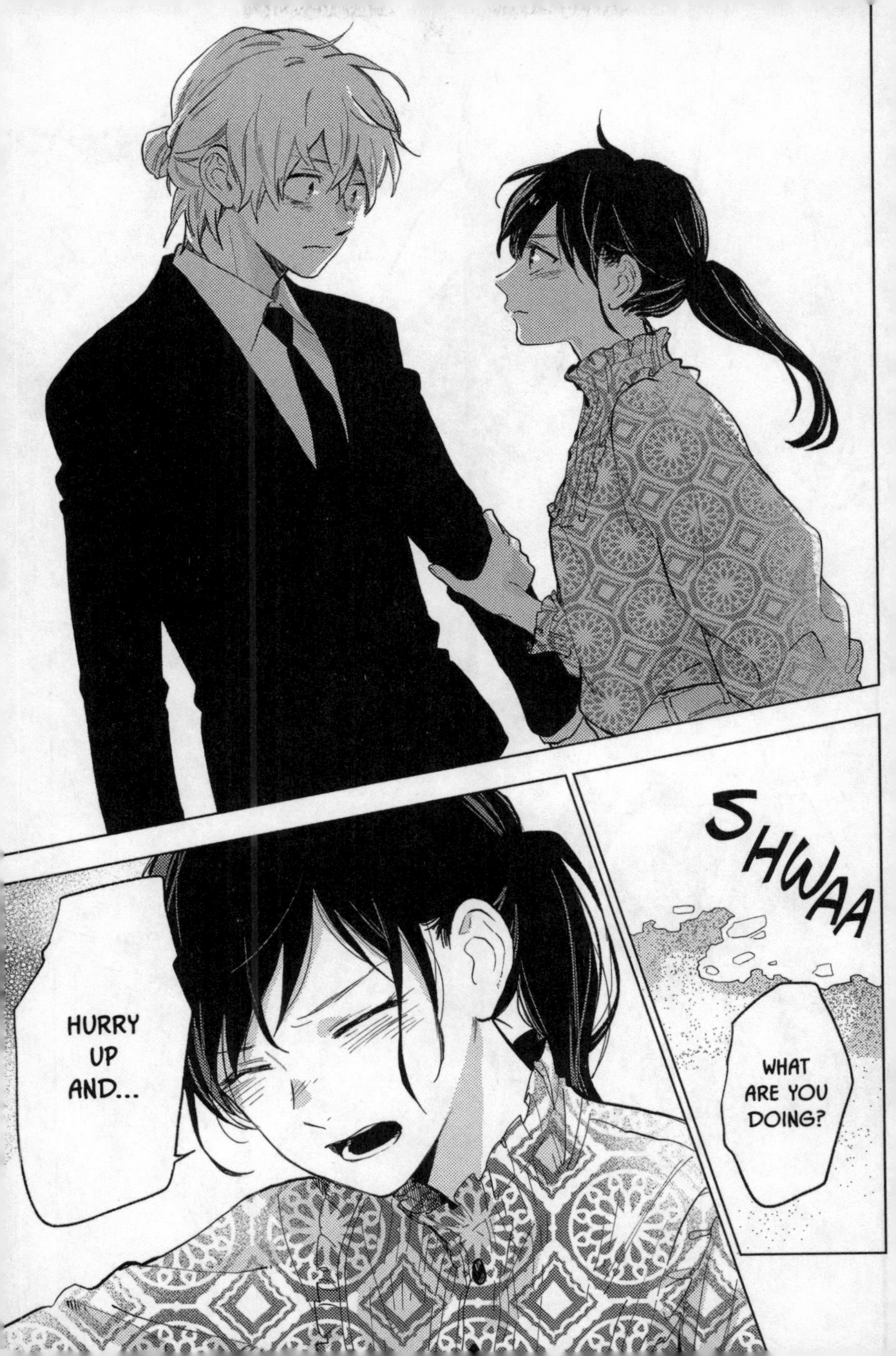
SHWAA
WHAT ARE YOU DOING?
HURRY UP AND...

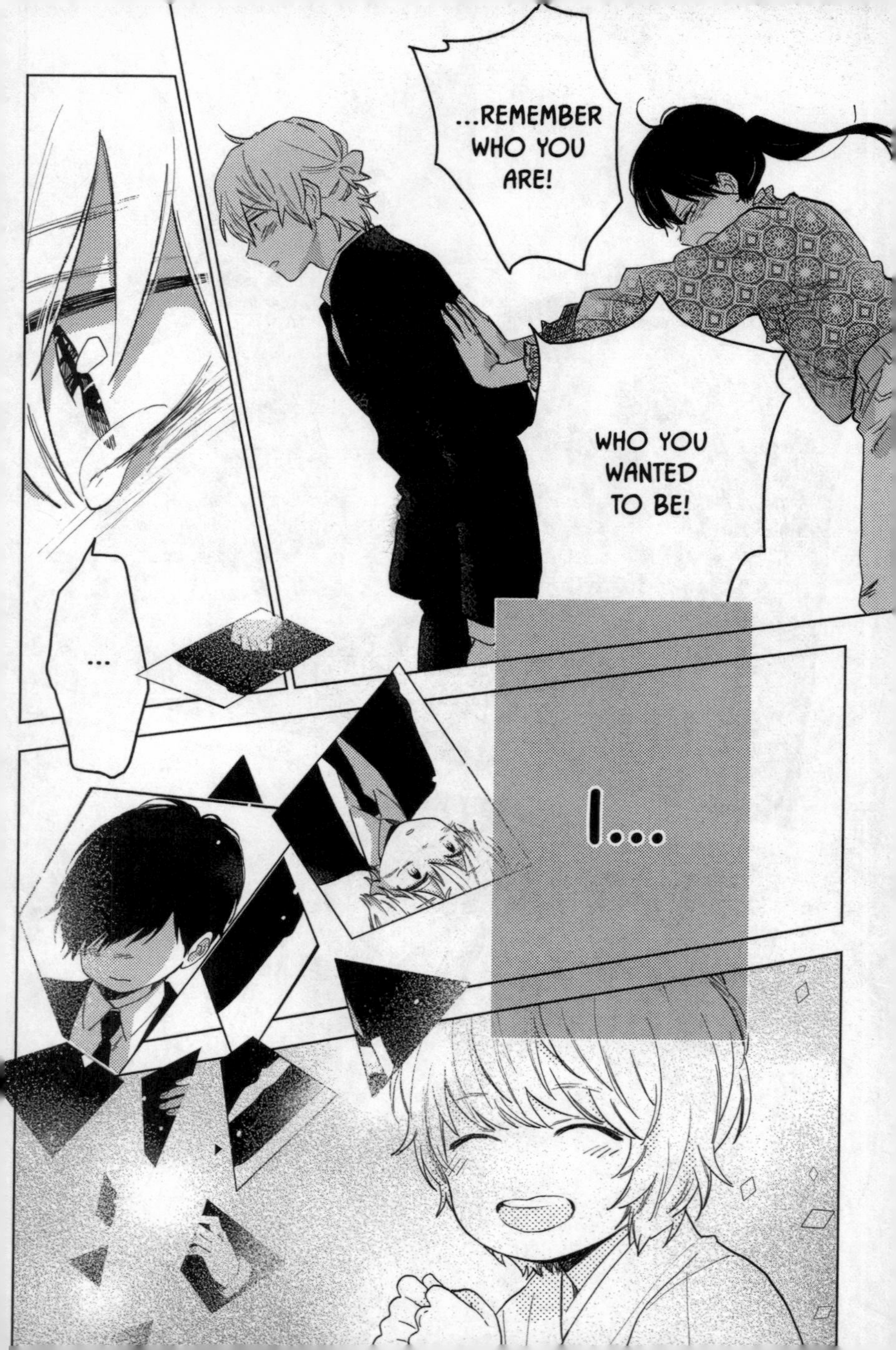
...REMEMBER WHO YOU ARE!
WHO YOU WANTED TO BE!
...
I...

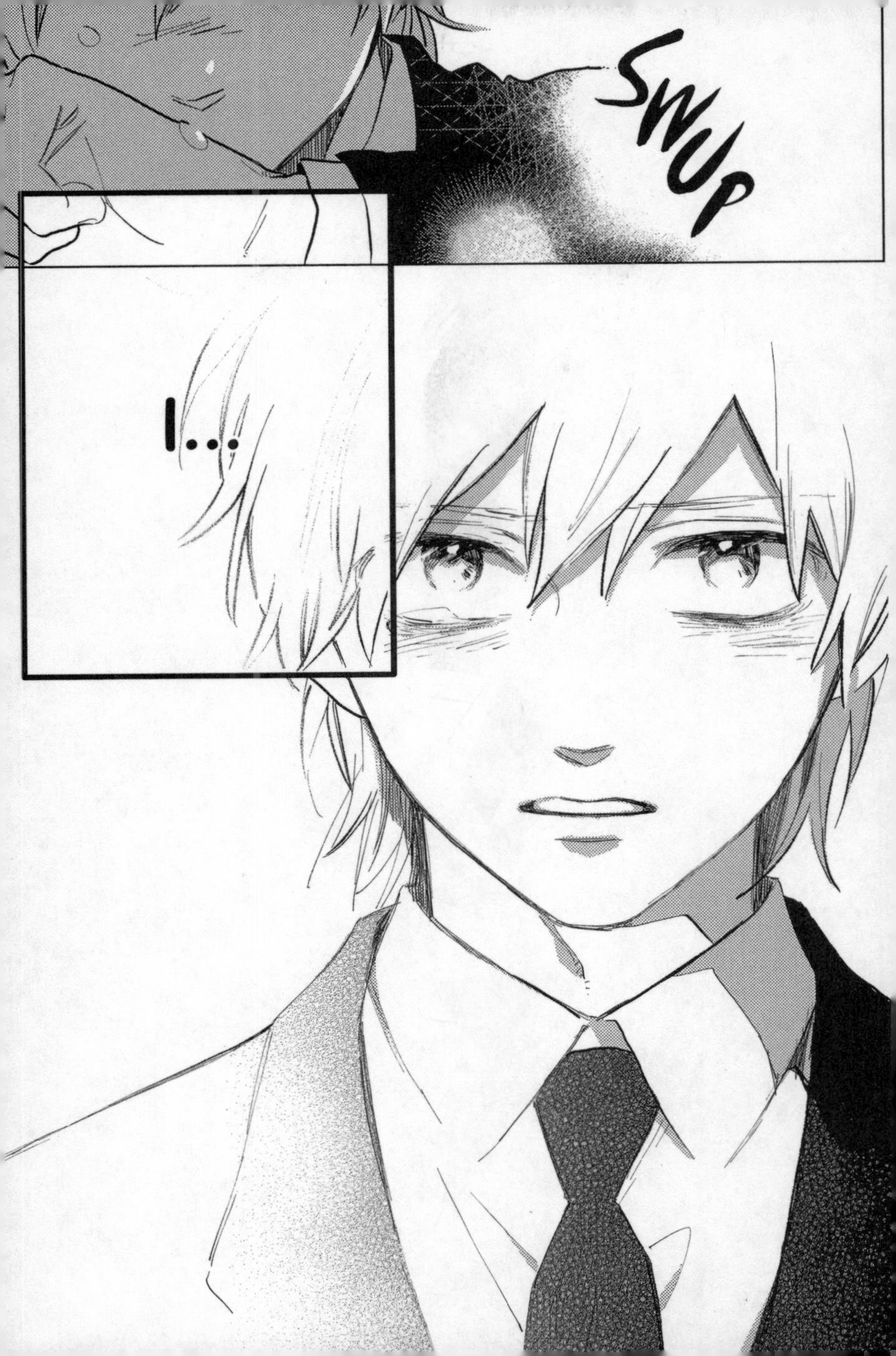
SNUP
I...

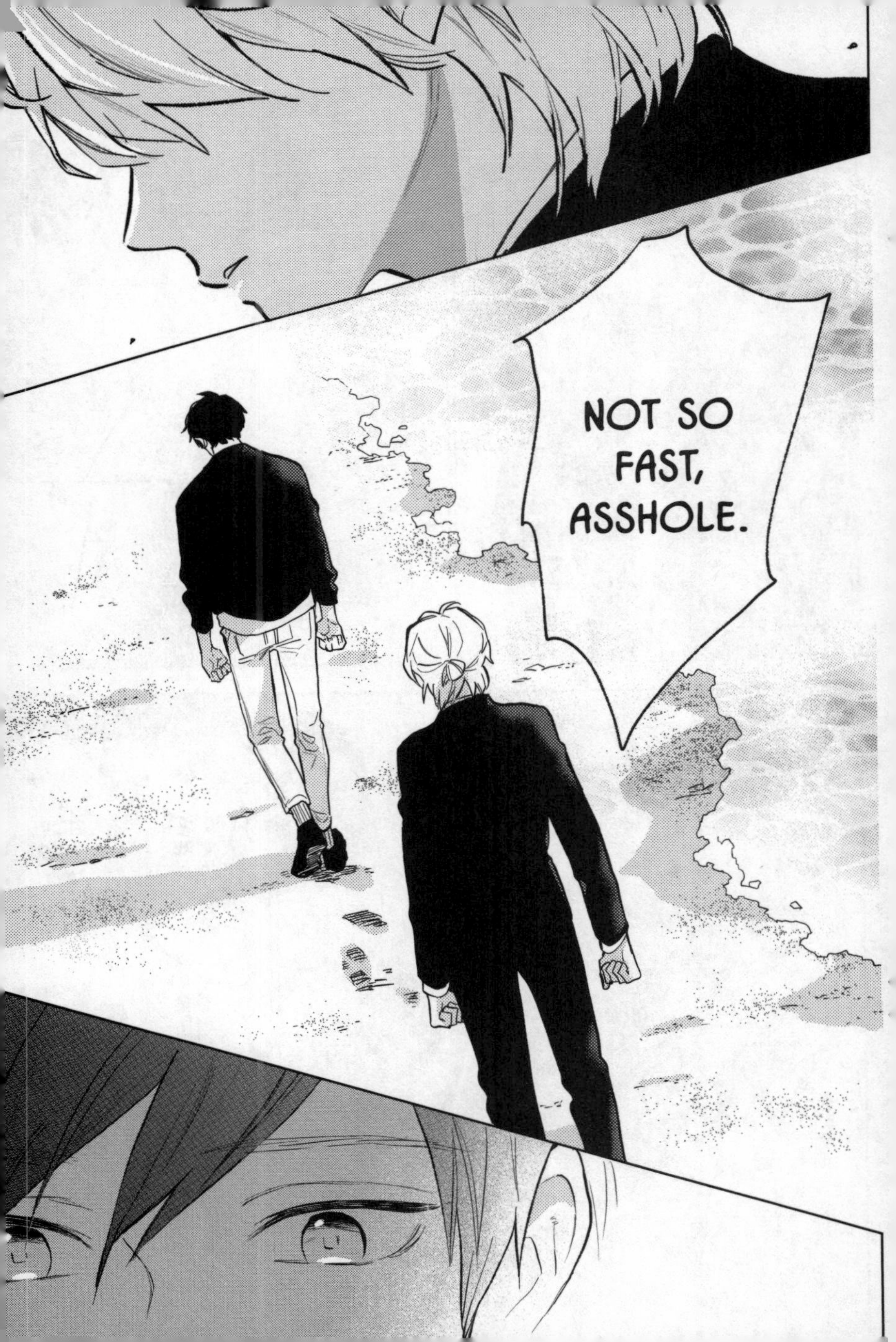
NOT SO FAST, ASSHOLE.

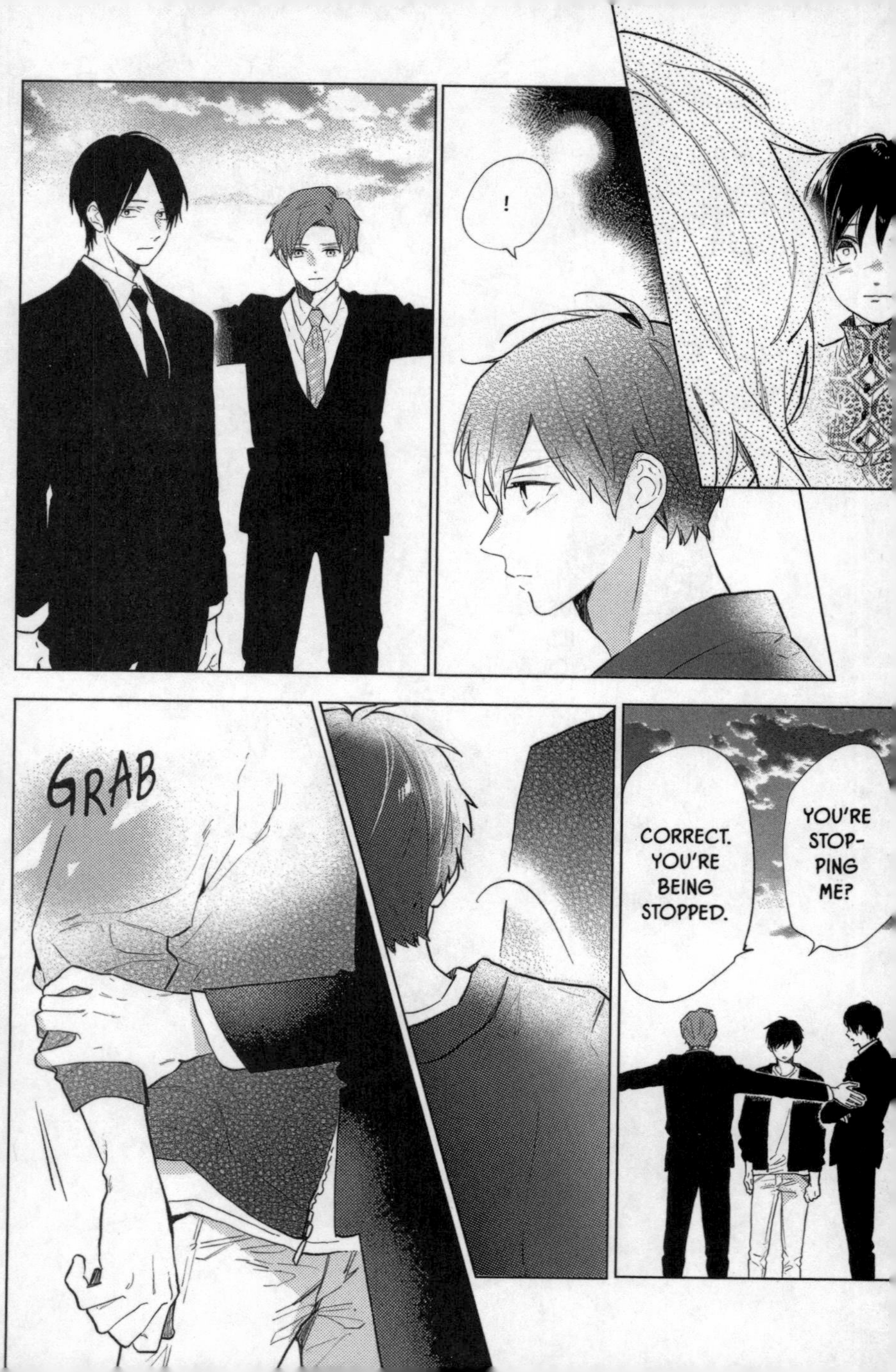
!
YOU'RE STOP-PING ME?
CORRECT. YOU'RE BEING STOPPED.
GRAB

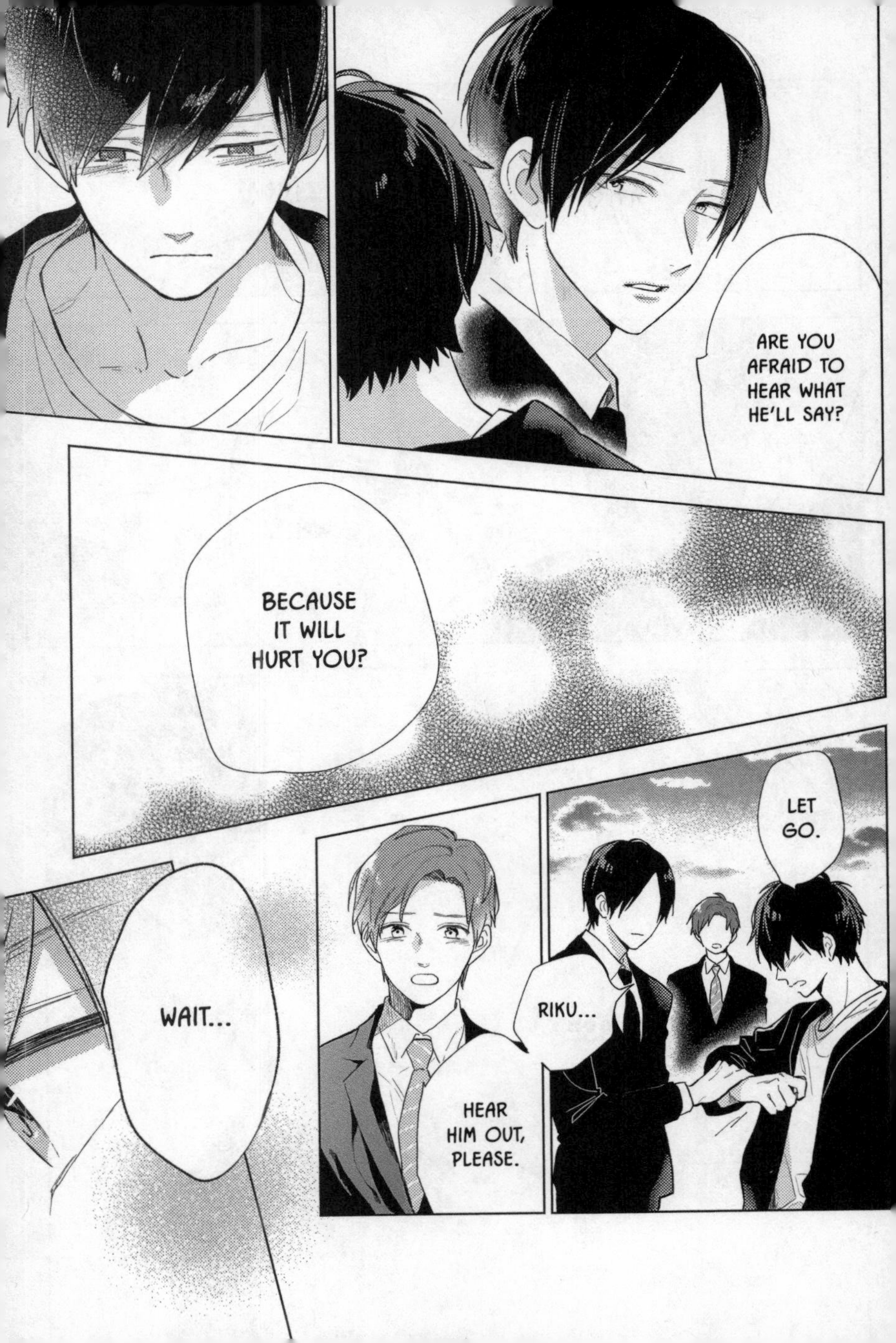
ARE YOU AFRAID TO HEAR WHAT HE'LL SAY?
BECAUSE IT WILL HURT YOU?
LET GO.
RIKU...
HEAR HIM OUT, PLEASE.
WAIT...

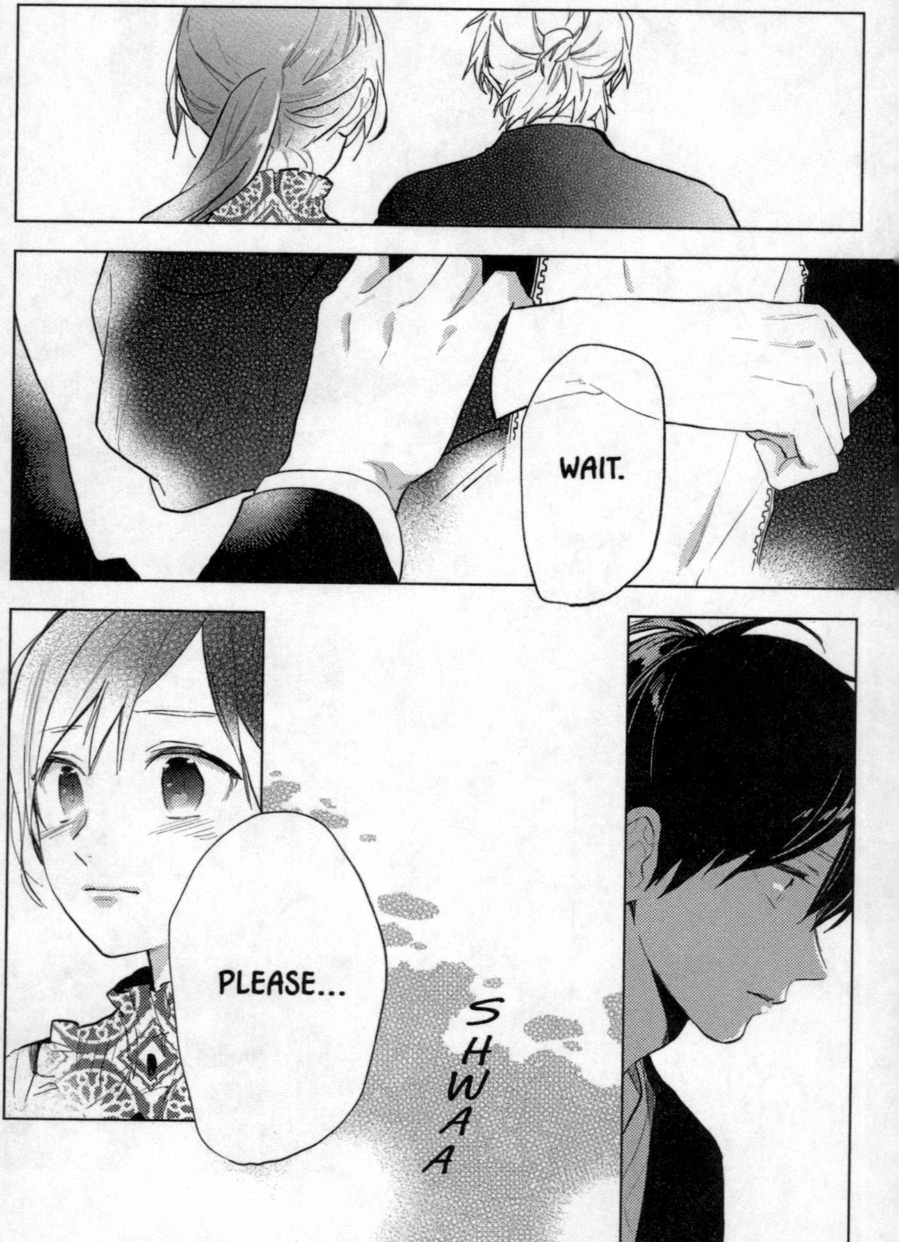
WAIT.
PLEASE...
SHWAA

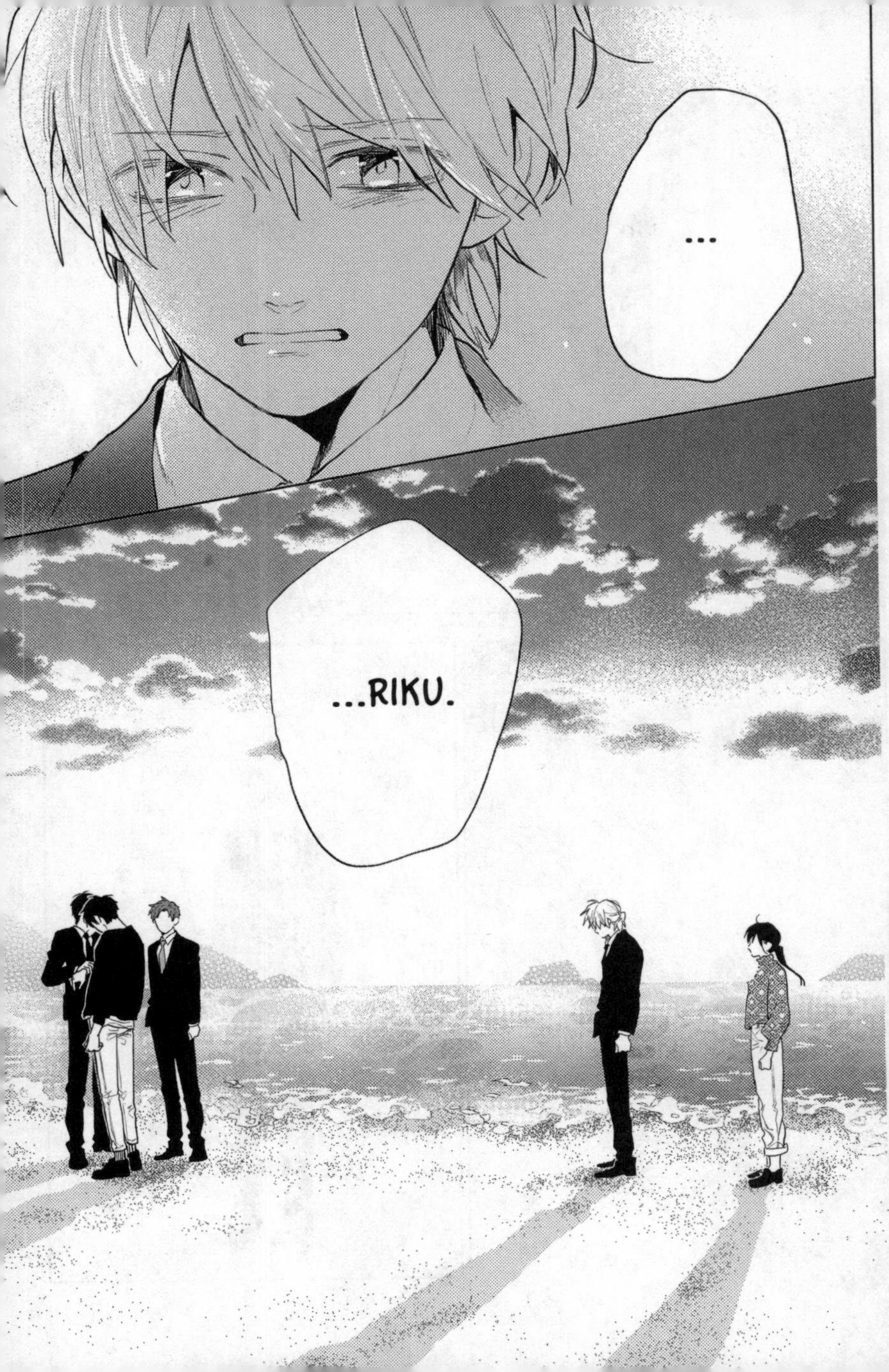
...
...RIKU.

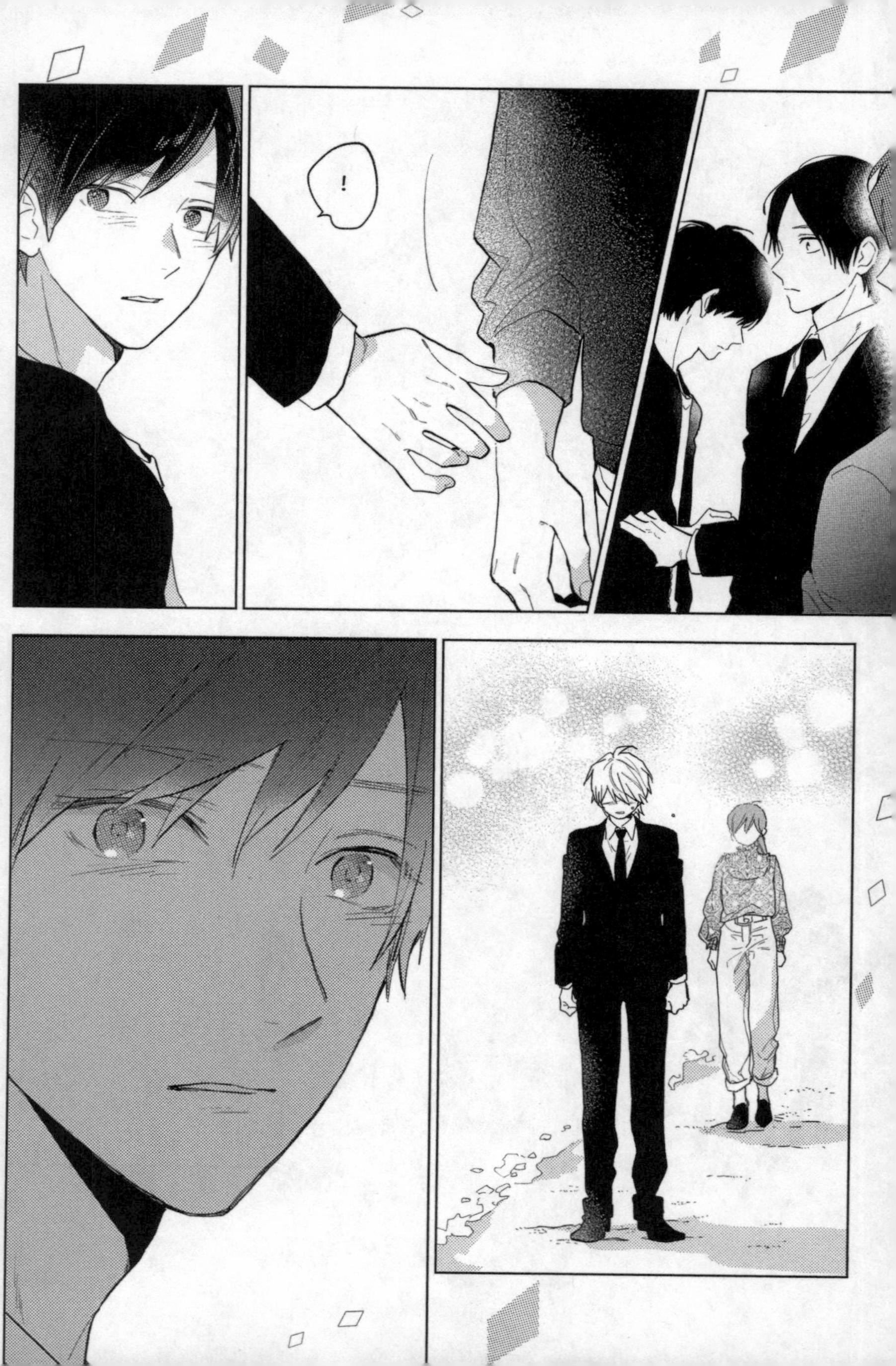
!

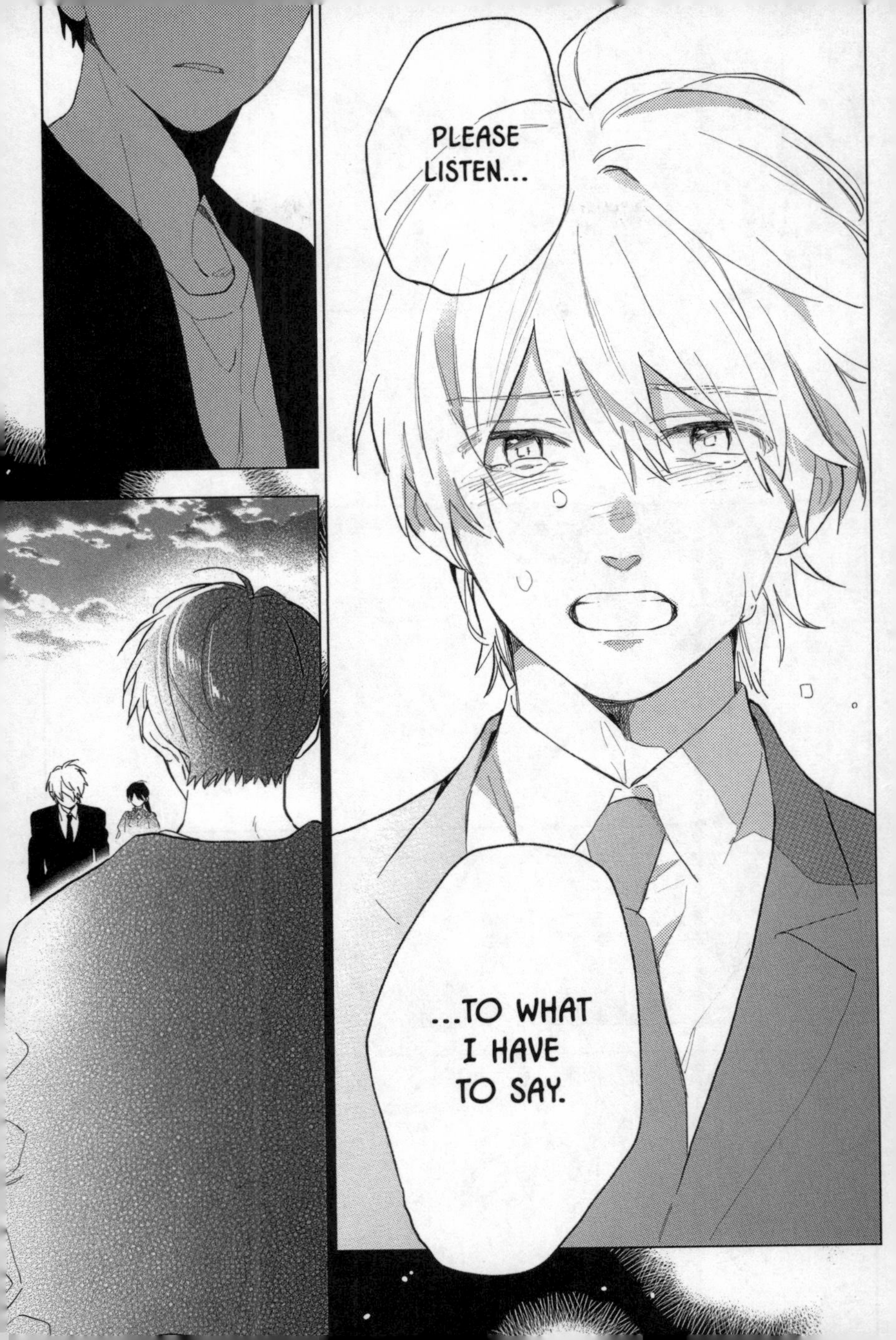
PLEASE LISTEN...
...TO WHAT I HAVE TO SAY.

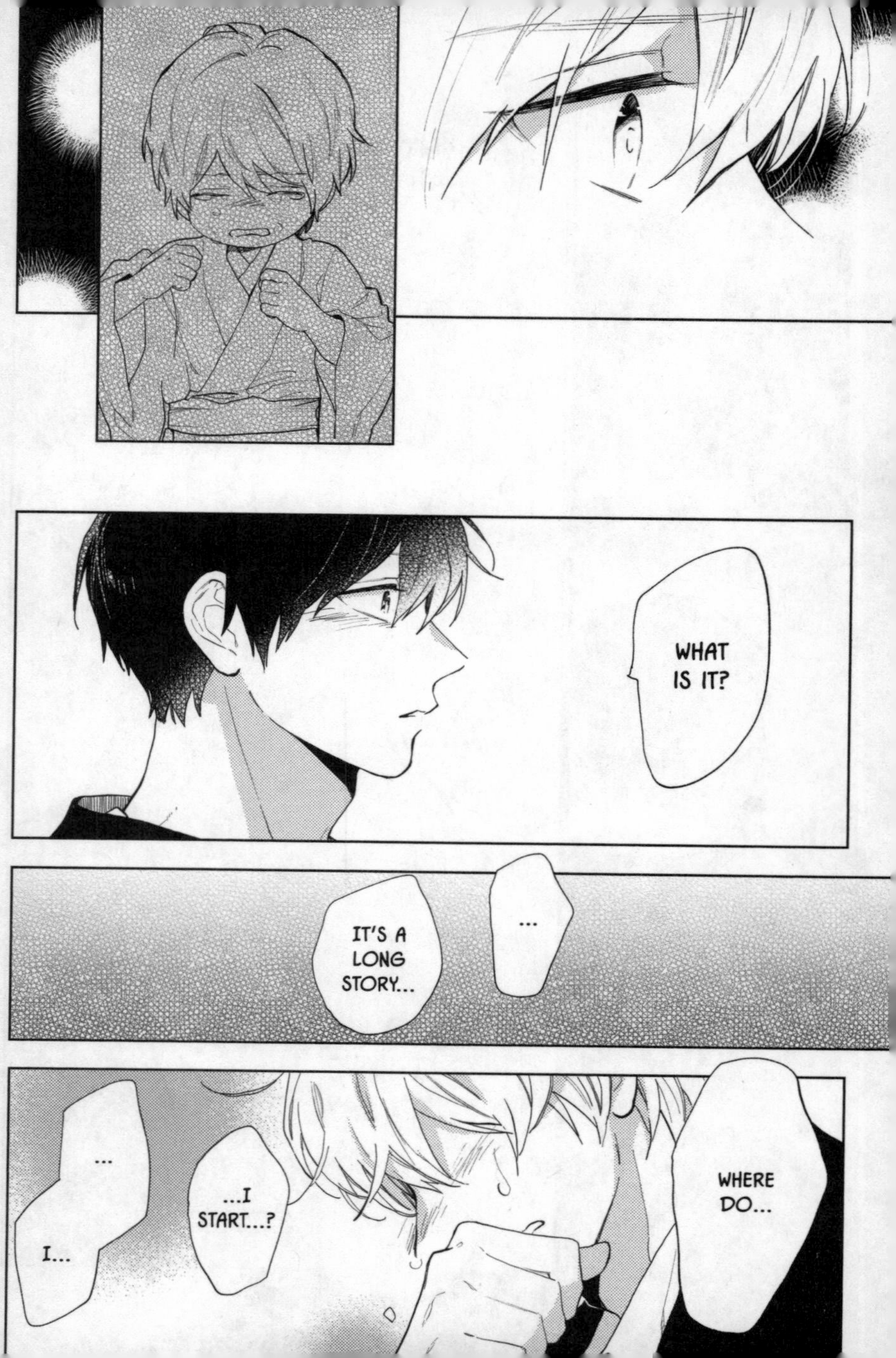
WHAT IS IT?
...
IT'S A LONG STORY...
WHERE DO...
...I START...?
... I...

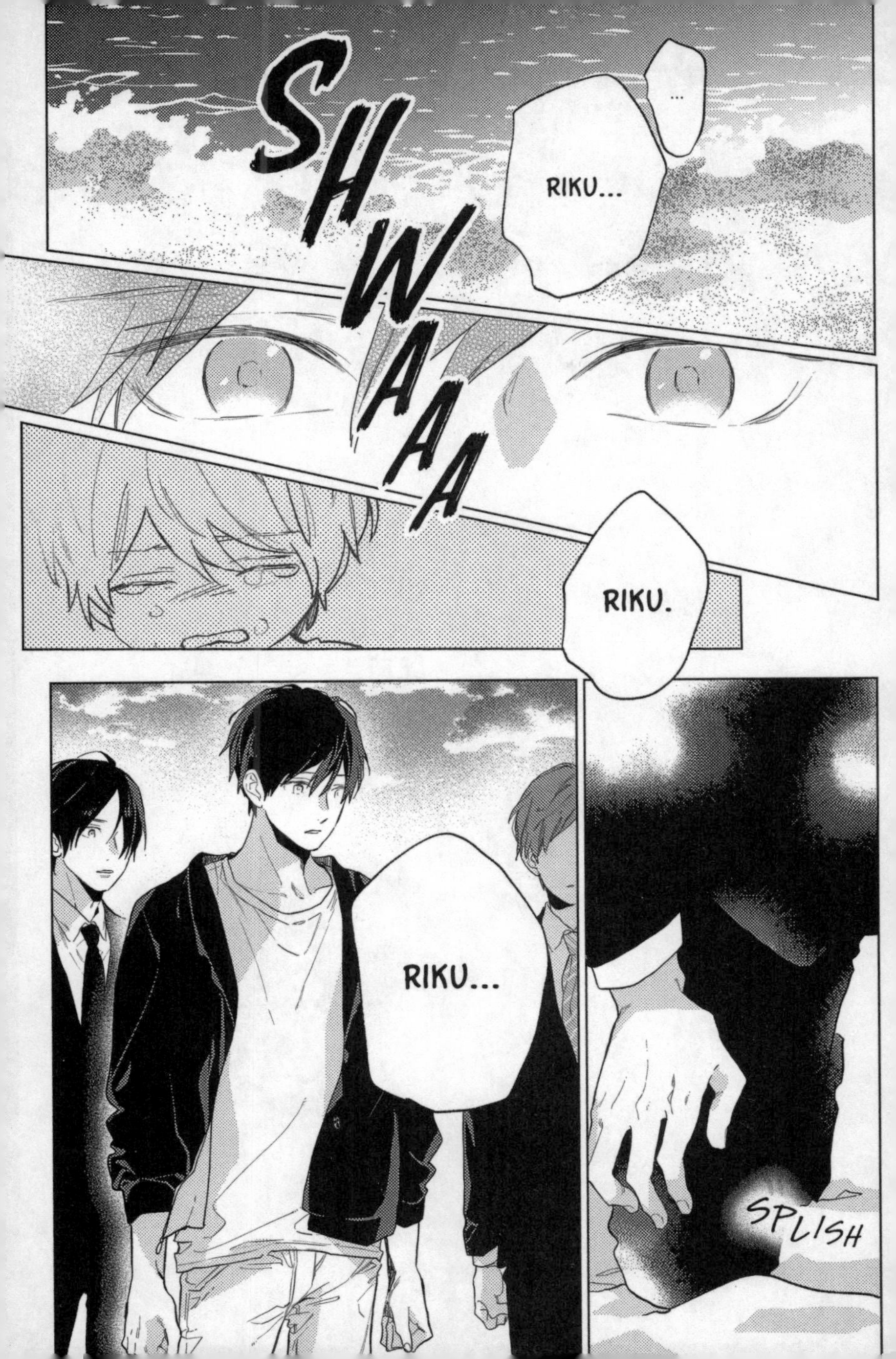
...
RIKU...
SHWAAAA
RIKU.
SPLISH
RIKU...

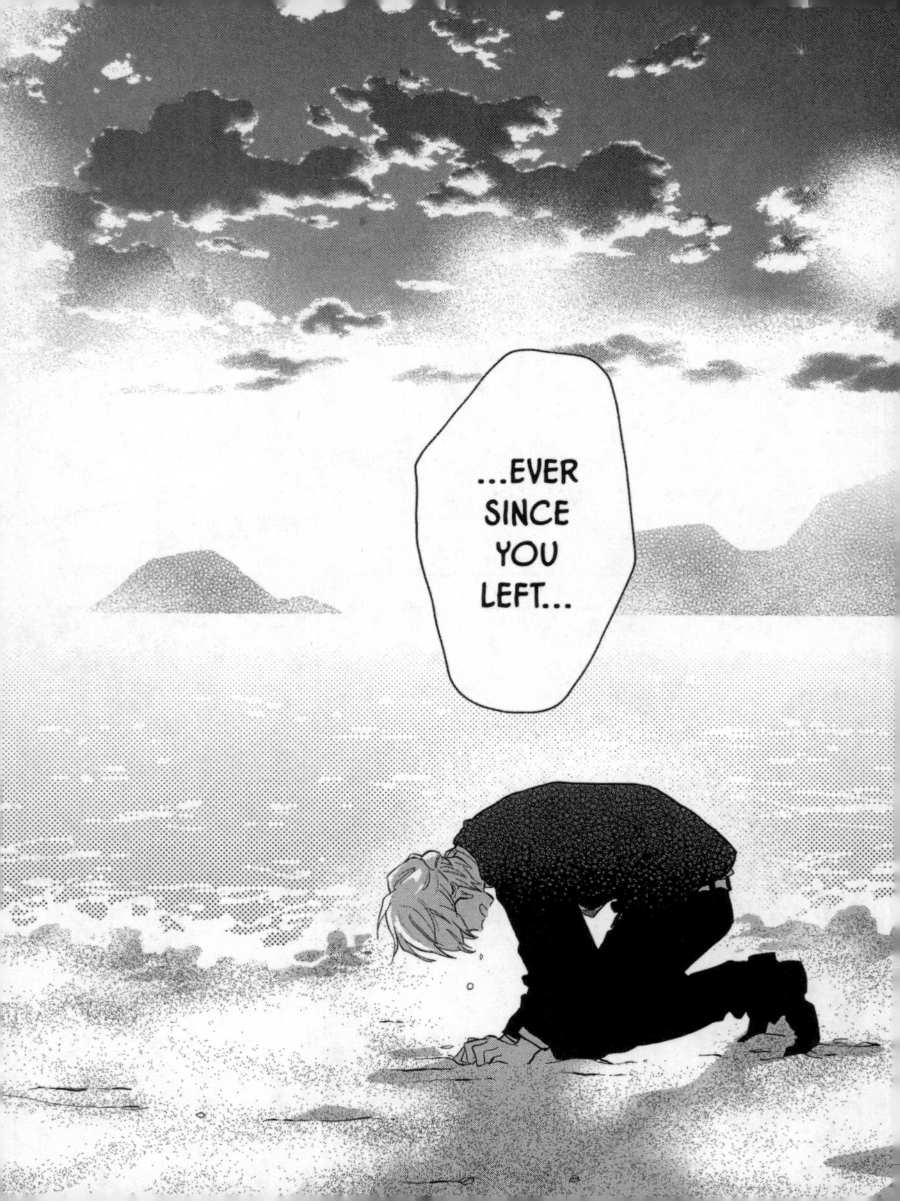
...EVER SINCE YOU LEFT...

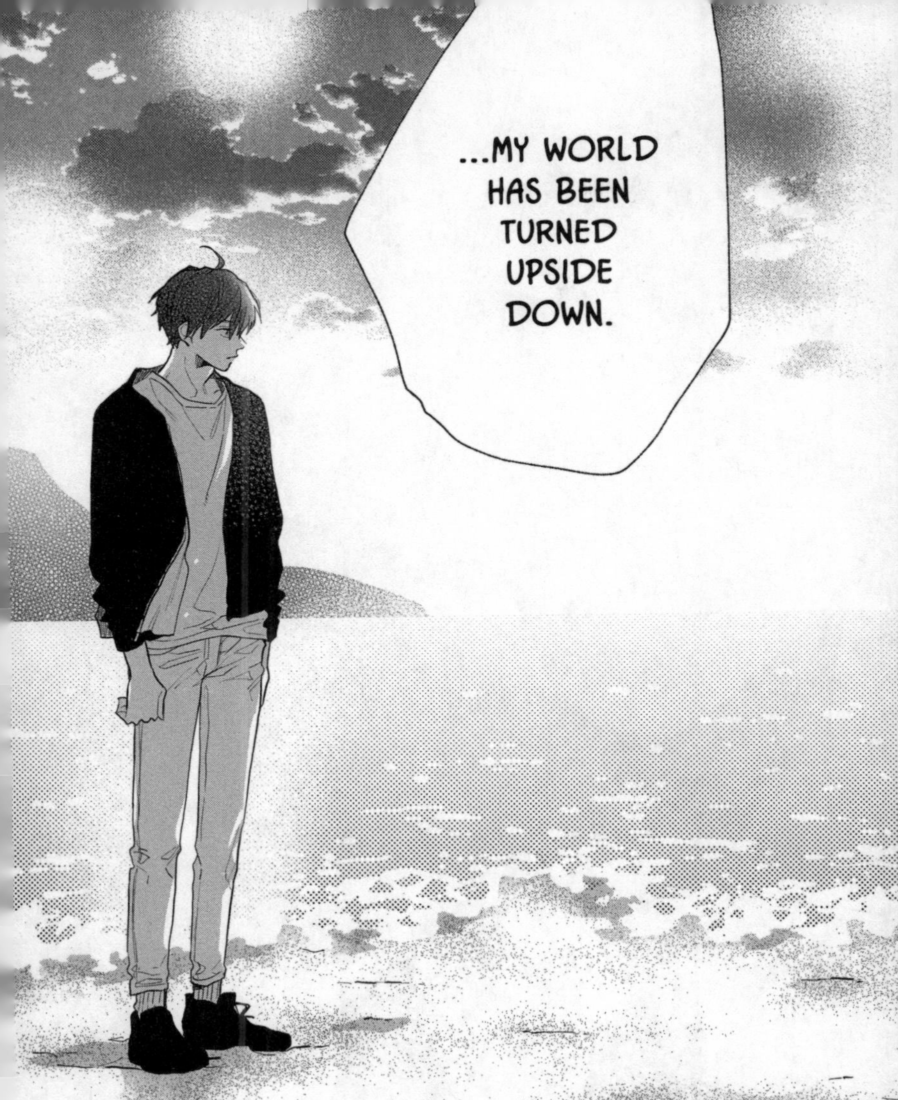
...MY WORLD HAS BEEN TURNED UPSIDE DOWN.

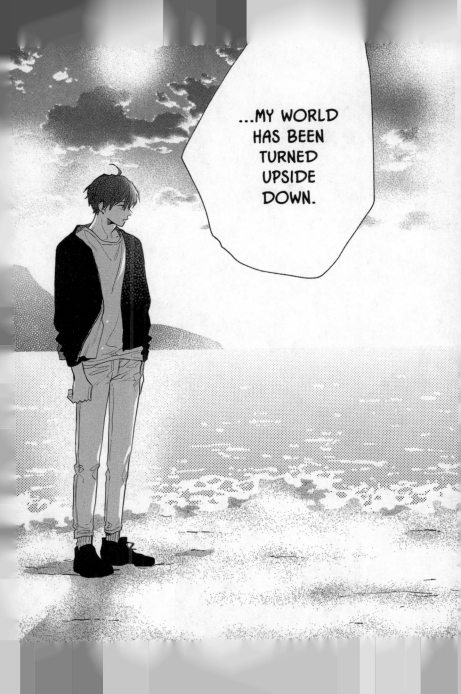

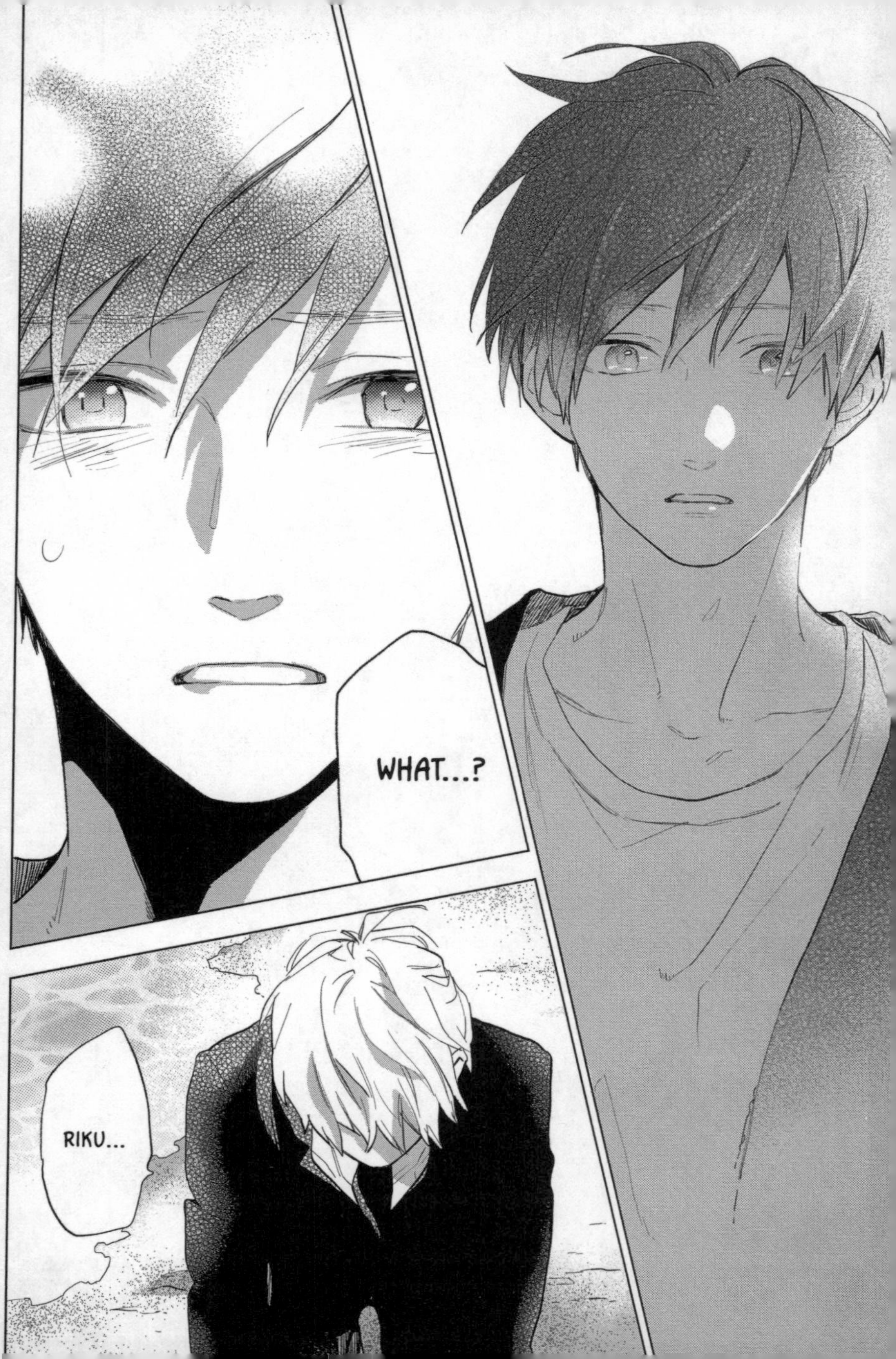
WHAT...?
RIKU...

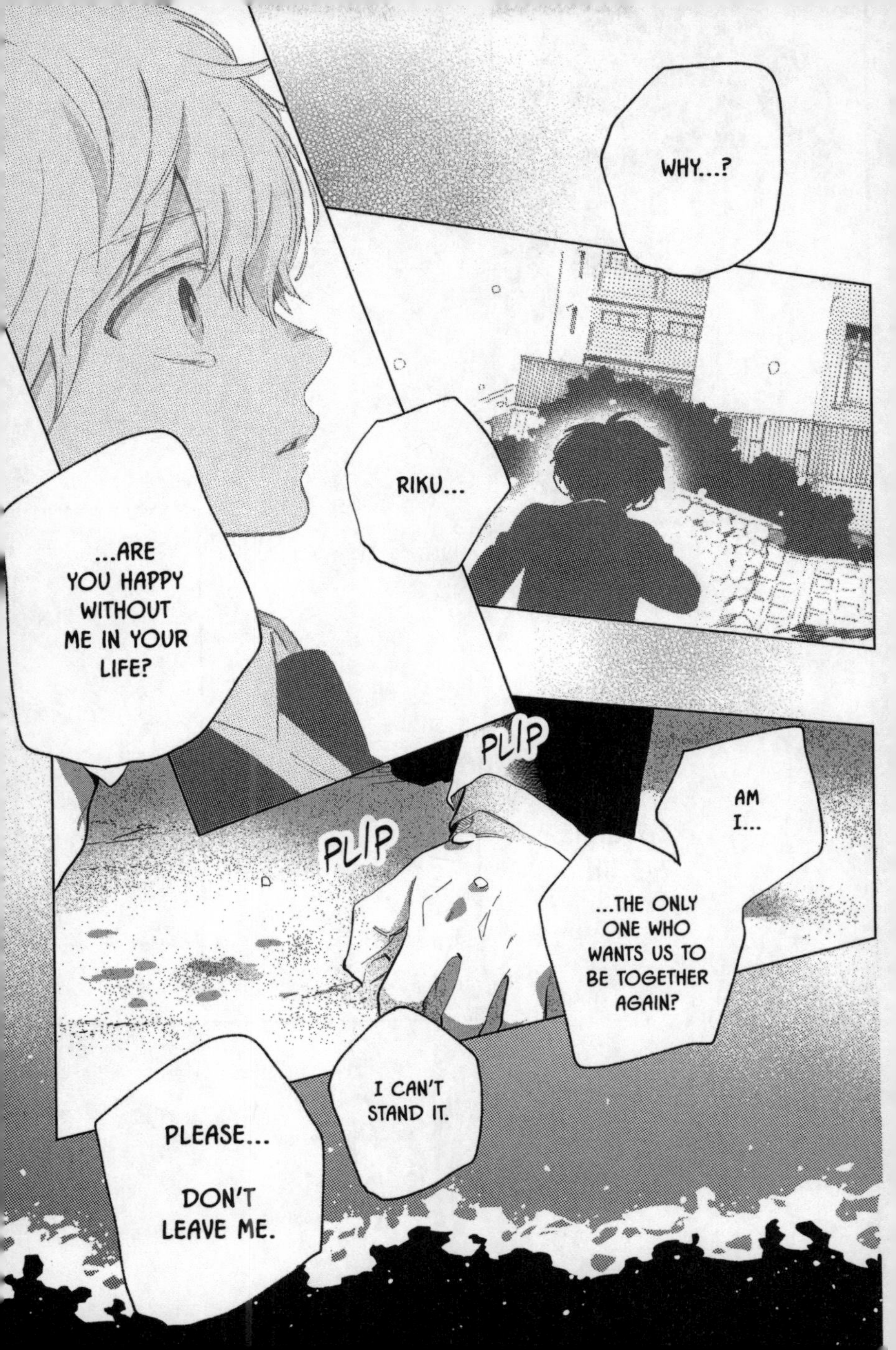
WHY...?
RIKU...
...ARE YOU HAPPY WITHOUT ME IN YOUR LIFE?
PLIP
PLIP
AM I...
...THE ONLY ONE WHO WANTS US TO BE TOGETHER AGAIN?
I CAN'T STAND IT.
PLEASE...
DON'T LEAVE ME.

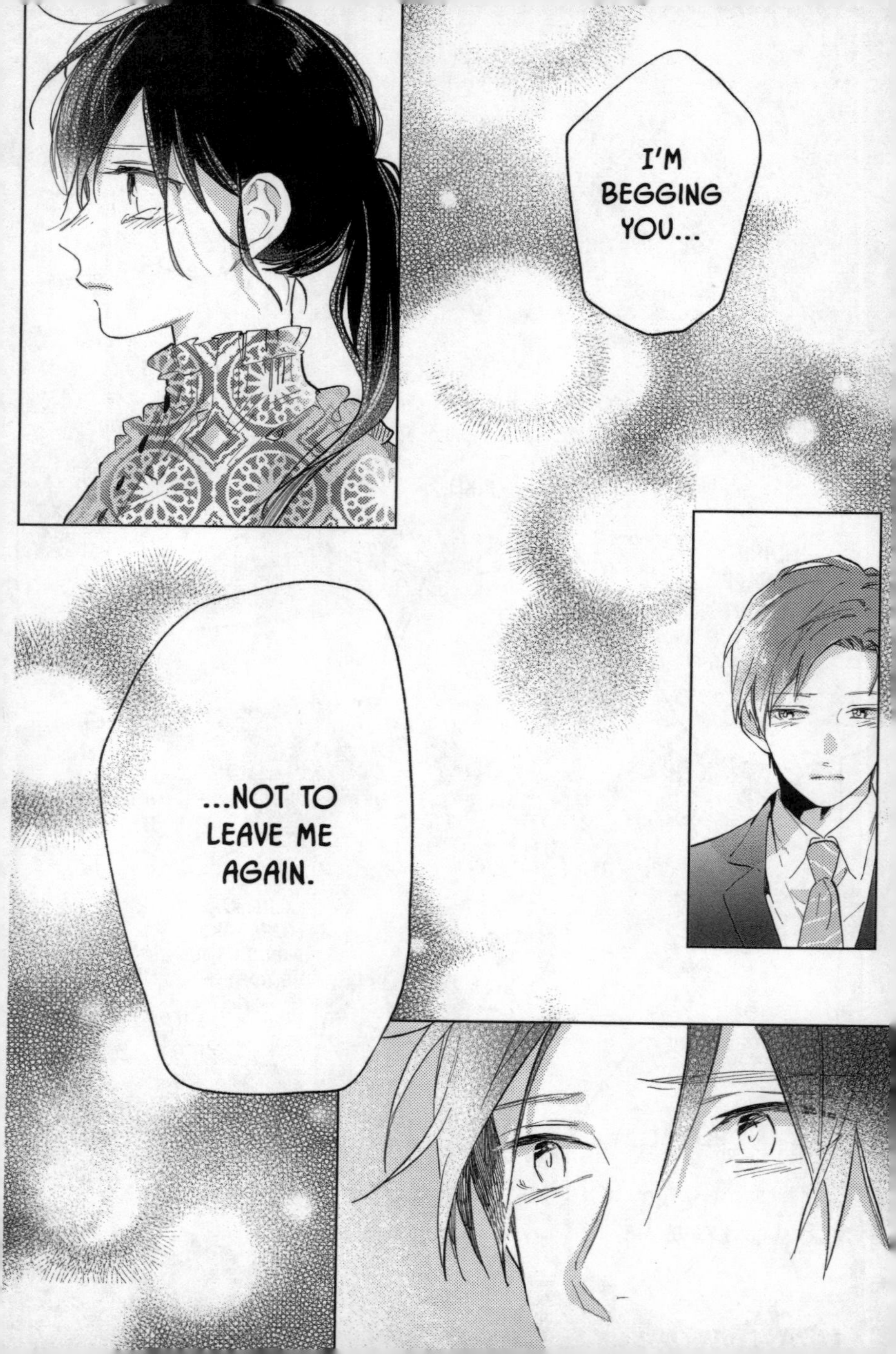
I'M BEGGING YOU...
...NOT TO LEAVE ME AGAIN.

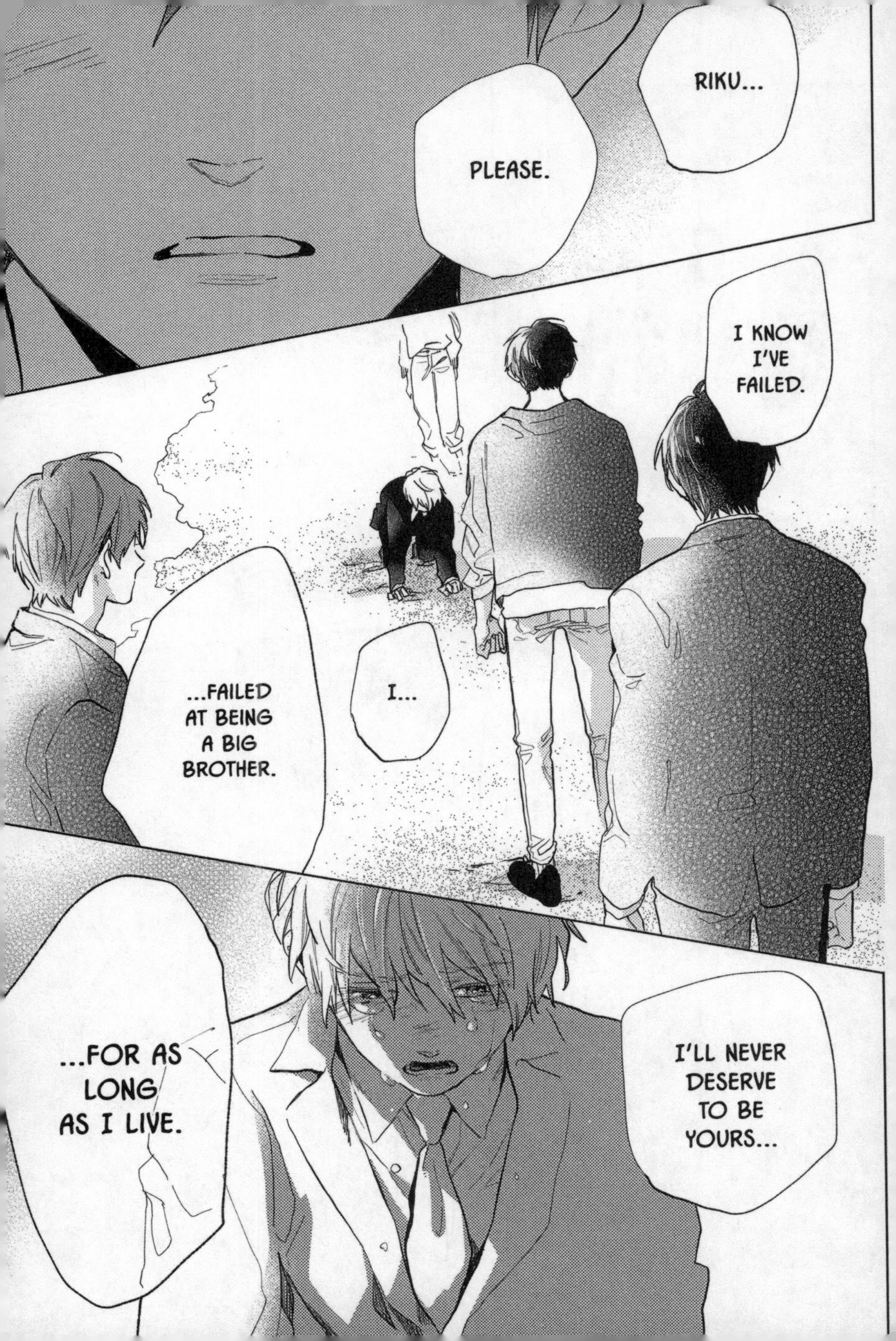
RIKU...
PLEASE.
I KNOW I'VE FAILED.
I...
...FAILED AT BEING A BIG BROTHER.
I'LL NEVER DESERVE TO BE YOURS...
...FOR AS LONG AS I LIVE.

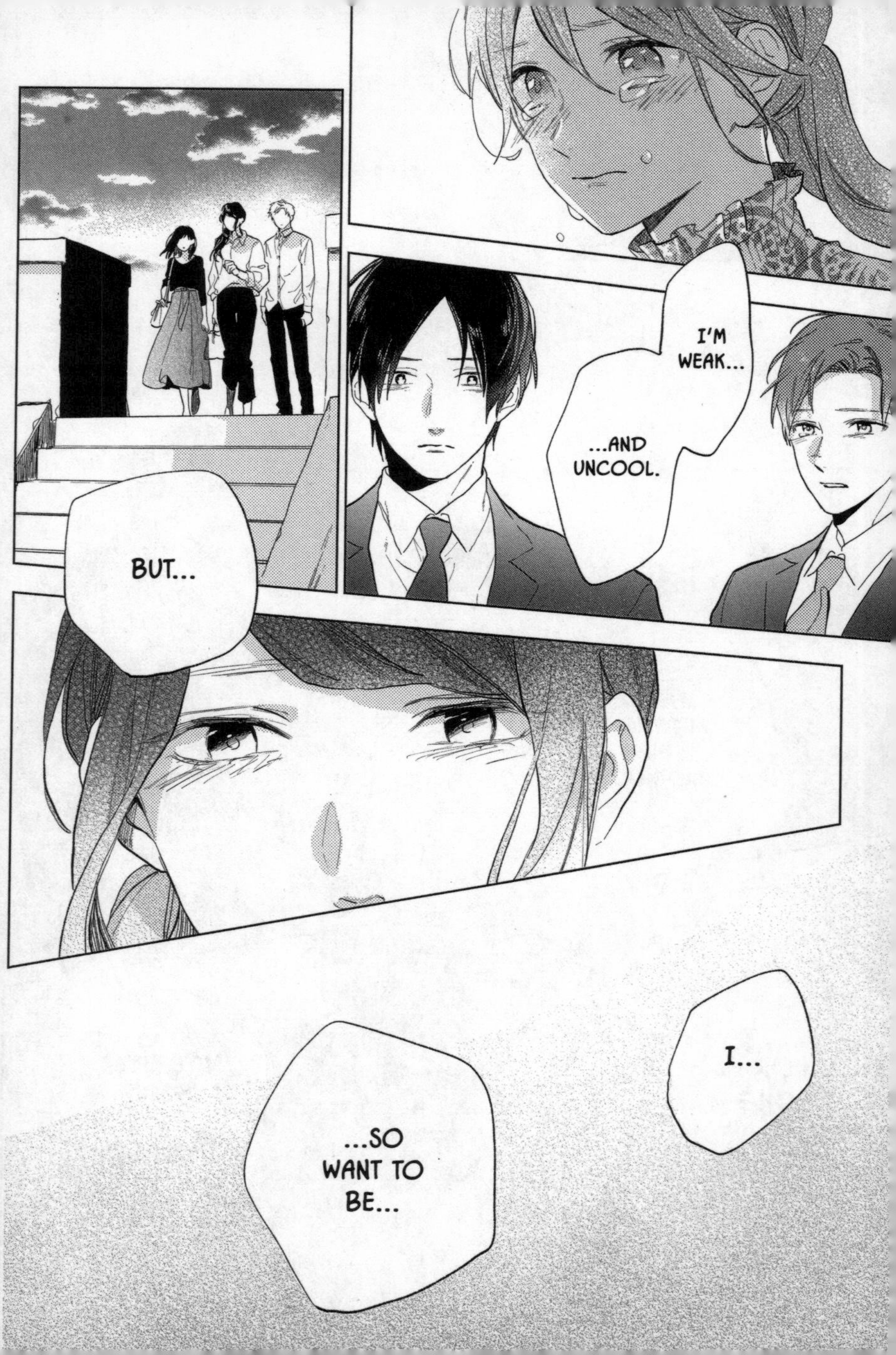
I'M WEAK...
...AND UNCOOL.
BUT...
I...
...SO WANT TO BE...

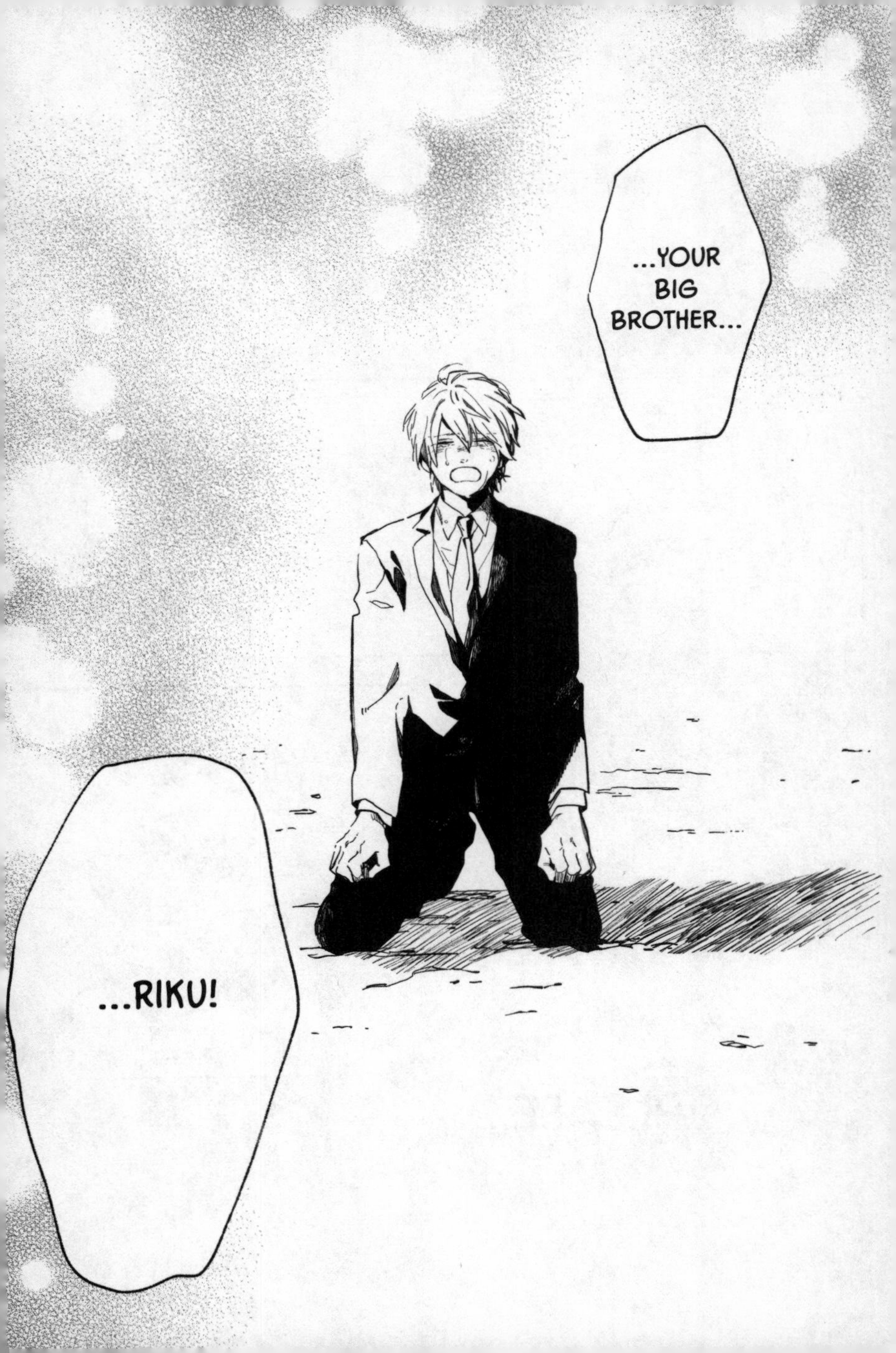
...YOUR BIG BROTHER...
...RIKU!

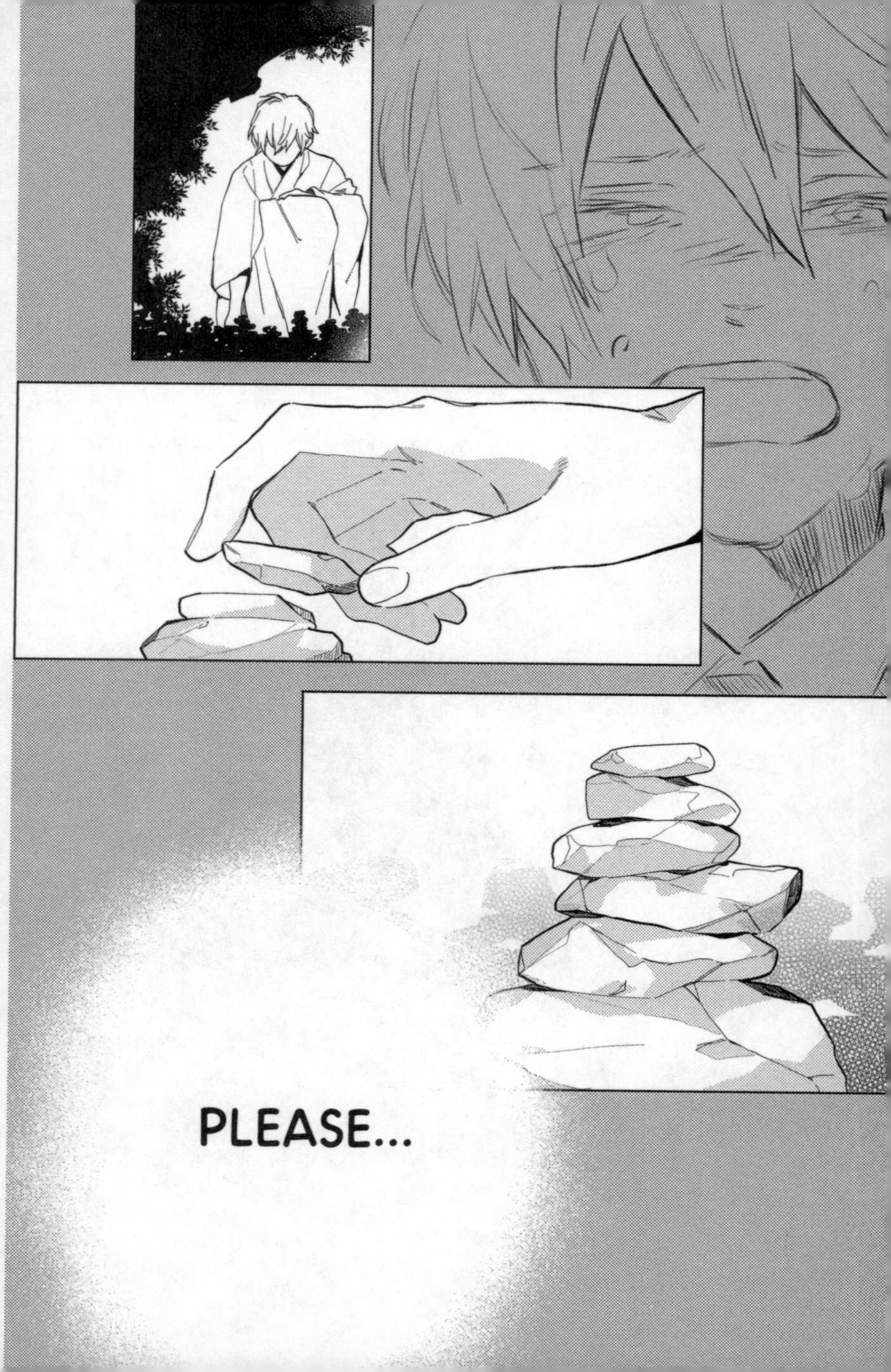
PLEASE...

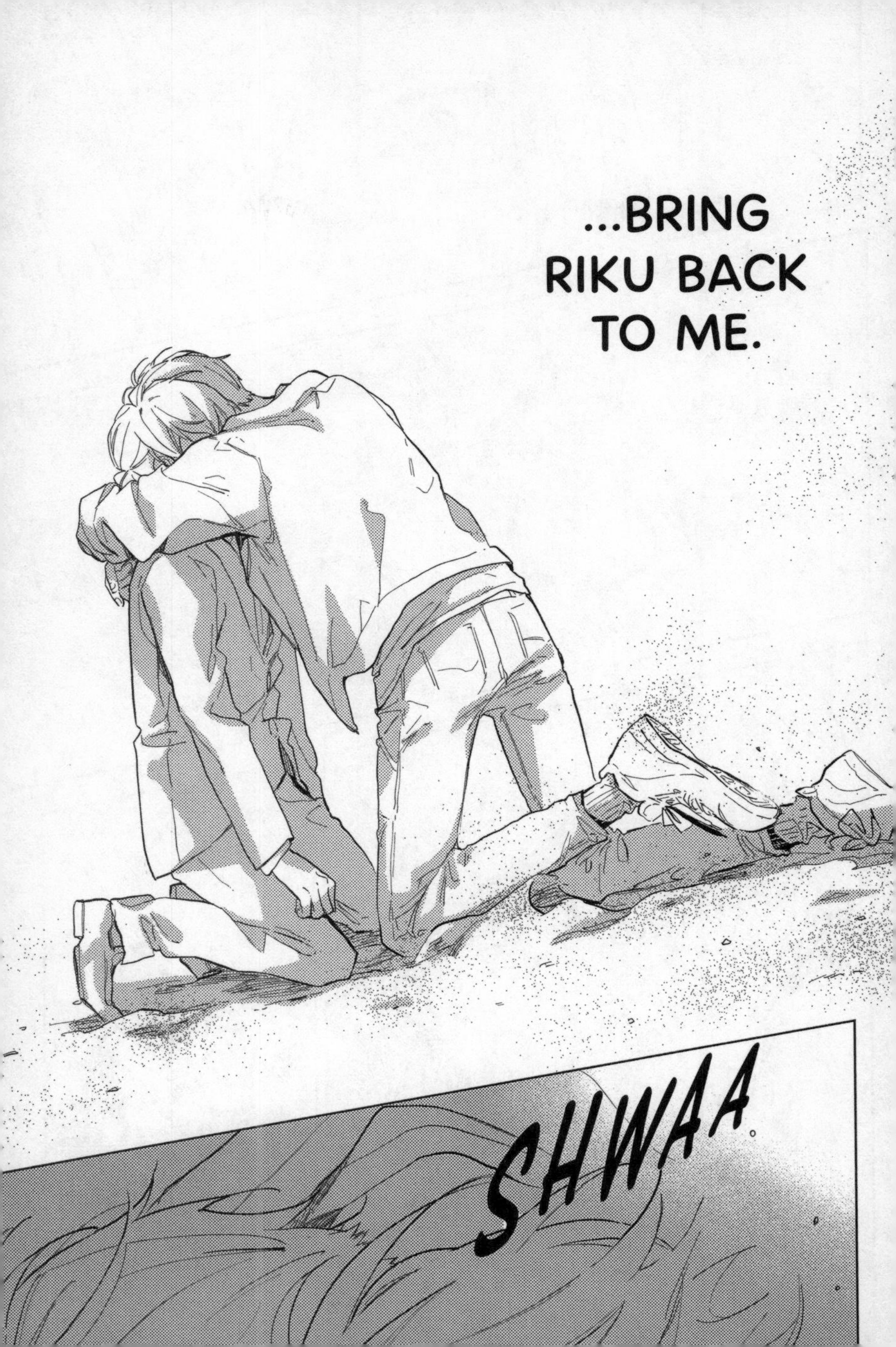
...BRING RIKU BACK TO ME.
SHWAA

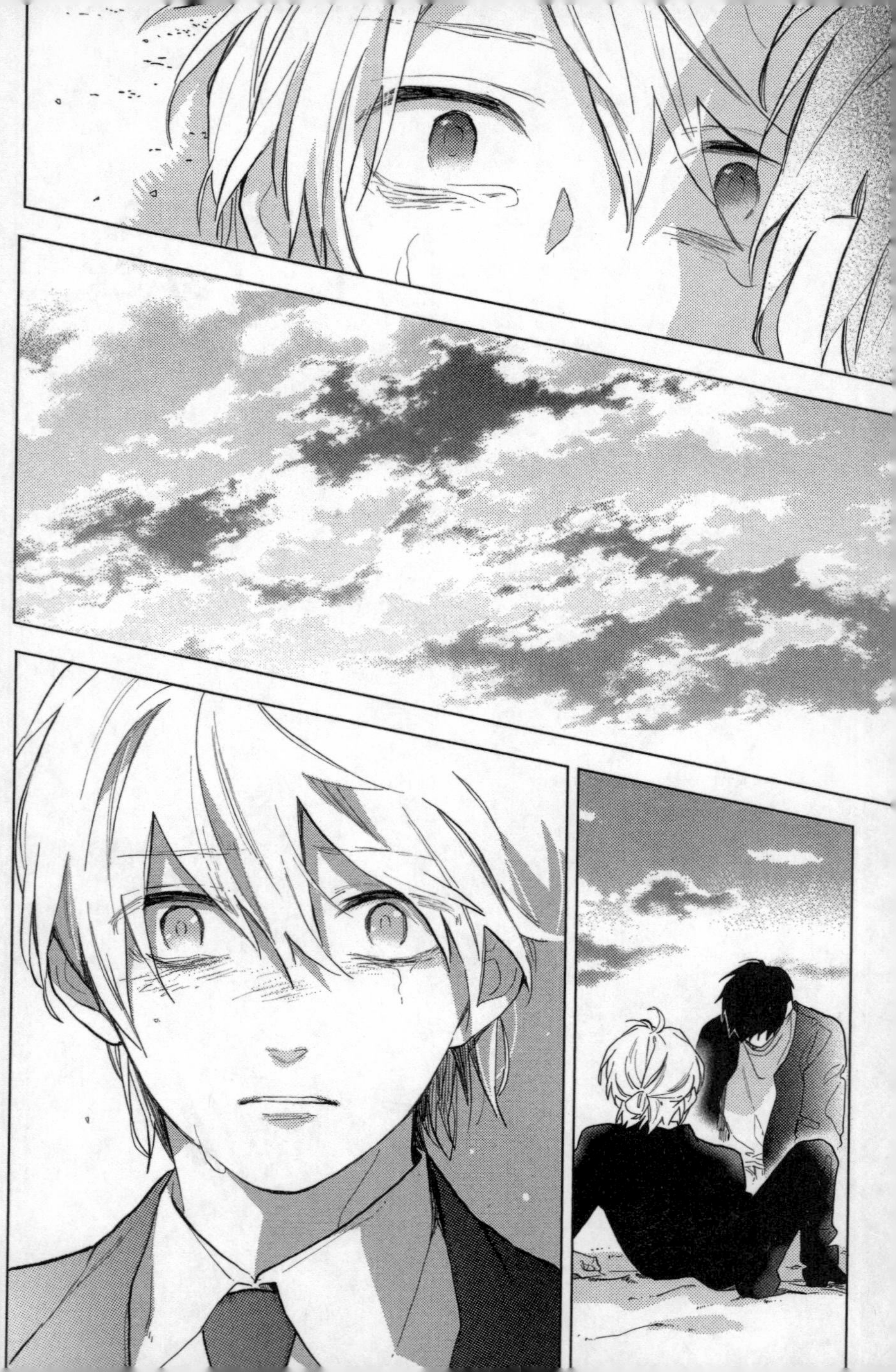

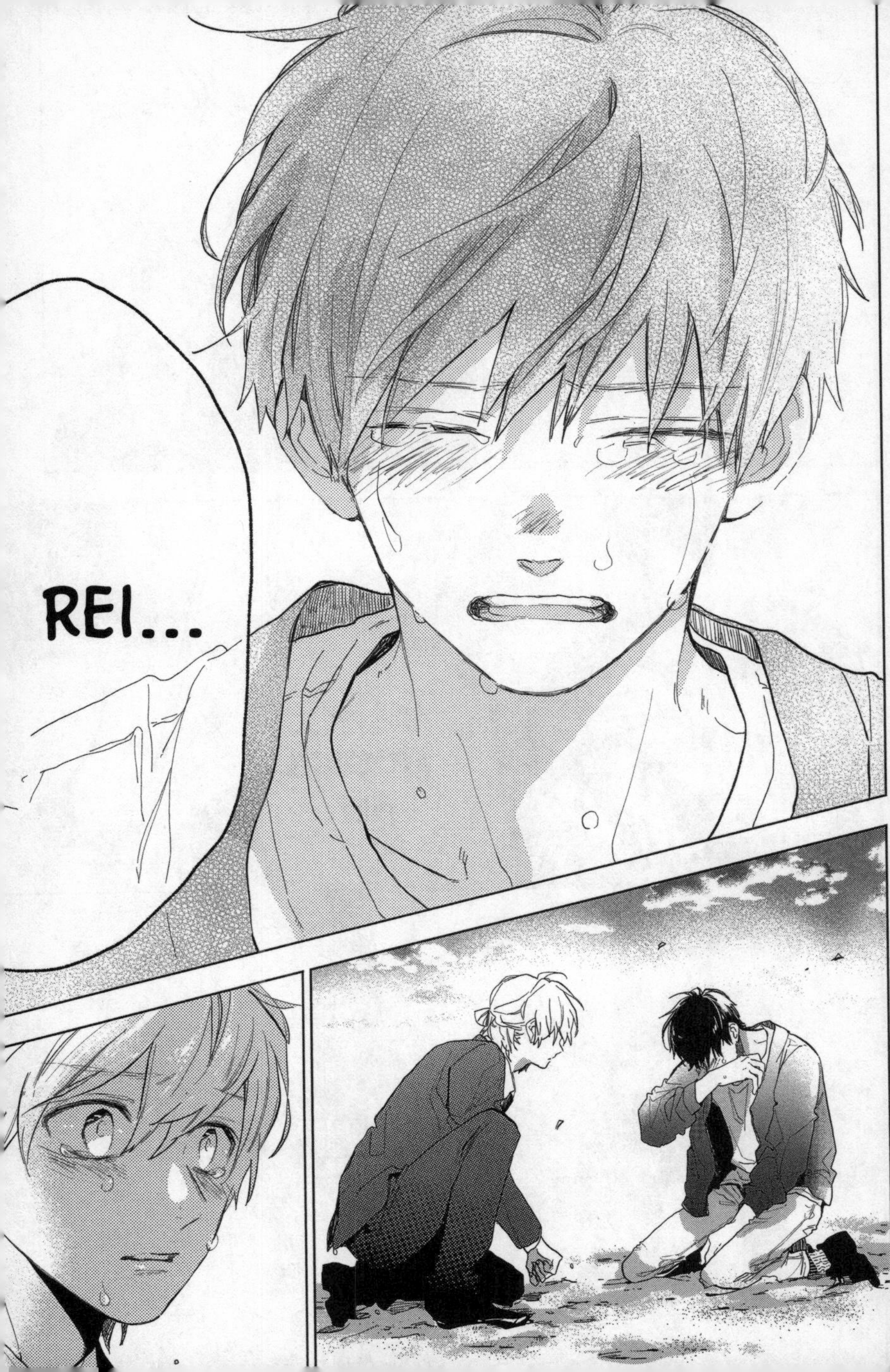
REI...

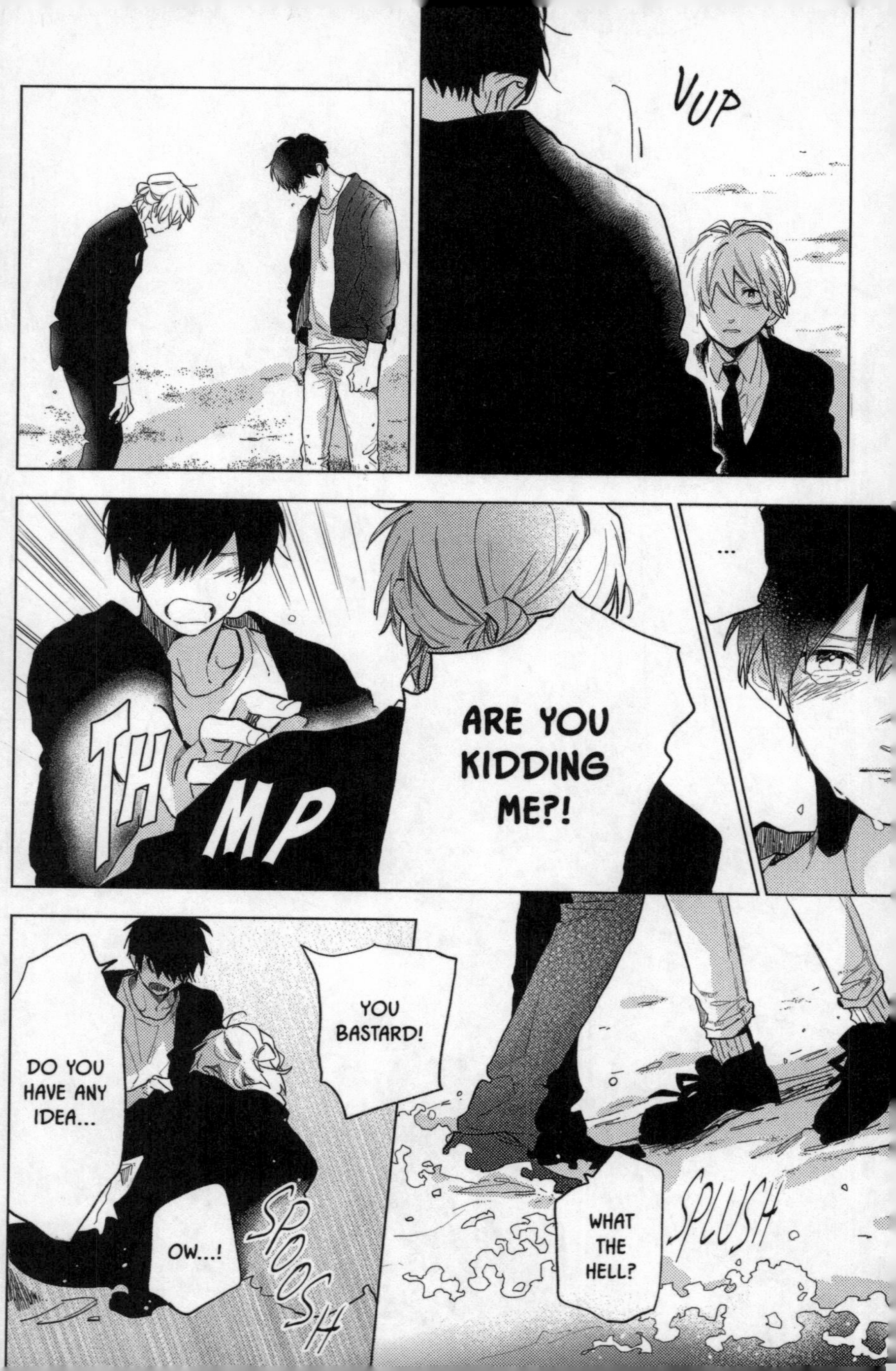
VUP
...
ARE YOU KIDDING ME?!
THMP
SPLUSH
WHAT THE HELL?
YOU BASTARD!
DO YOU HAVE ANY IDEA...
OW...!
SPOOSH

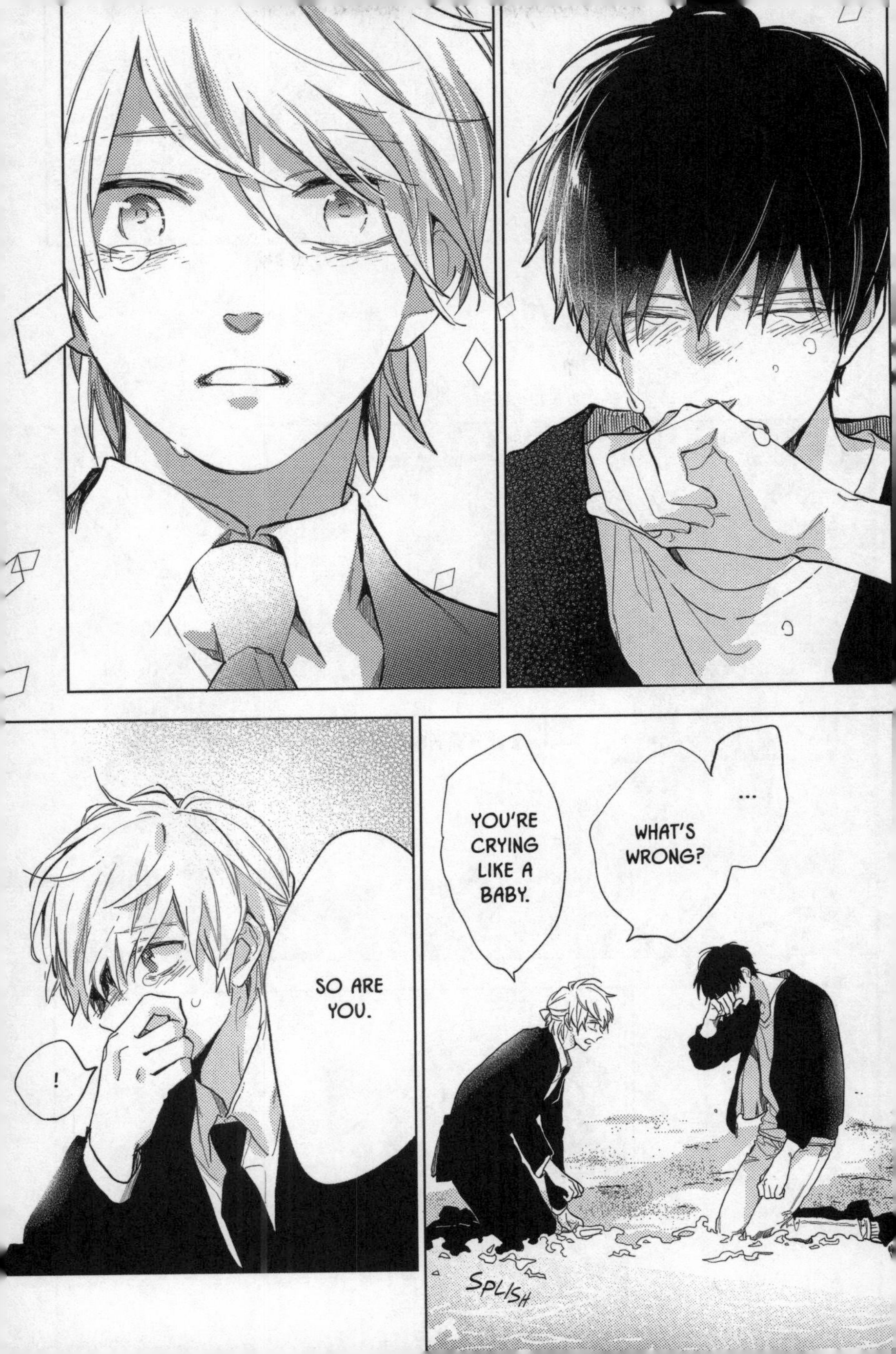
...
WHAT'S WRONG?
YOU'RE CRYING LIKE A BABY.
SPLISH
SO ARE YOU.
!

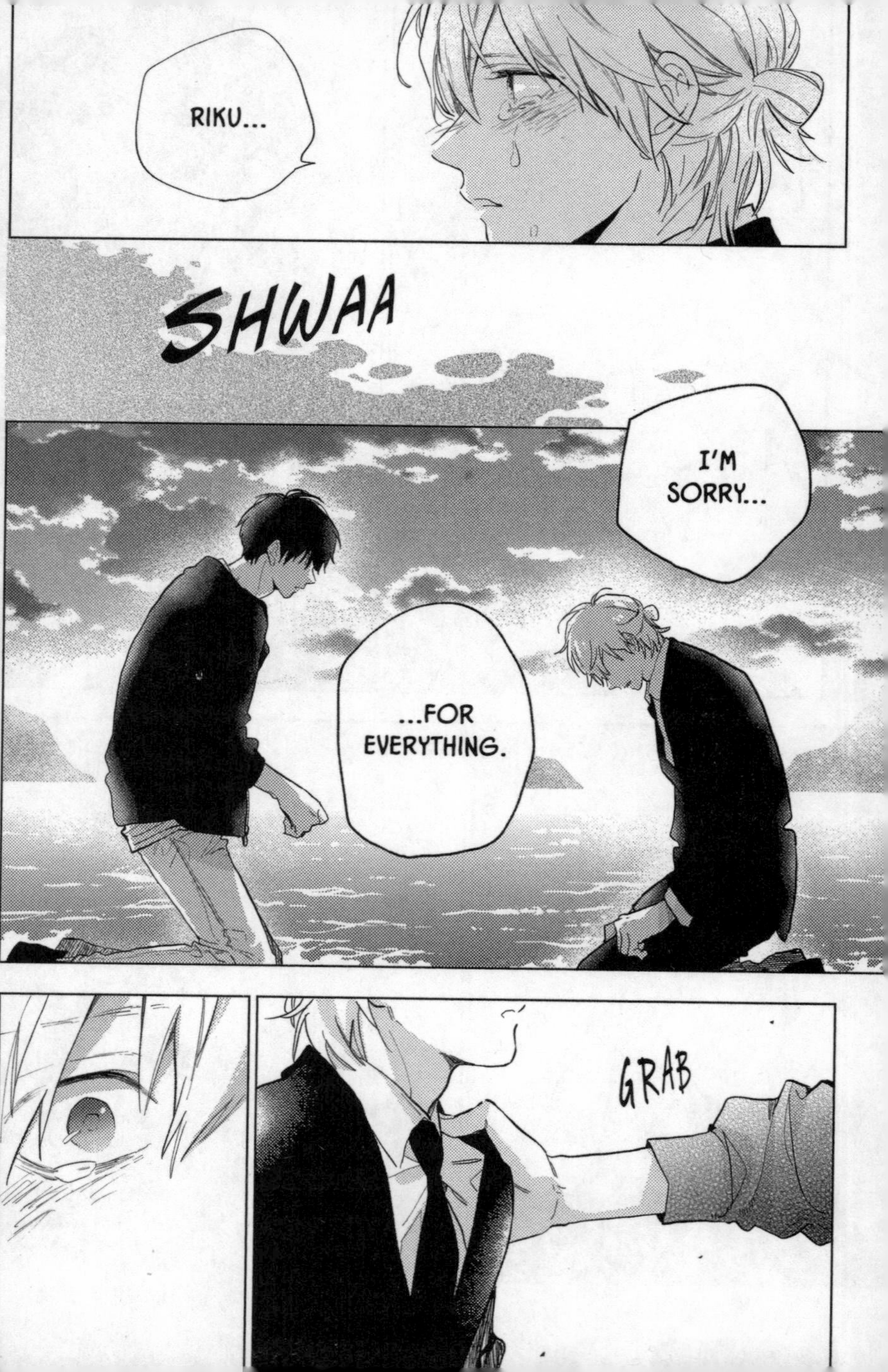
RIKU...
SHWAA
I'M SORRY...
...FOR EVERYTHING.
GRAB

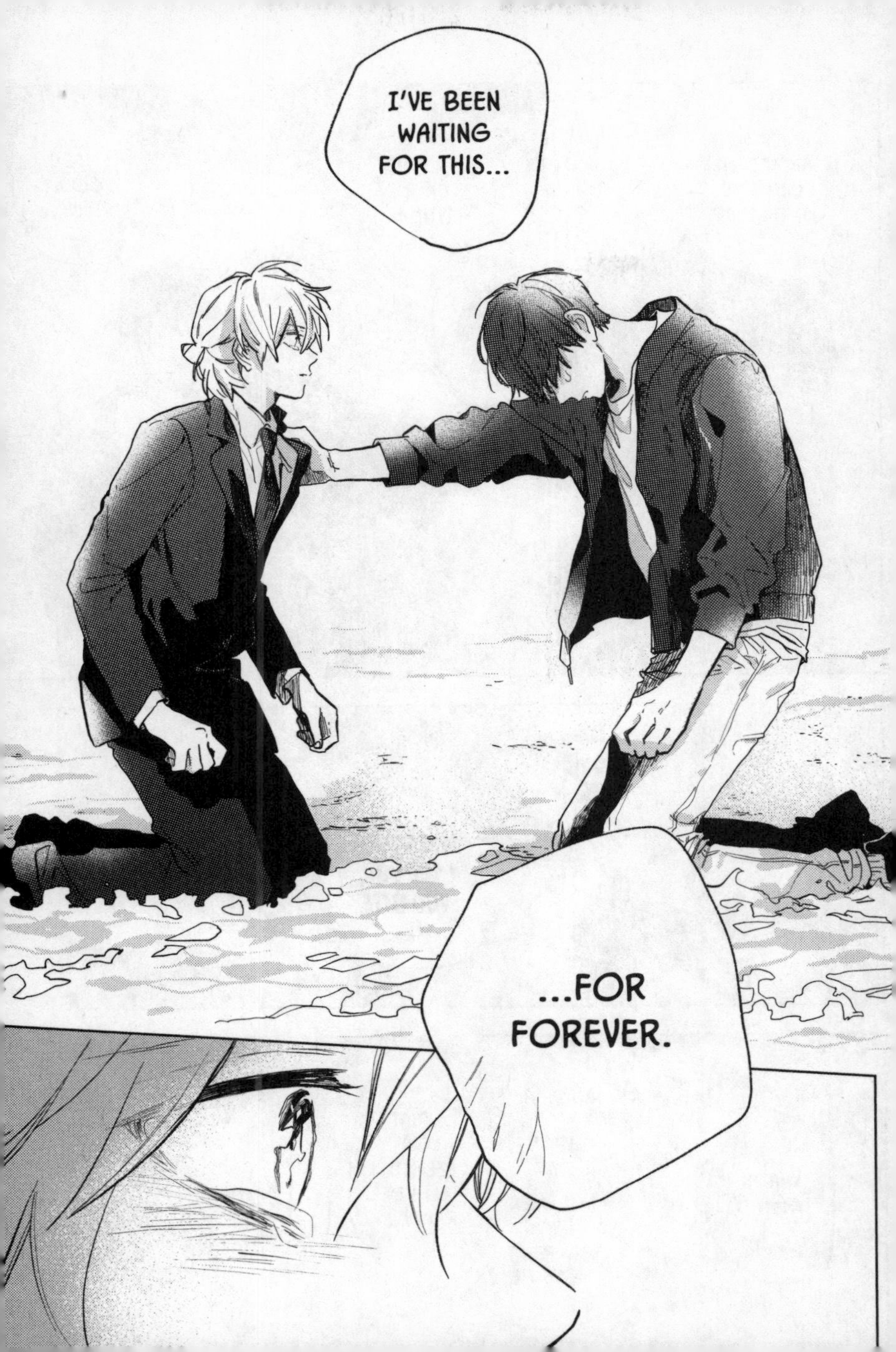
I'VE BEEN WAITING FOR THIS...
...FOR FOREVER.

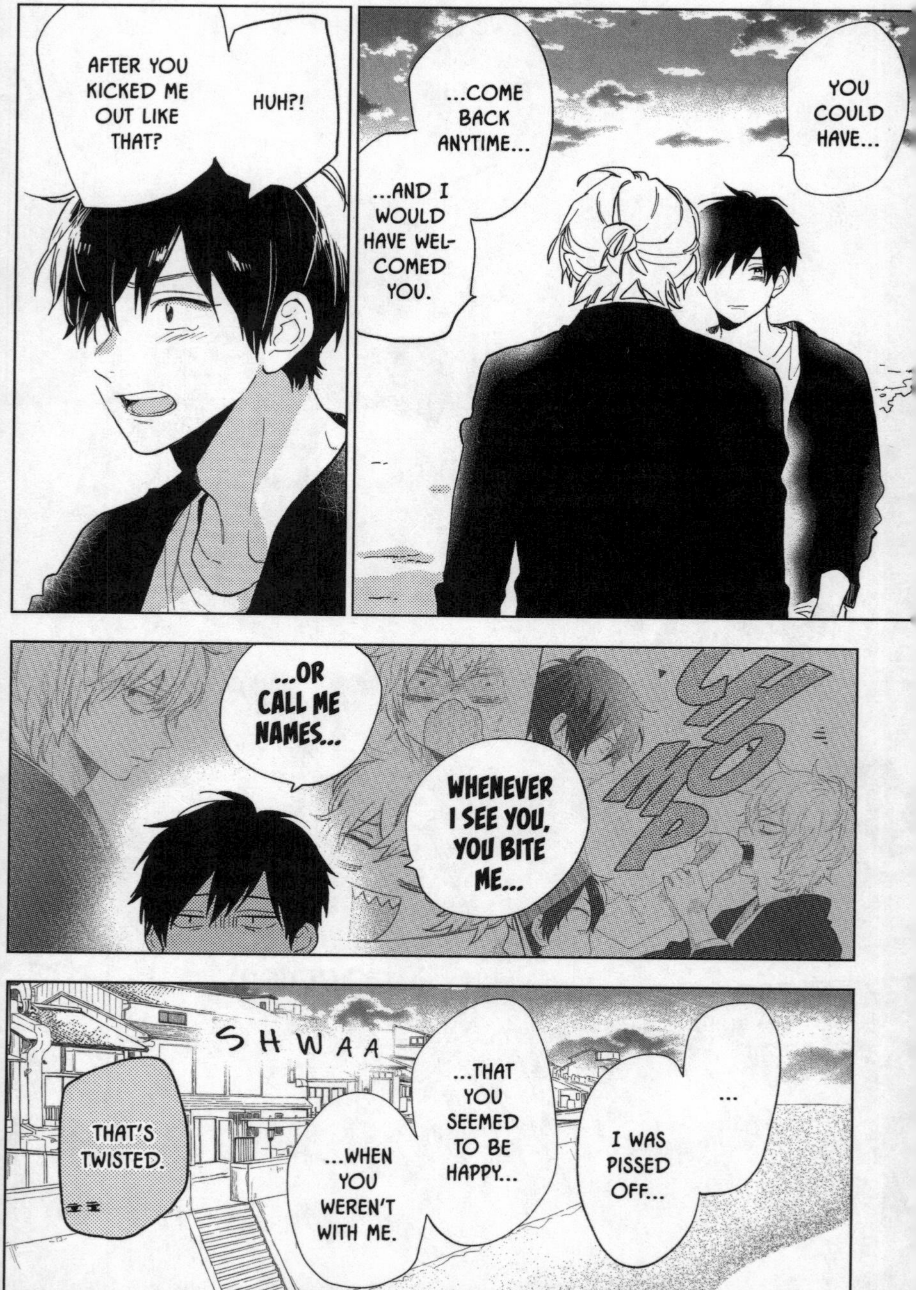
YOU COULD HAVE...
...COME BACK ANYTIME...
...AND I WOULD HAVE WEL-COMED YOU.
HUH?!
AFTER YOU KICKED ME OUT LIKE THAT?
CHOMP
WHENEVER I SEE YOU, YOU BITE ME...
...OR CALL ME NAMES...
...
I WAS PISSED OFF...
...THAT YOU SEEMED TO BE HAPPY...
...WHEN YOU WEREN'T WITH ME.
SHWAA
THAT'S TWISTED.

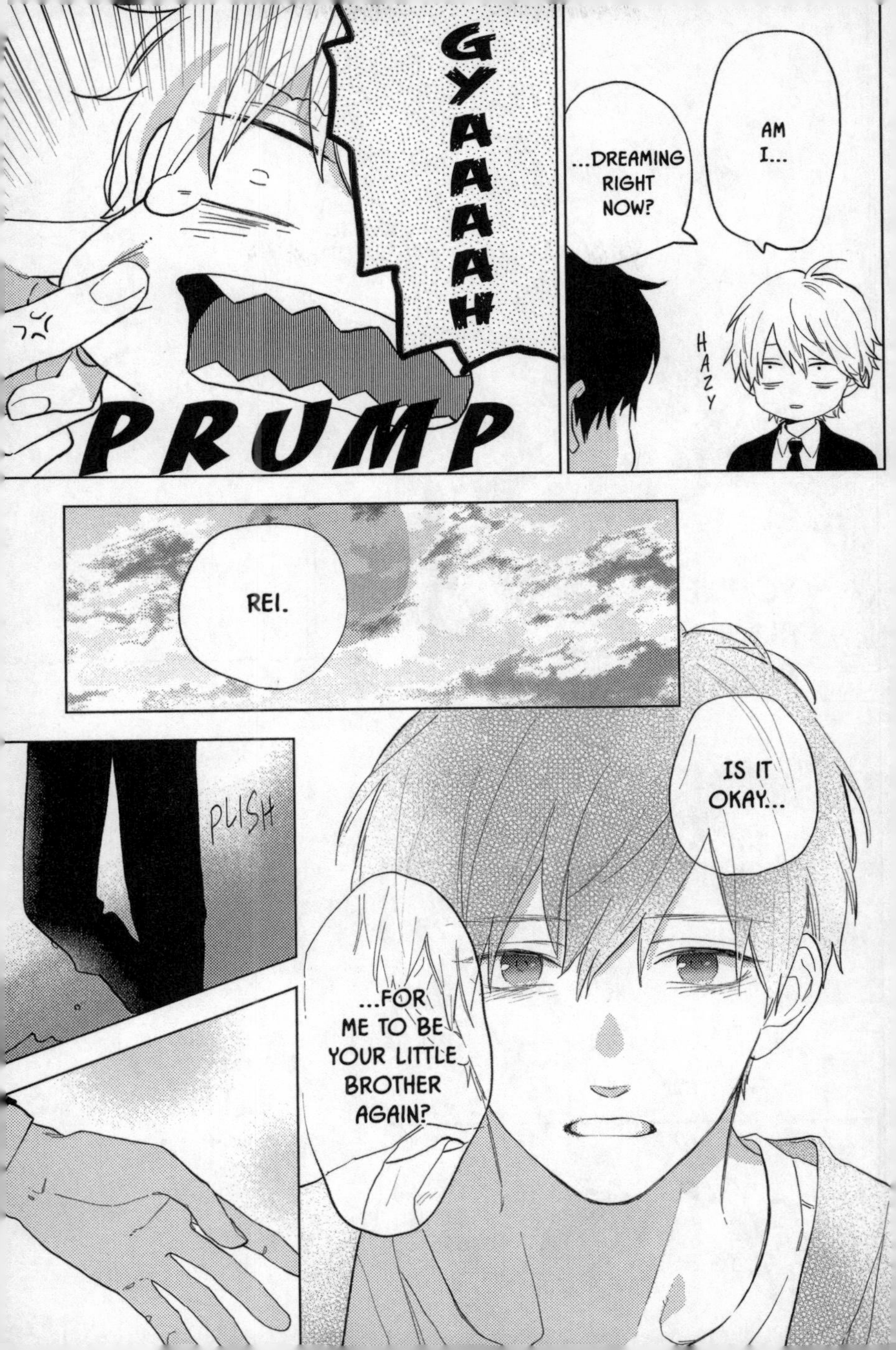
AM I...
...DREAMING RIGHT NOW?
HAZY
GYAAAAH
PRUMP
REI.
IS IT OKAY...
...FOR ME TO BE YOUR LITTLE BROTHER AGAIN?
PLISH

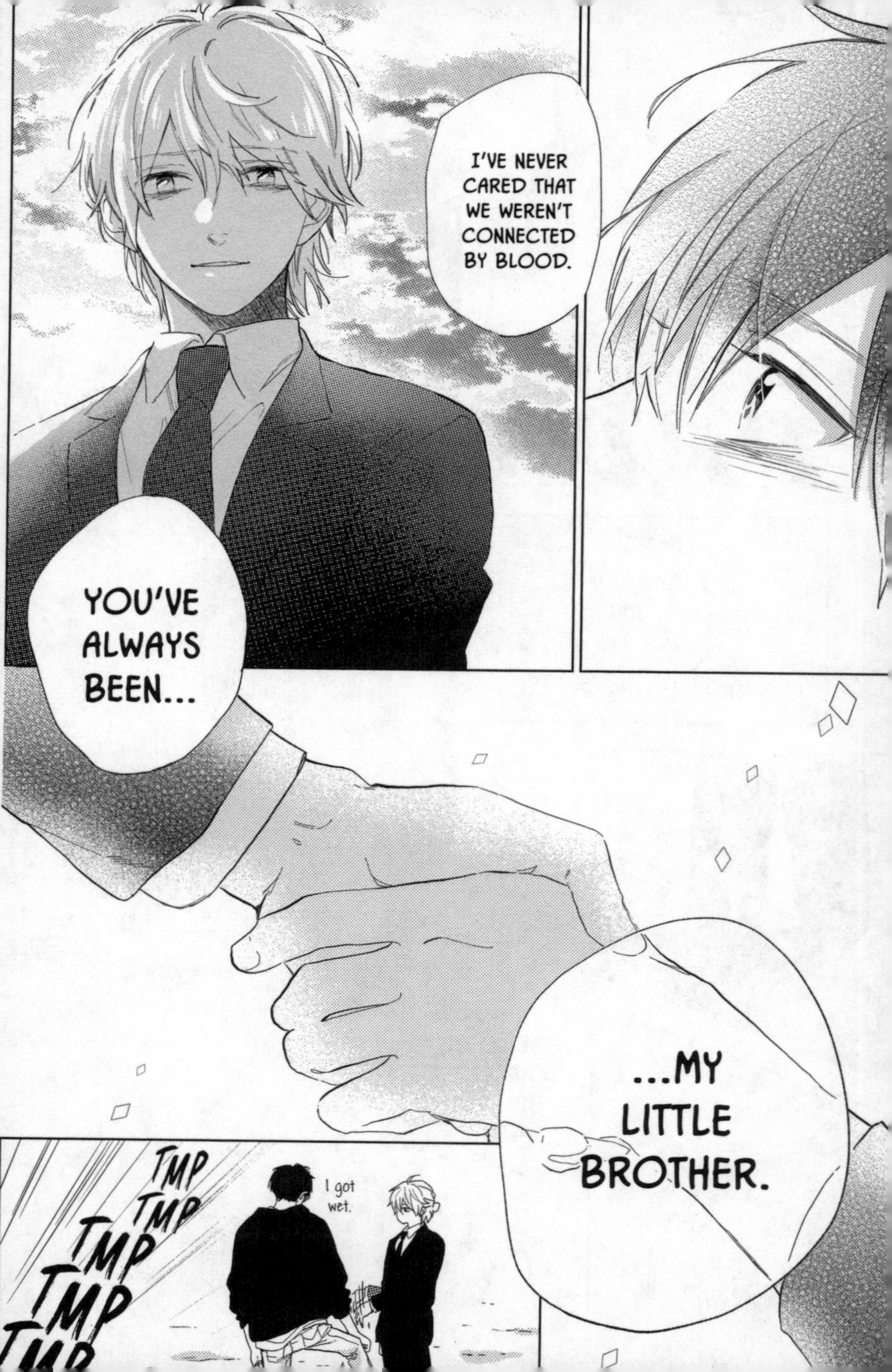
I'VE NEVER CARED THAT WE WEREN'T CONNECTED BY BLOOD.
YOU'VE ALWAYS BEEN...
...MY LITTLE BROTHER.
I got wet.
TMP TMP TMP TMP TMP TMP

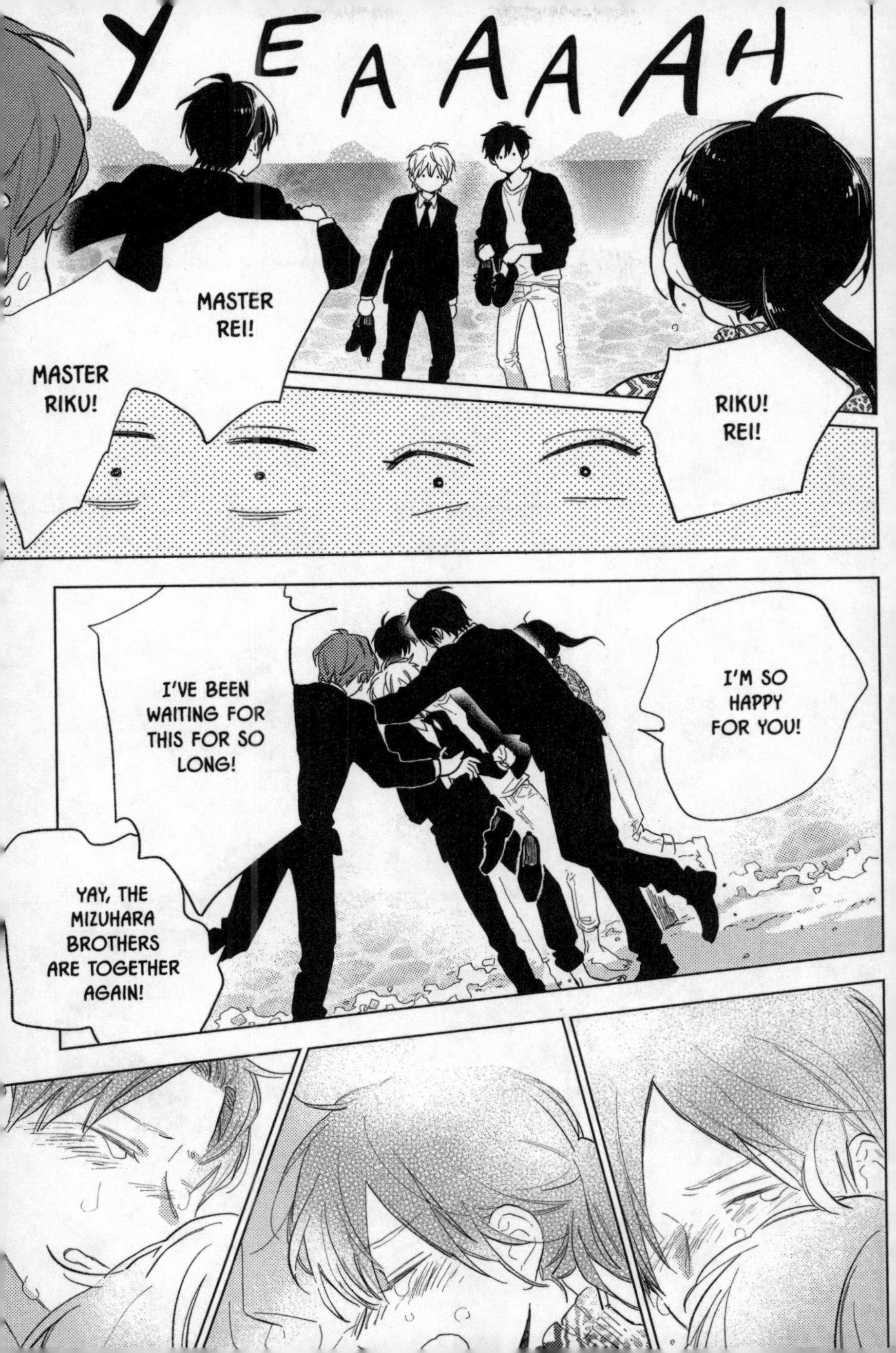
YEAAAAH
RIKU! REI!
MASTER REI!
MASTER RIKU!
I'M SO HAPPY FOR YOU!
I'VE BEEN WAITING FOR THIS FOR SO LONG!
YAY, THE MIZUHARA BROTHERS ARE TOGETHER AGAIN!

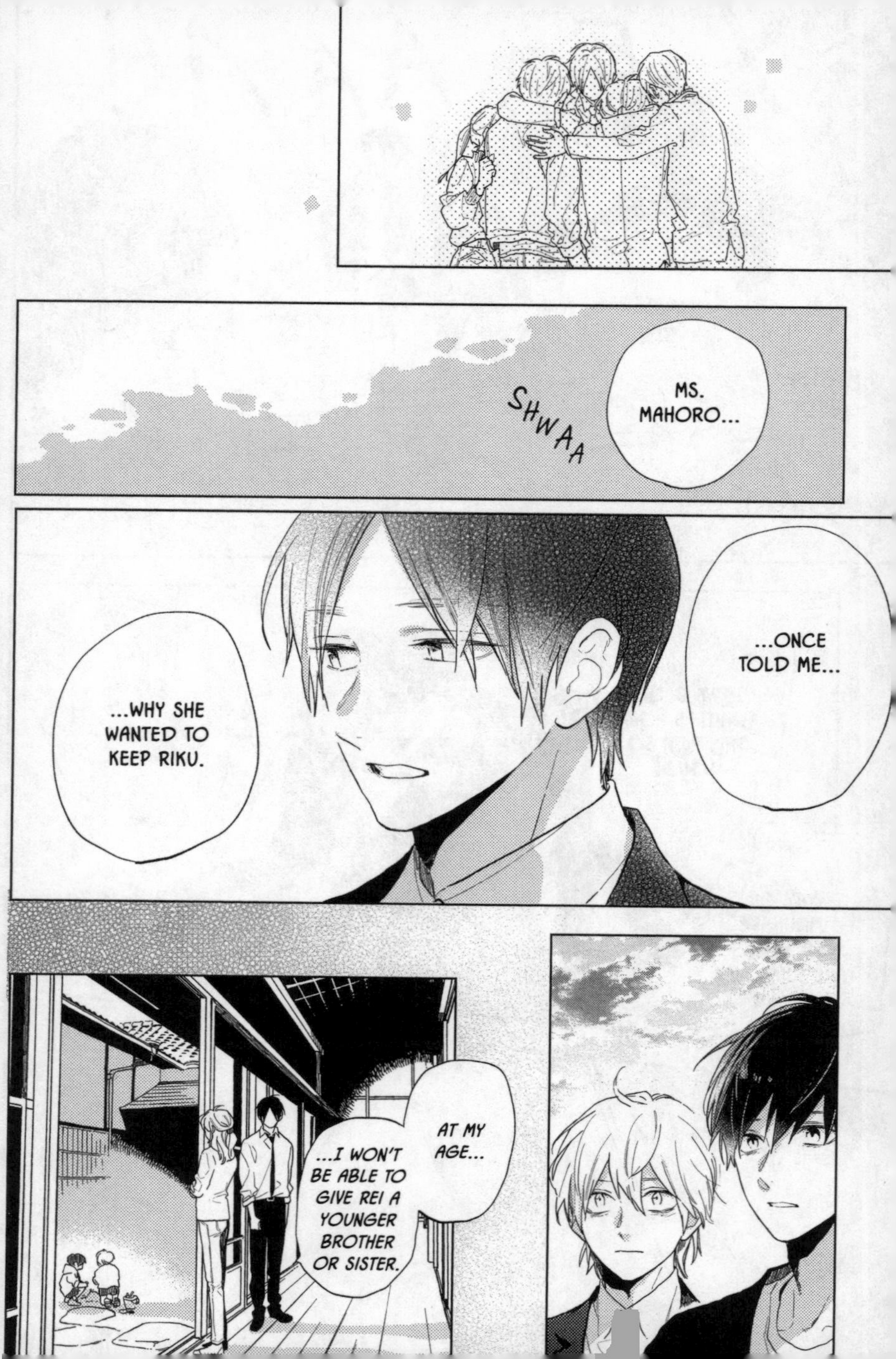
MS. MAHORO...
SHWAA
...ONCE TOLD ME...
...WHY SHE WANTED TO KEEP RIKU.
AT MY AGE...
...I WON'T BE ABLE TO GIVE REI A YOUNGER BROTHER OR SISTER.

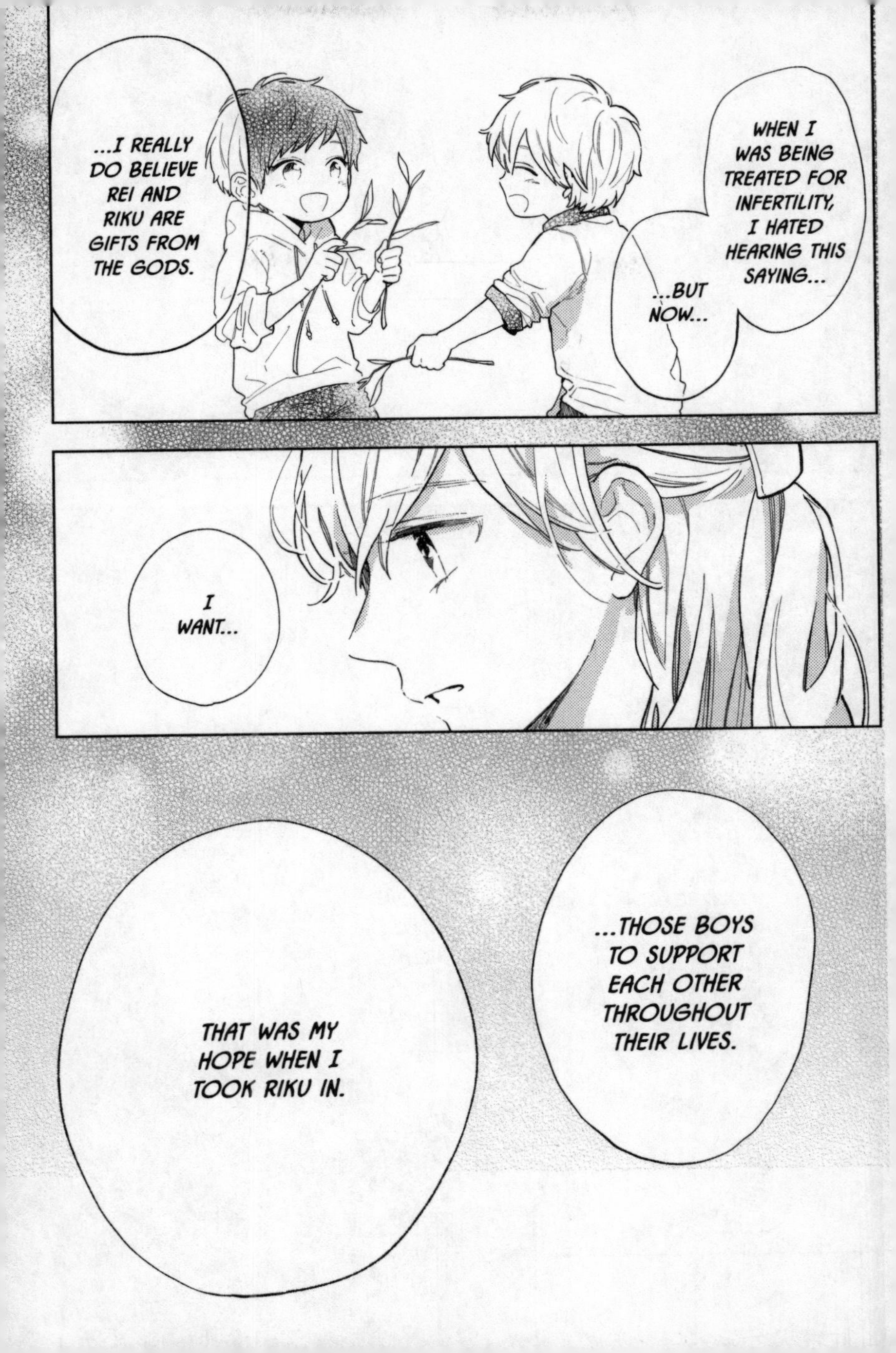
WHEN I WAS BEING TREATED FOR INFERTILITY, I HATED HEARING THIS SAYING...
...BUT NOW...
...I REALLY DO BELIEVE REI AND RIKU ARE GIFTS FROM THE GODS.
I WANT...
...THOSE BOYS TO SUPPORT EACH OTHER THROUGHOUT THEIR LIVES.
THAT WAS MY HOPE WHEN I TOOK RIKU IN.

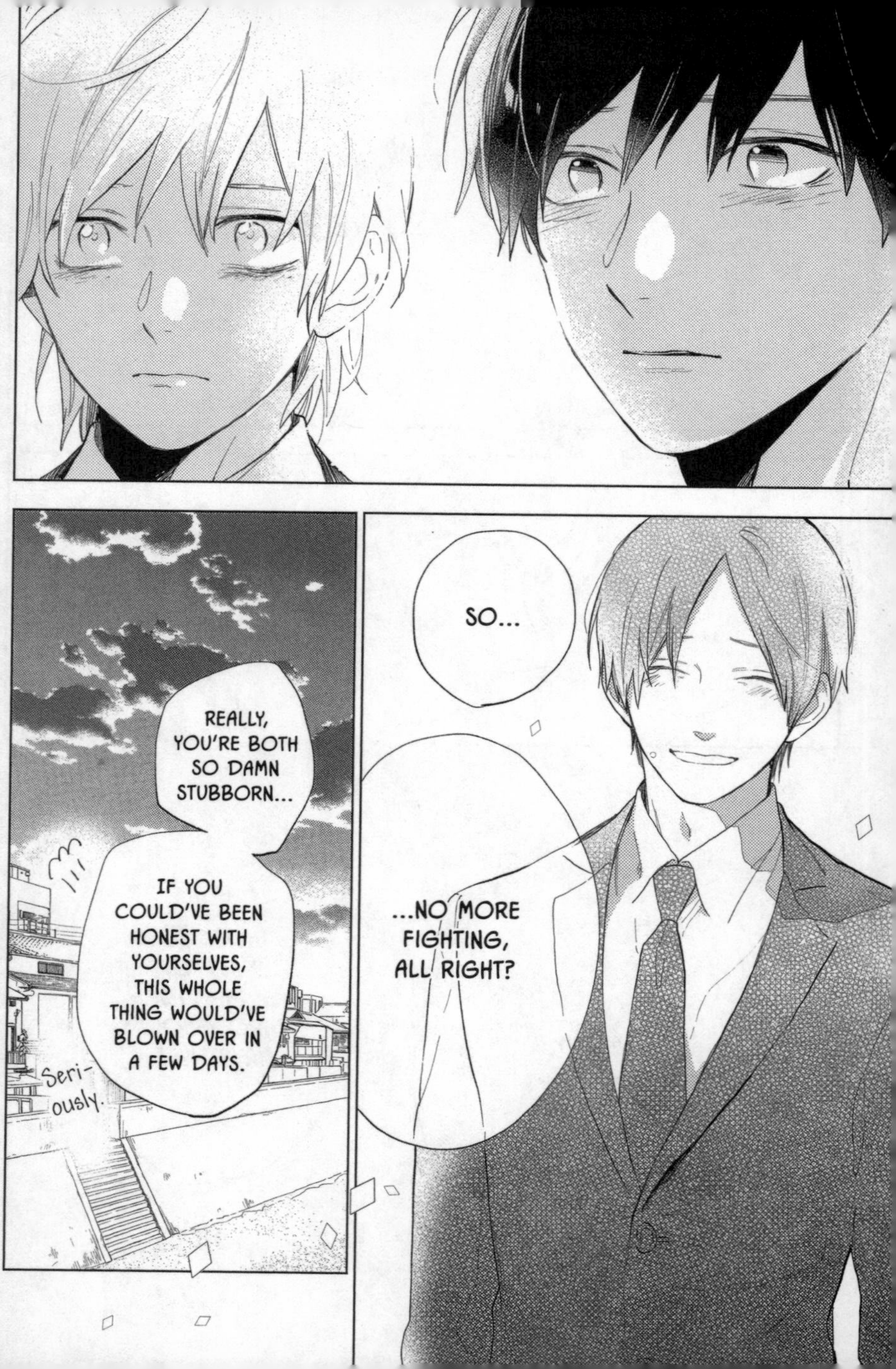
SO...
...NO MORE FIGHTING, ALL RIGHT?
REALLY, YOU'RE BOTH SO DAMN STUBBORN...
IF YOU COULD'VE BEEN HONEST WITH YOURSELVES, THIS WHOLE THING WOULD'VE BLOWN OVER IN A FEW DAYS.
Seri-ously.

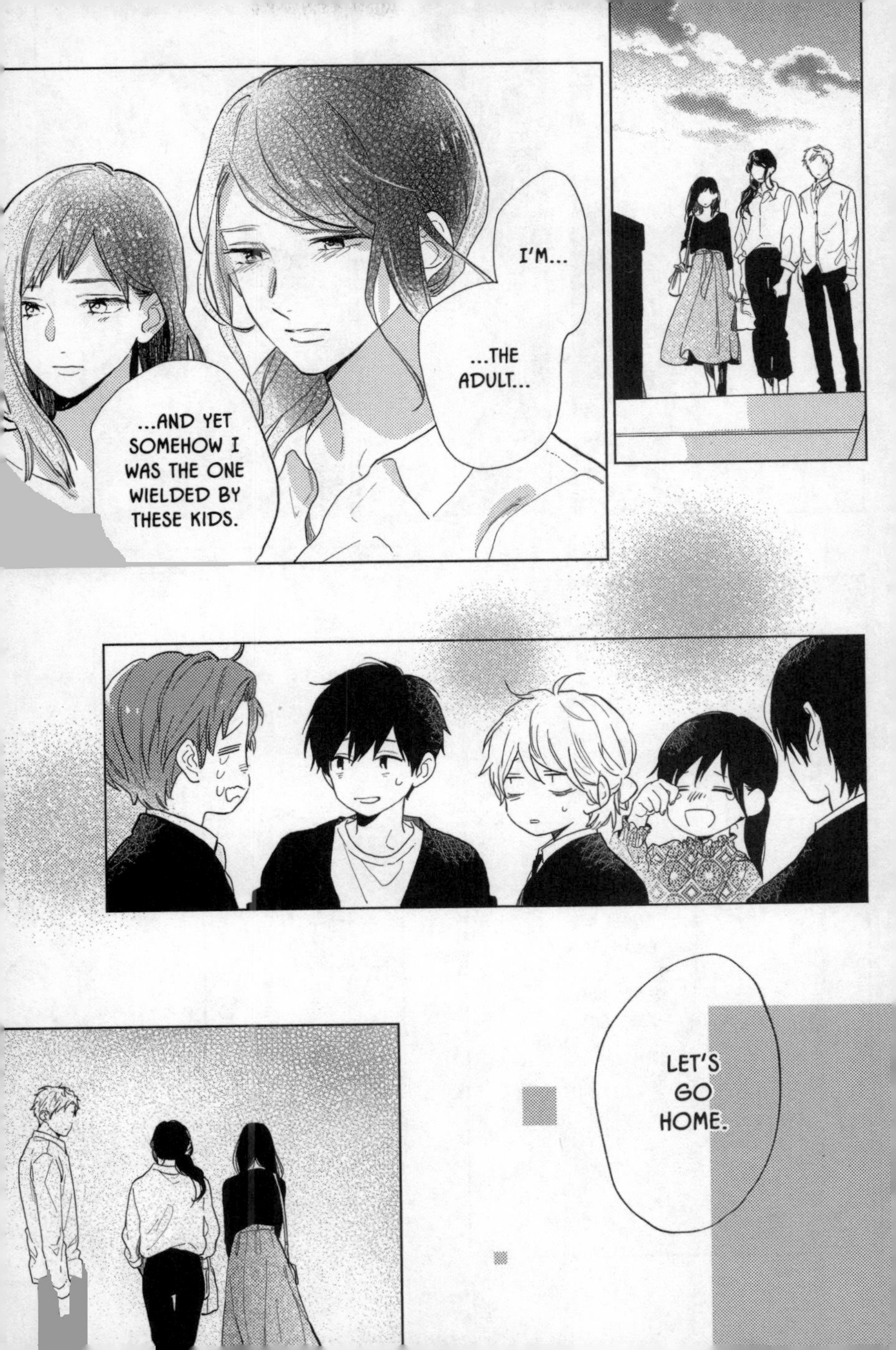
I'M...
...THE ADULT...
...AND YET SOMEHOW I WAS THE ONE WIELDED BY THESE KIDS.
LET'S GO HOME.

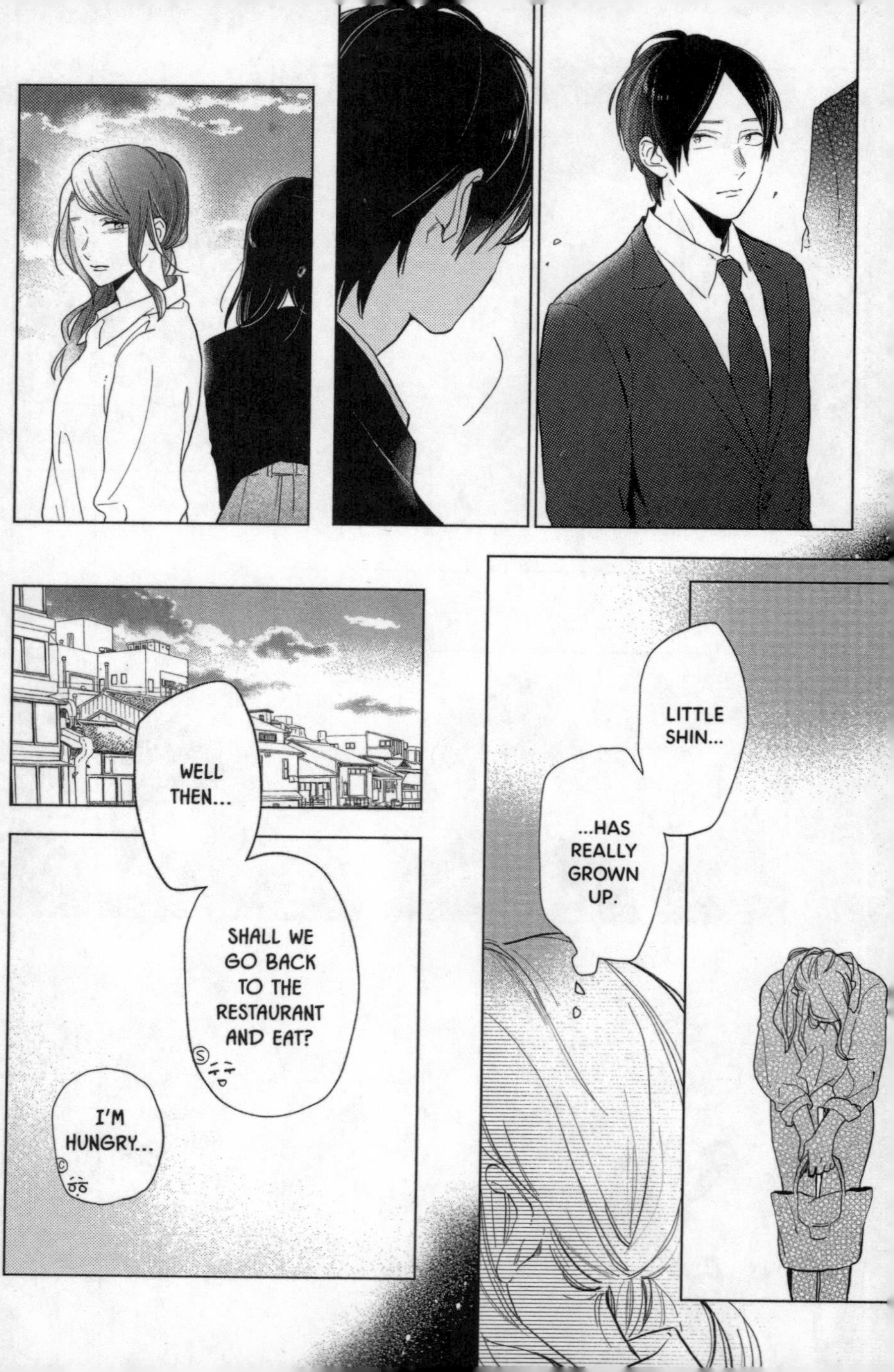
LITTLE SHIN...
...HAS REALLY GROWN UP.
WELL THEN...
SHALL WE GO BACK TO THE RESTAURANT AND EAT?
I'M HUNGRY...

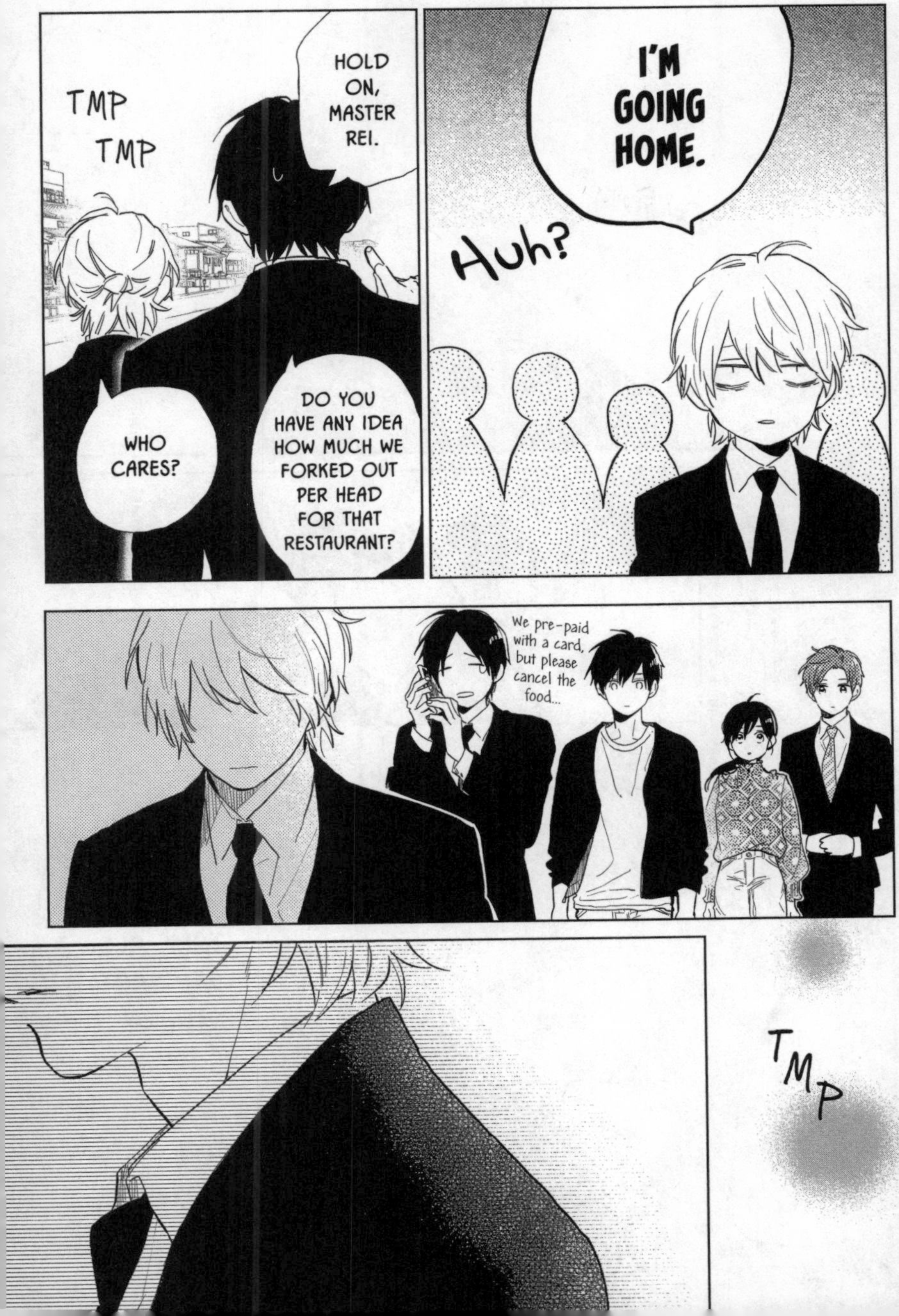
I'M GOING HOME.
Huh?
HOLD ON, MASTER REI.
TMP TMP
DO YOU HAVE ANY IDEA HOW MUCH WE FORKED OUT PER HEAD FOR THAT RESTAURANT?
WHO CARES?
We pre-paid with a card, but please cancel the food...
TMP

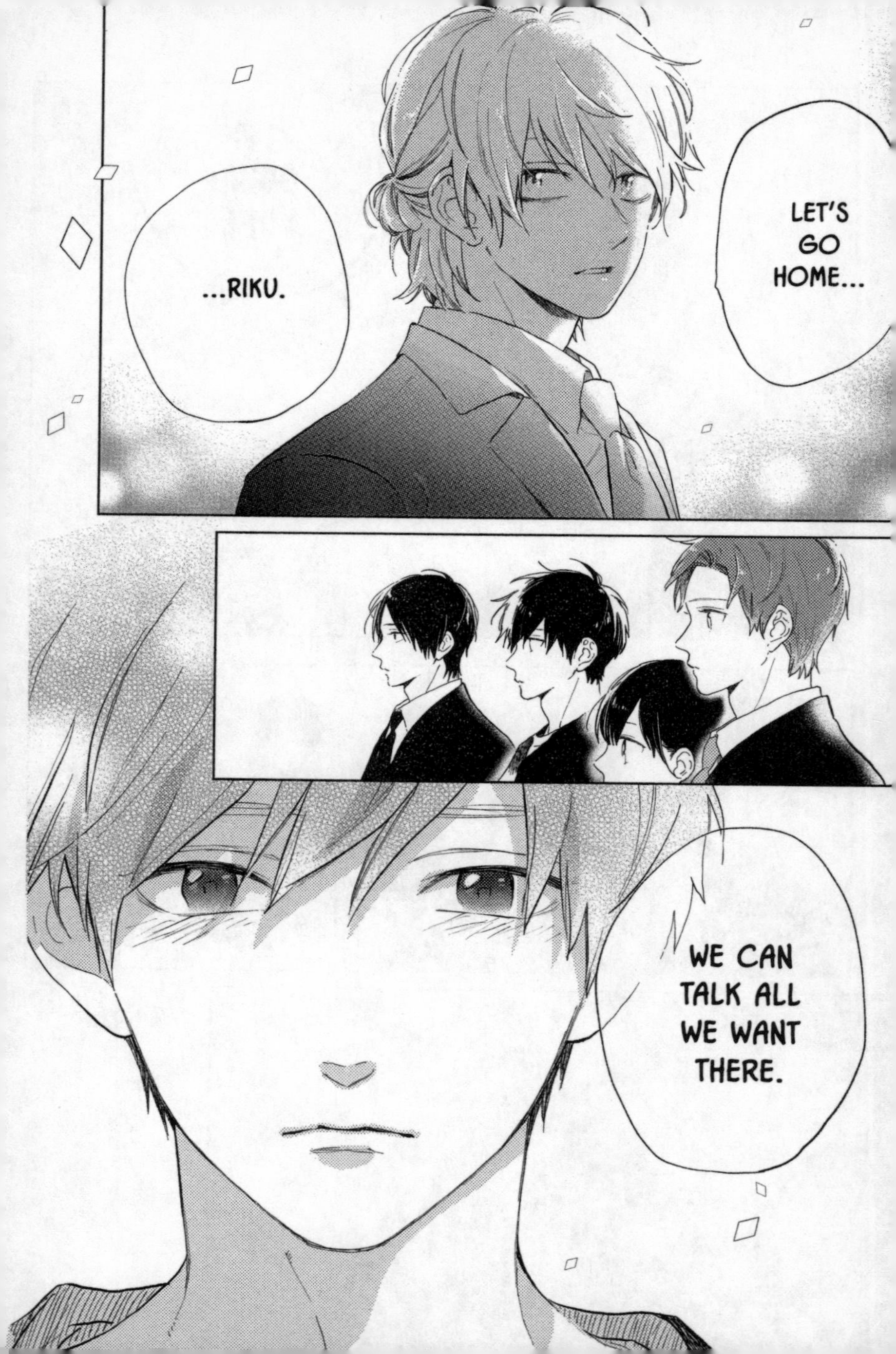
LET'S GO HOME...
...RIKU.
WE CAN TALK ALL WE WANT THERE.

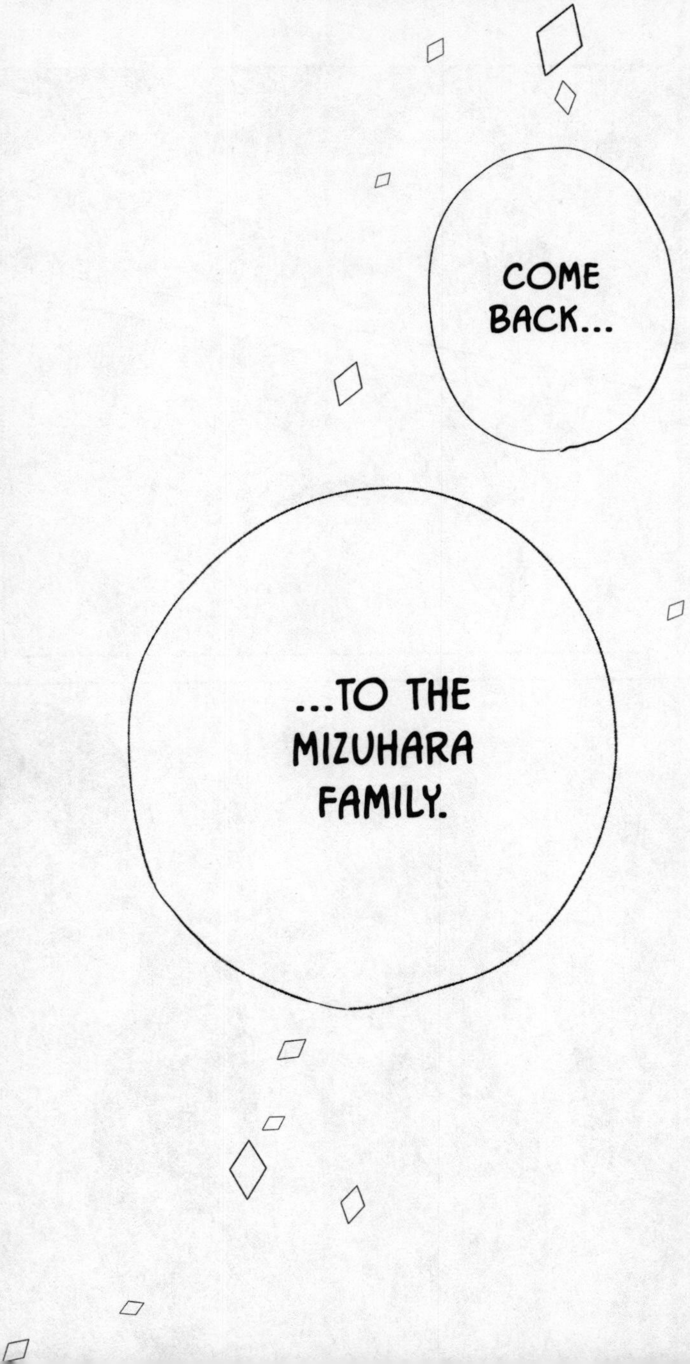
COME BACK...
...TO THE MIZUHARA FAMILY.

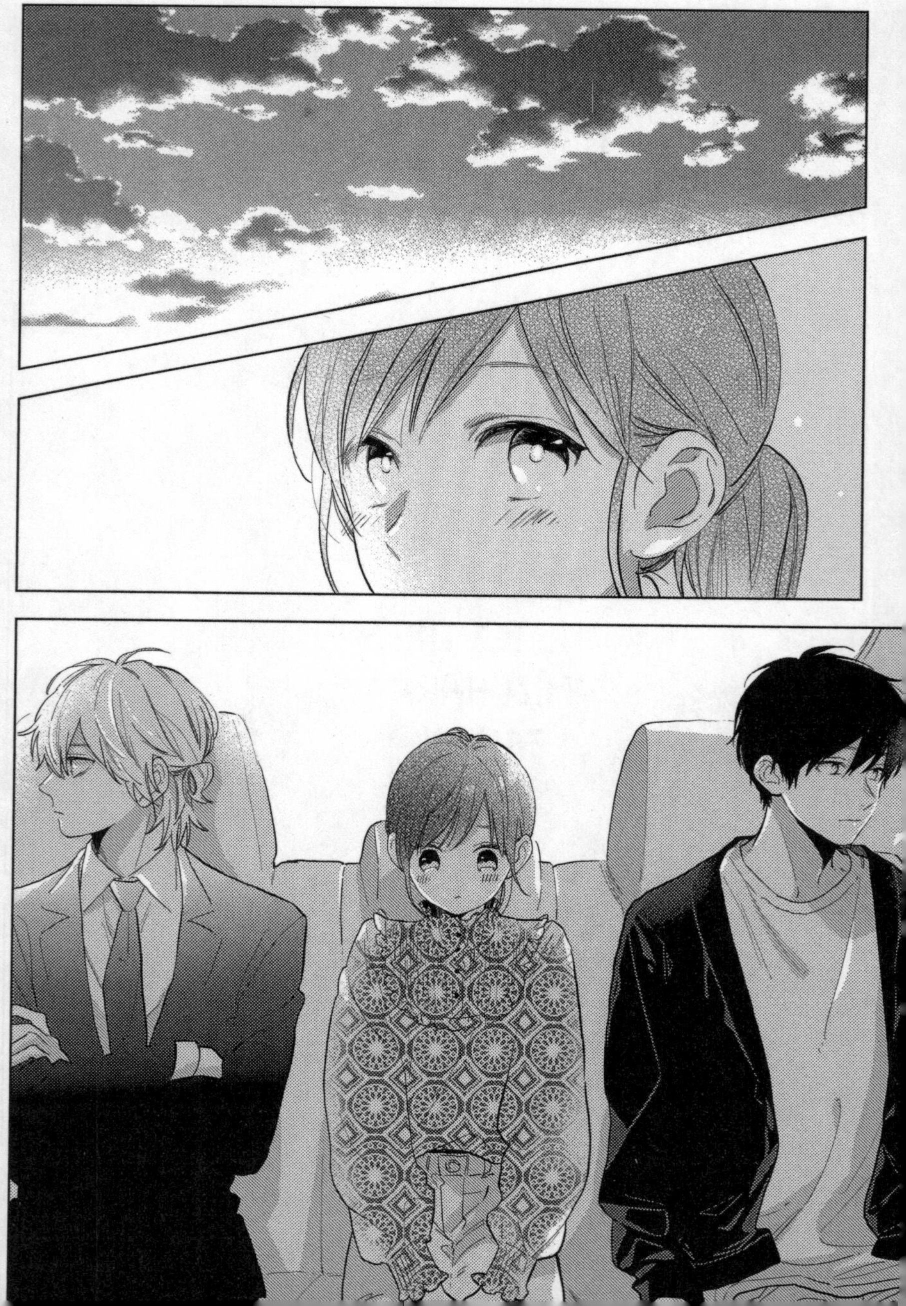

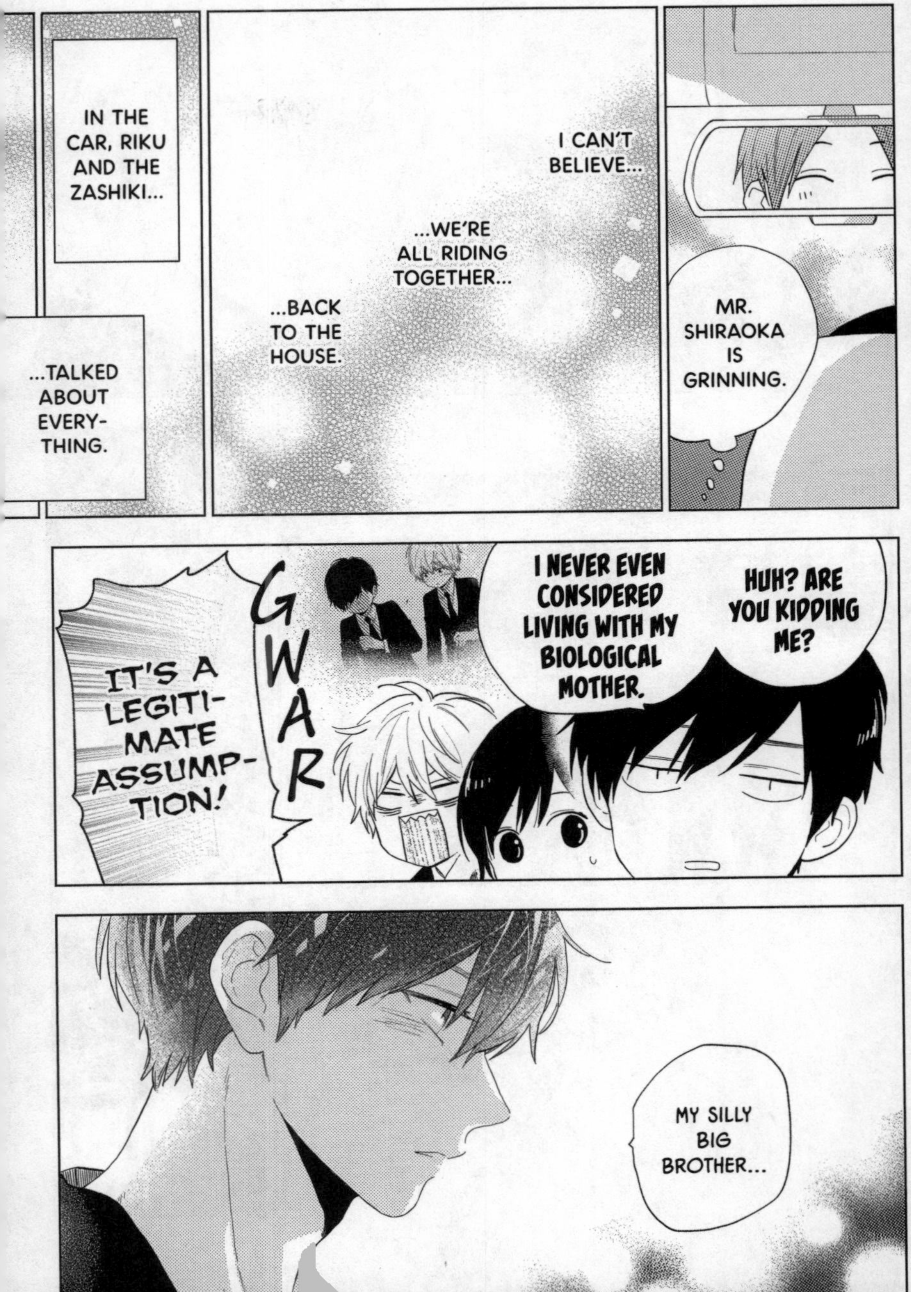
MR. SHIRAOKA IS GRINNING.
I CAN'T BELIEVE...
...WE'RE ALL RIDING TOGETHER...
...BACK TO THE HOUSE.
IN THE CAR, RIKU AND THE ZASHIKI...
...TALKED ABOUT EVERY-THING.
HUH? ARE YOU KIDDING ME?
I NEVER EVEN CONSIDERED LIVING WITH MY BIOLOGICAL MOTHER.
GWAR
IT'S A LEGITI-MATE ASSUMP-TION!
MY SILLY BIG BROTHER...

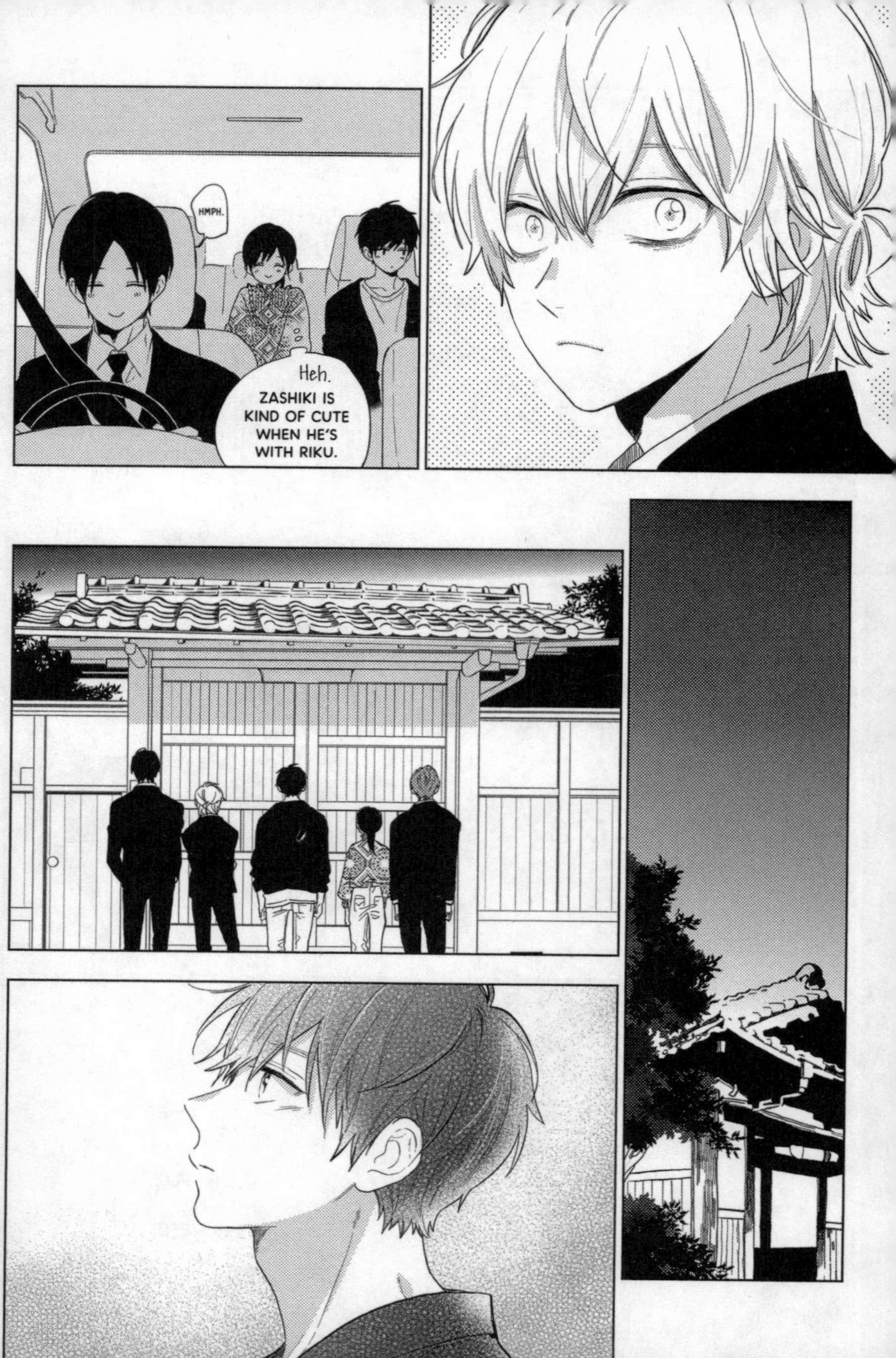

HMPH.
Heh.
ZASHIKI IS KIND OF CUTE WHEN HE'S WITH RIKU.

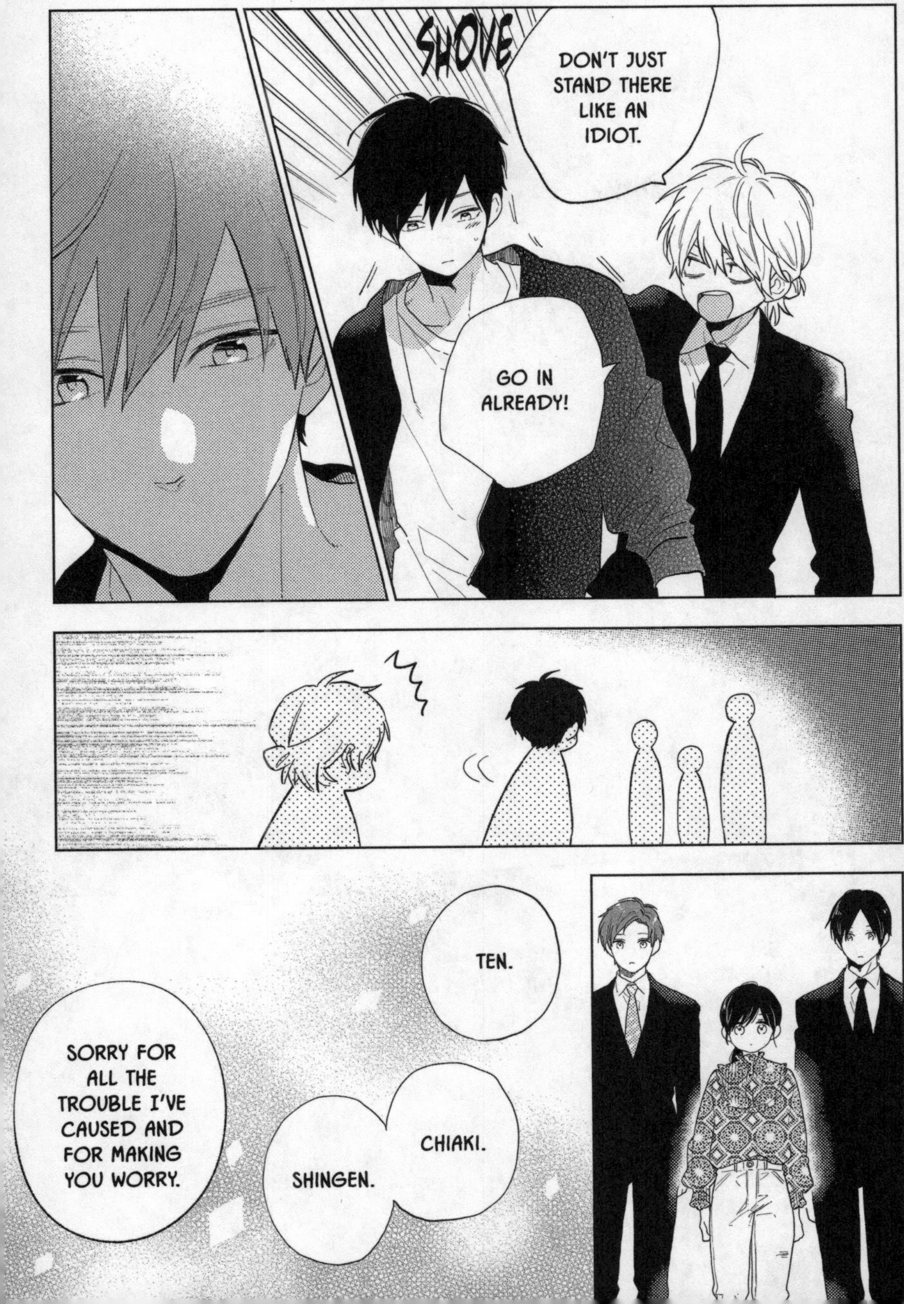
SHOVE
DON'T JUST STAND THERE LIKE AN IDIOT.
GO IN ALREADY!
TEN.
CHIAKI.
SHINGEN.
SORRY FOR ALL THE TROUBLE I'VE CAUSED AND FOR MAKING YOU WORRY.

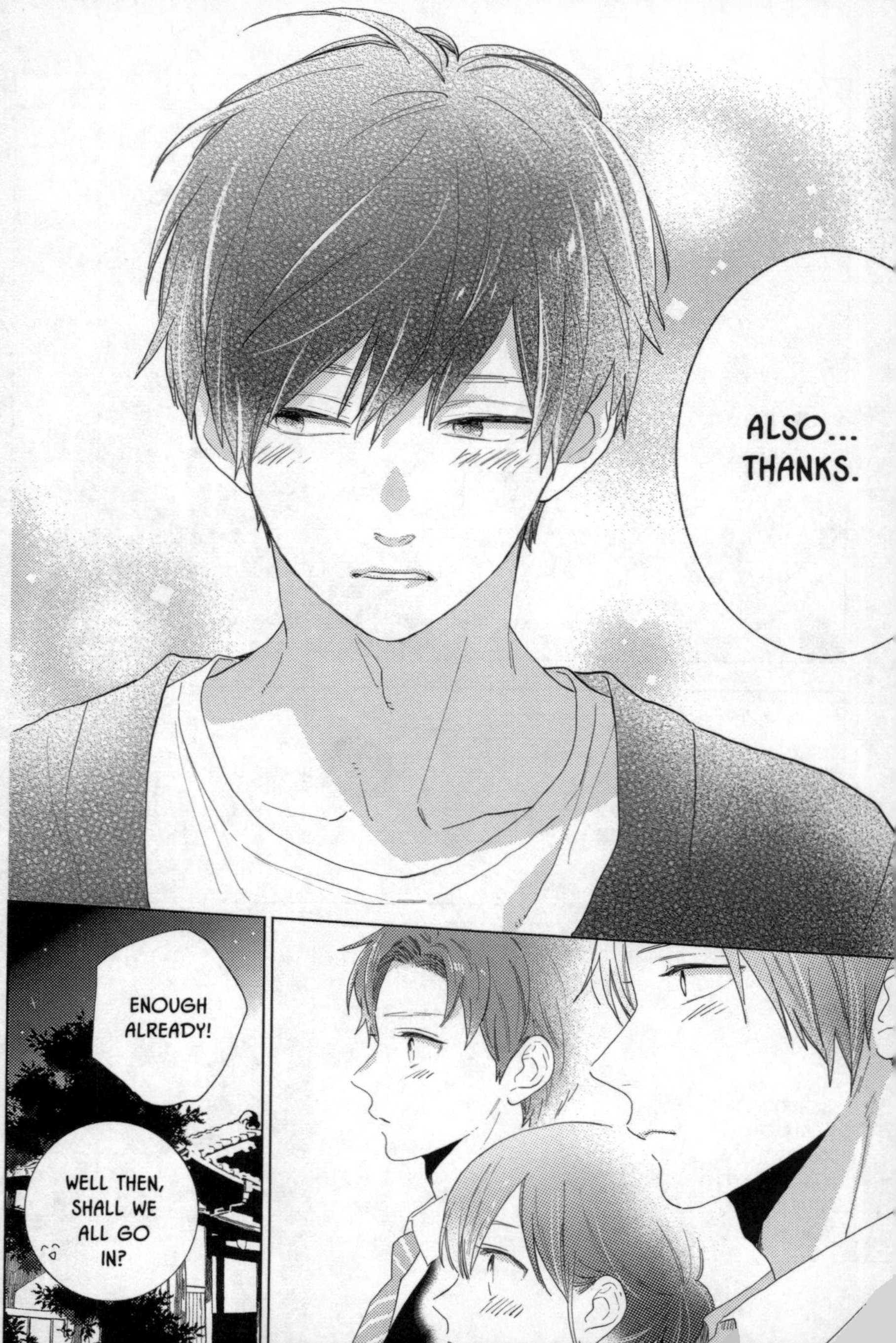
ALSO... THANKS.
ENOUGH ALREADY!
WELL THEN, SHALL WE ALL GO IN?

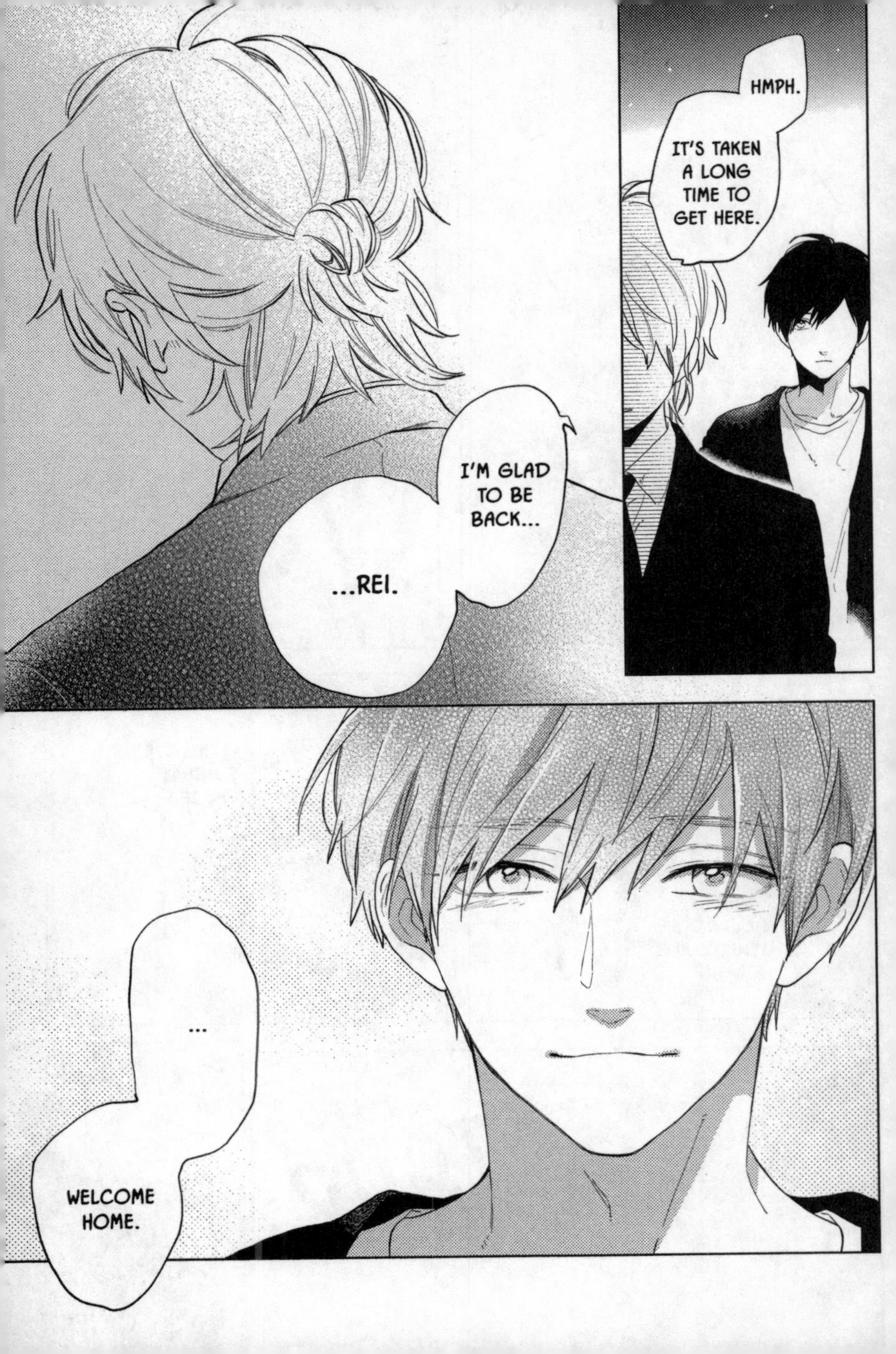
HMPH.
IT'S TAKEN A LONG TIME TO GET HERE.
I'M GLAD TO BE BACK...
...REI.
...
WELCOME HOME.

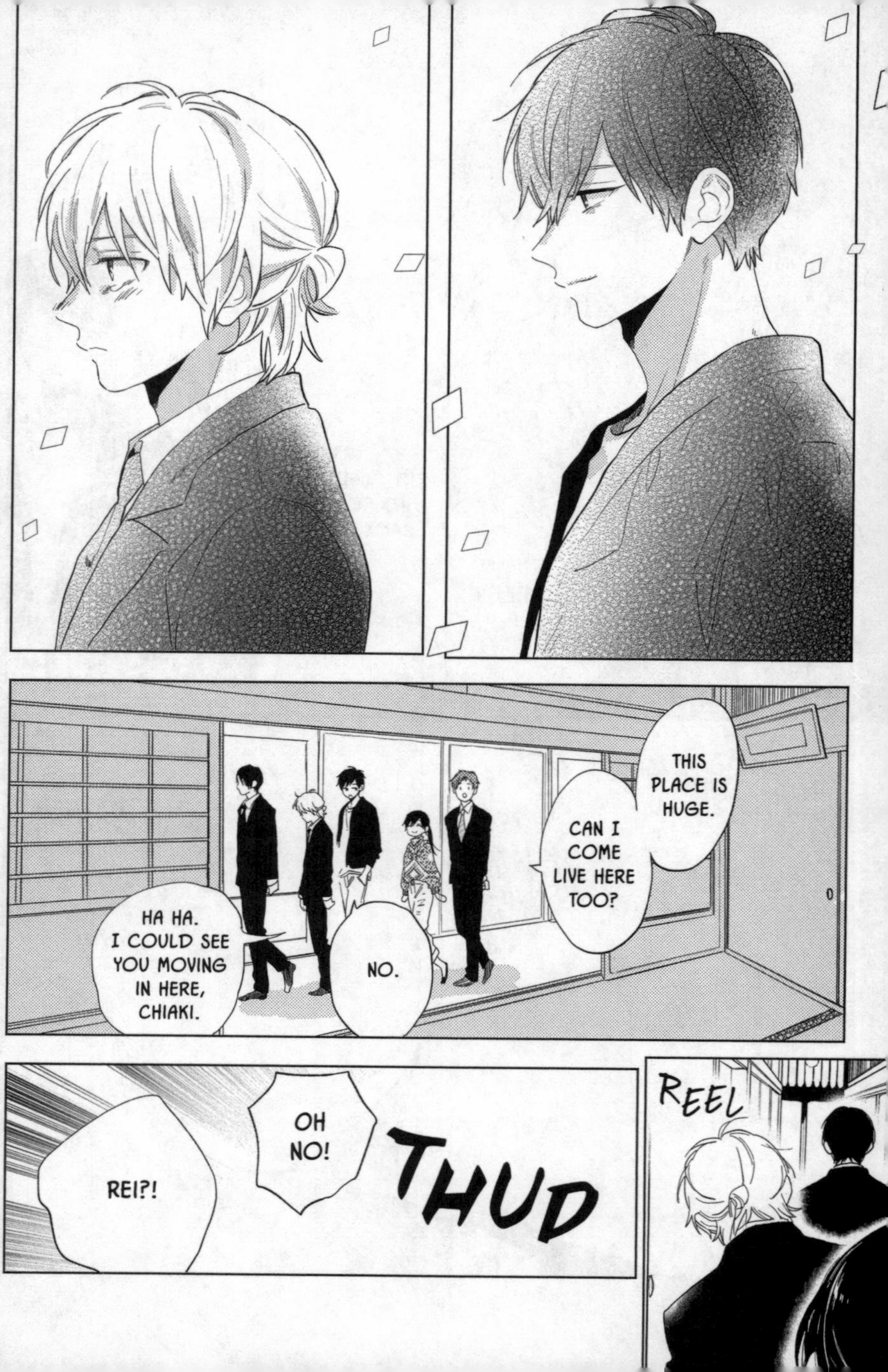
THIS PLACE IS HUGE.
CAN I COME LIVE HERE TOO?
NO.
HA HA. I COULD SEE YOU MOVING IN HERE, CHIAKI.
REEL
THUD
OH NO!
REI?!

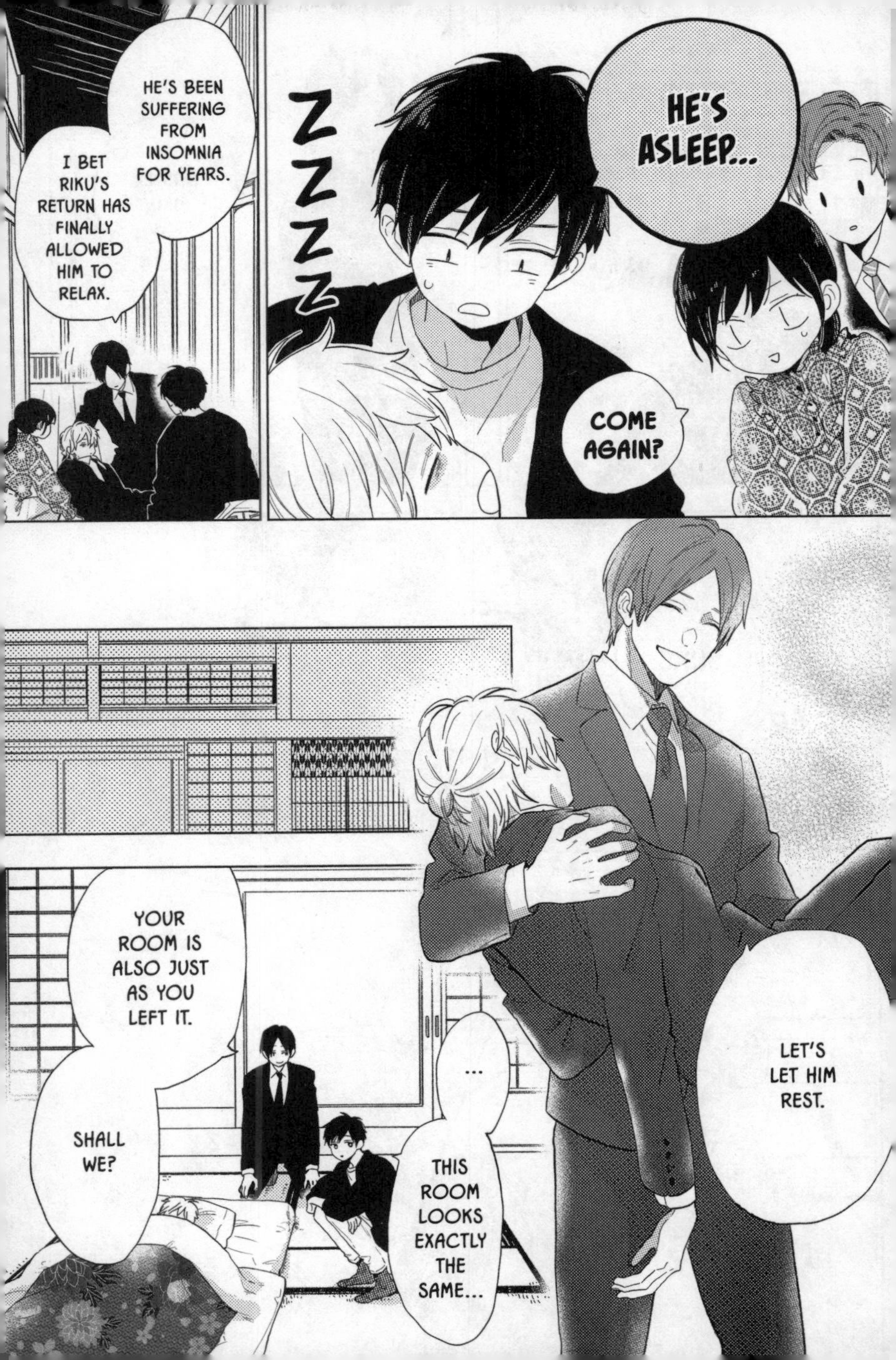
HE'S ASLEEP...
ZZZZ
COME AGAIN?
HE'S BEEN SUFFERING FROM INSOMNIA FOR YEARS.
I BET RIKU'S RETURN HAS FINALLY ALLOWED HIM TO RELAX.
LET'S LET HIM REST.
...
THIS ROOM LOOKS EXACTLY THE SAME...
YOUR ROOM IS ALSO JUST AS YOU LEFT IT.
SHALL WE?

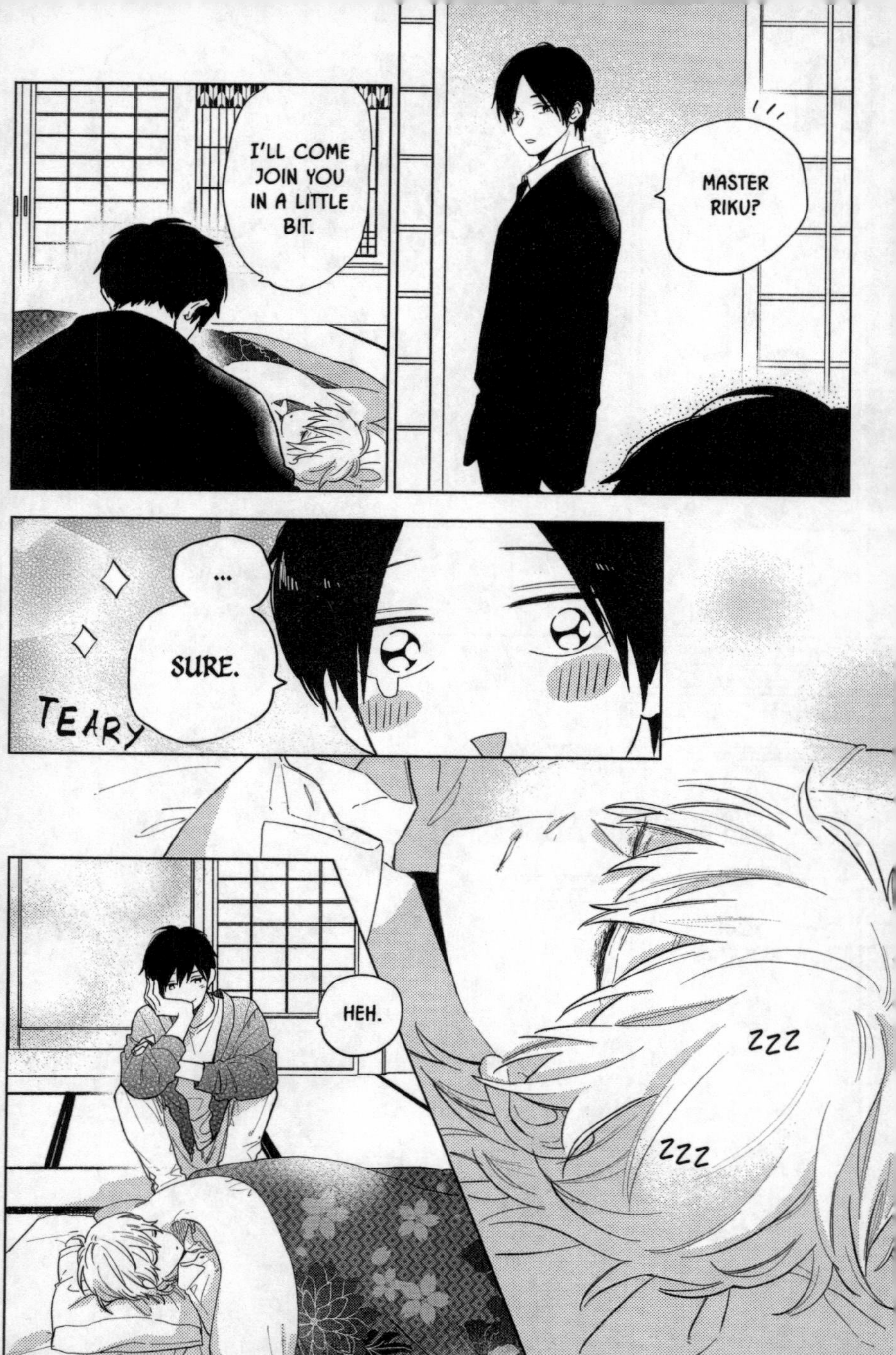
MASTER RIKU?
I'LL COME JOIN YOU IN A LITTLE BIT.
... SURE.
TEARY
ZZZ
ZZZ
HEH.

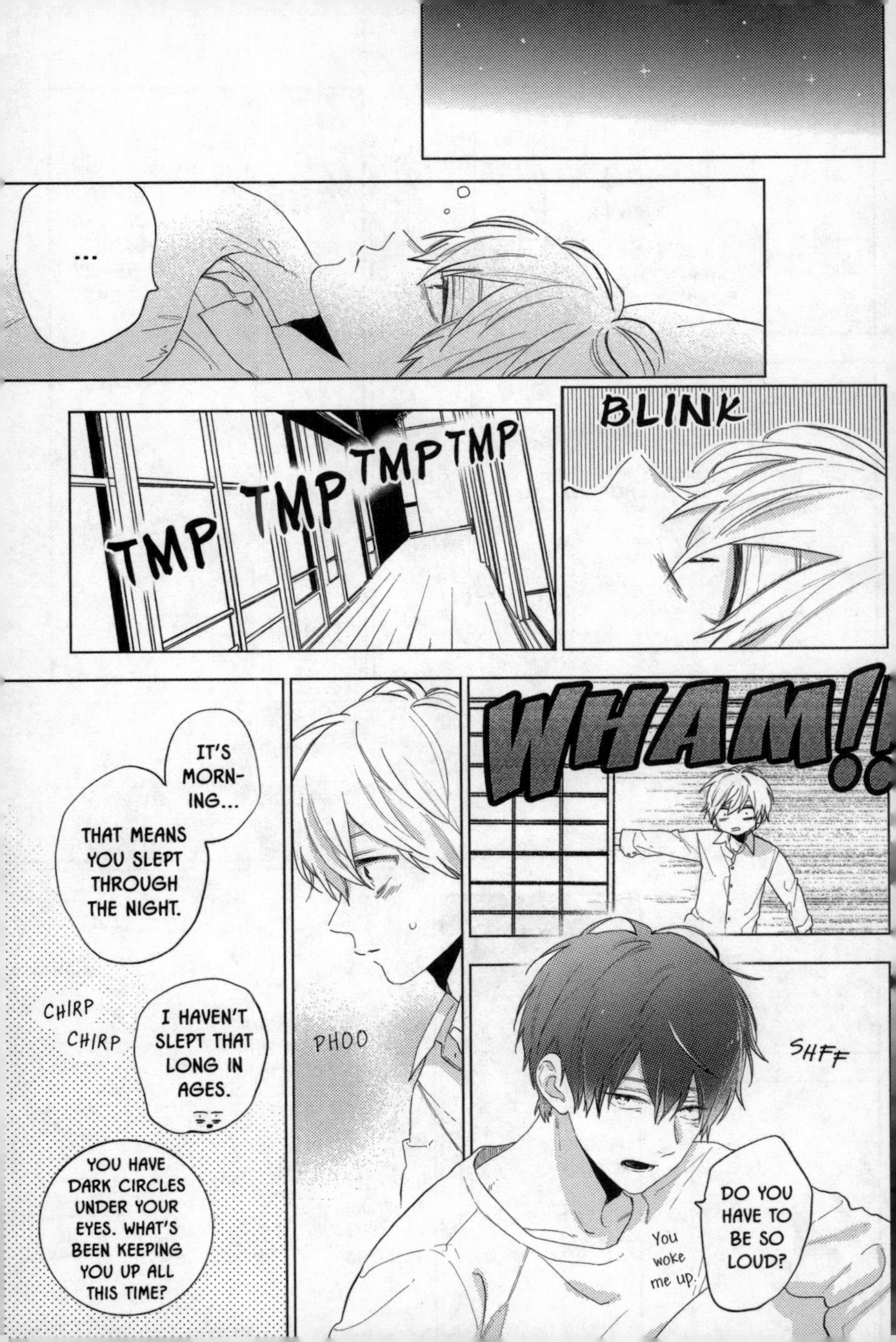
...
BLINK
TMP TMP TMPTMP
WHAM!!
SHFF
DO YOU HAVE TO BE SO LOUD?
You woke me up.
PHOO
IT'S MORNING...
THAT MEANS YOU SLEPT THROUGH THE NIGHT.
CHIRP CHIRP
I HAVEN'T SLEPT THAT LONG IN AGES.
YOU HAVE DARK CIRCLES UNDER YOUR EYES. WHAT'S BEEN KEEPING YOU UP ALL THIS TIME?

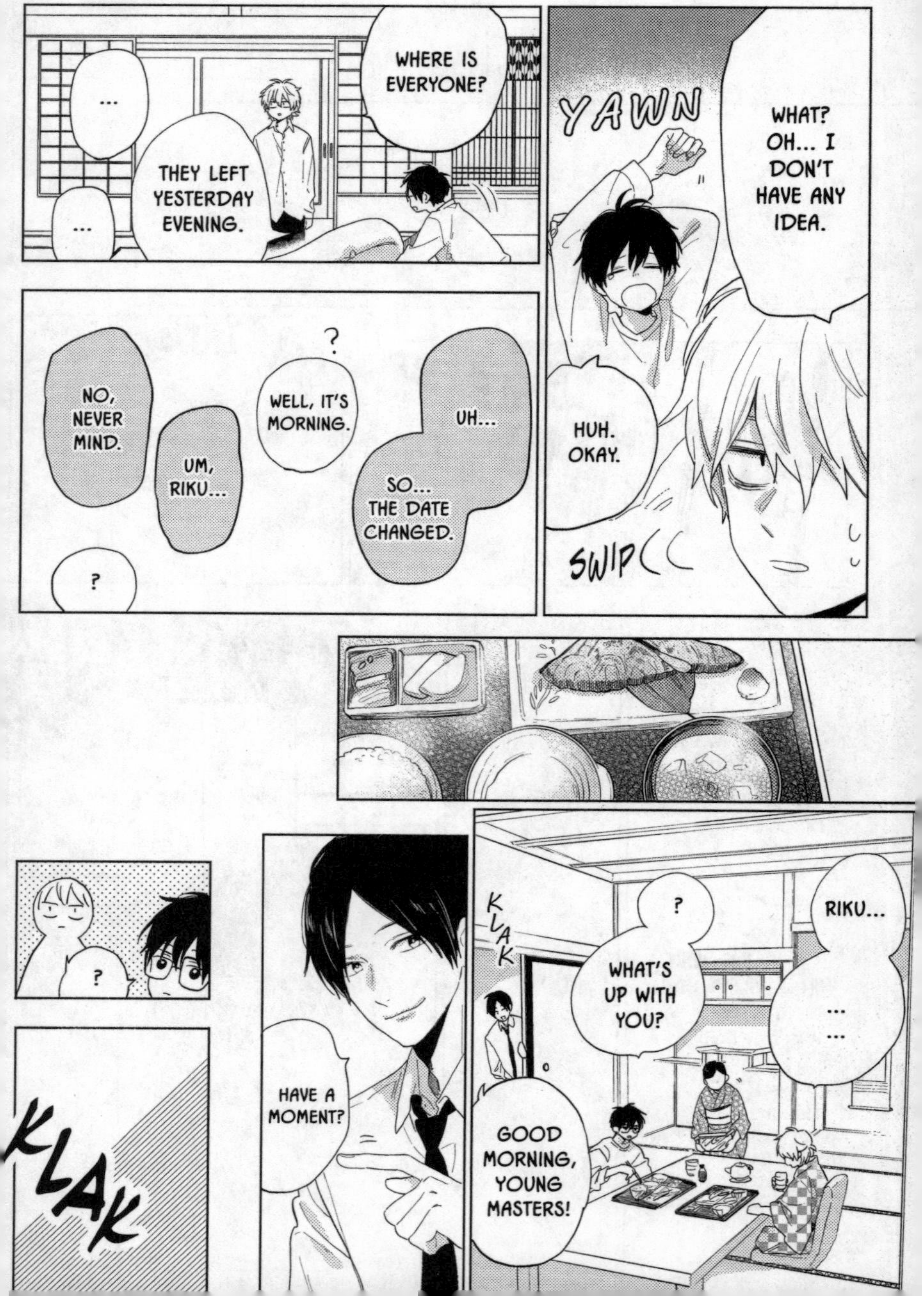
YAWN
WHAT? OH... I DON'T HAVE ANY IDEA.
HUH. OKAY.
SWIP
WHERE IS EVERYONE?
THEY LEFT YESTERDAY EVENING.
...
...
UH...
SO... THE DATE CHANGED.
?
WELL, IT'S MORNING.
UM, RIKU...
NO, NEVER MIND.
?
RIKU...
...
...
?
WHAT'S UP WITH YOU?
KLAK
GOOD MORNING, YOUNG MASTERS!
HAVE A MOMENT?
?
KLAK

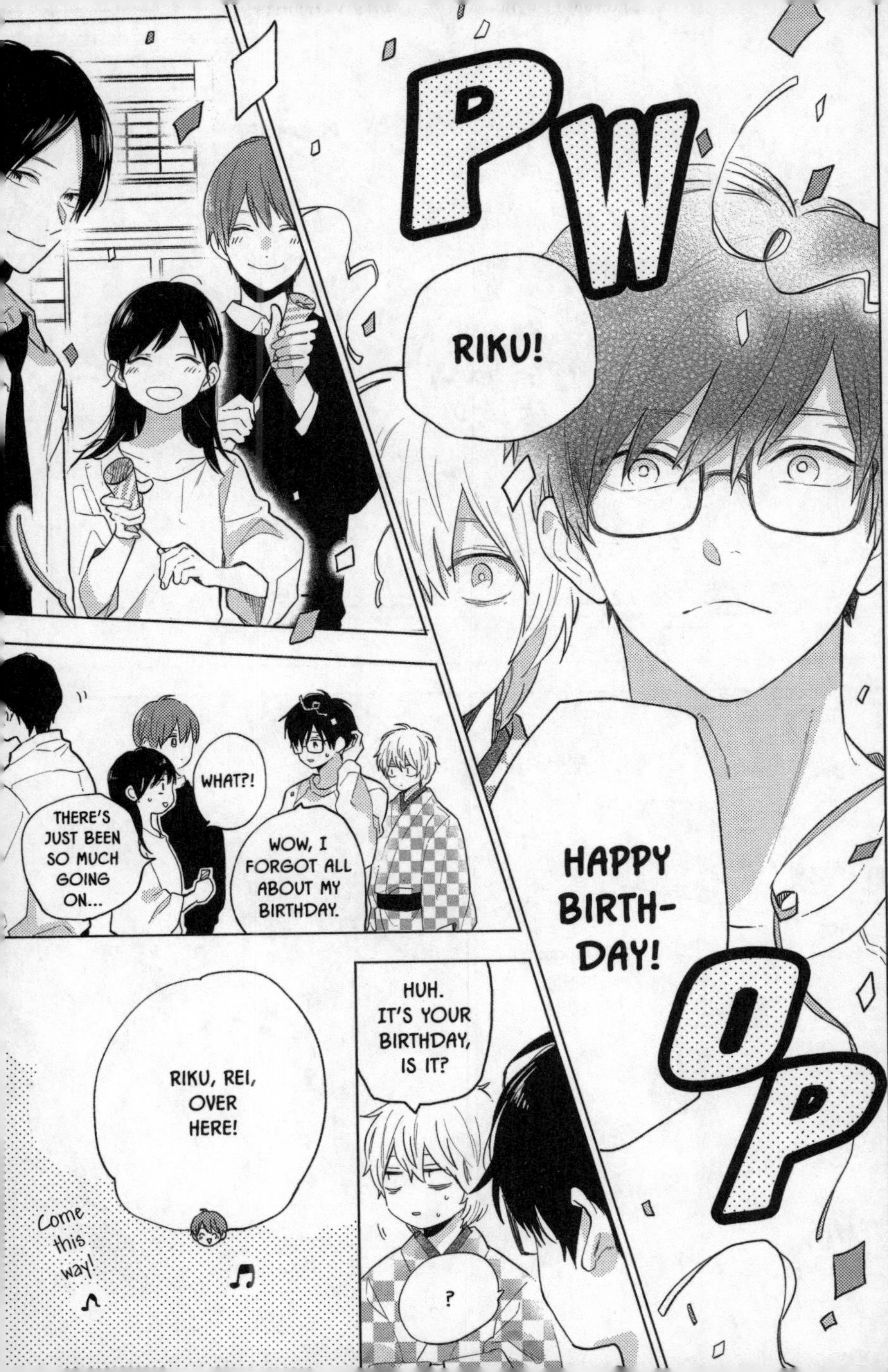

PW
RIKU!
HAPPY BIRTH-DAY!
OP
WHAT?!
WOW, I FORGOT ALL ABOUT MY BIRTHDAY.
THERE'S JUST BEEN SO MUCH GOING ON...
HUH. IT'S YOUR BIRTHDAY, IS IT?
?
RIKU, REI, OVER HERE!
Come this way!

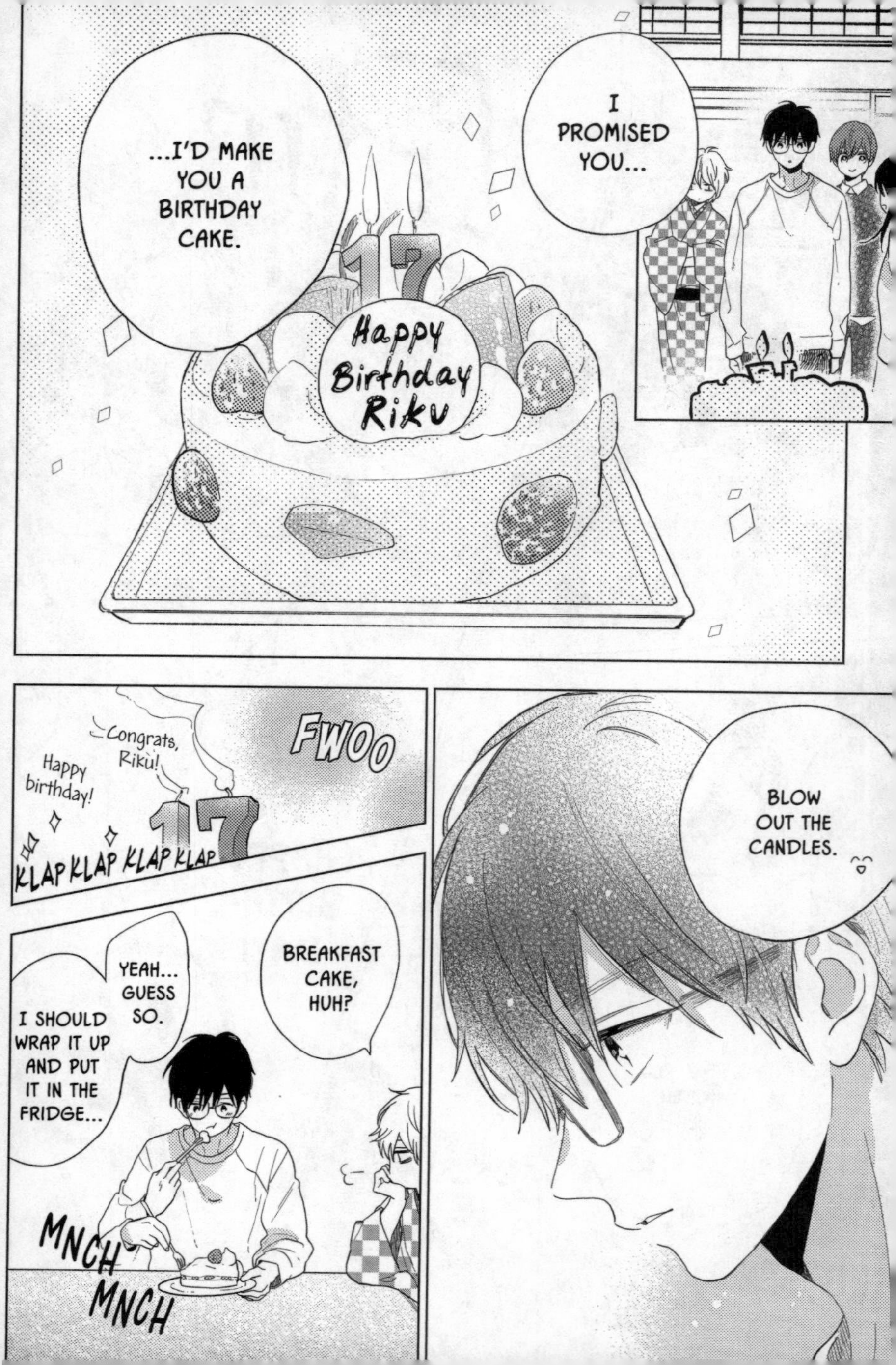
I PROMISED YOU...
...I'D MAKE YOU A BIRTHDAY CAKE.
Happy Birthday Riku
BLOW OUT THE CANDLES.
FWOO
Congrats, Riku!
Happy birthday!
KLAP KLAP KLAP KLAP
BREAKFAST CAKE, HUH?
YEAH... GUESS SO.
I SHOULD WRAP IT UP AND PUT IT IN THE FRIDGE...
MNCH MNCH

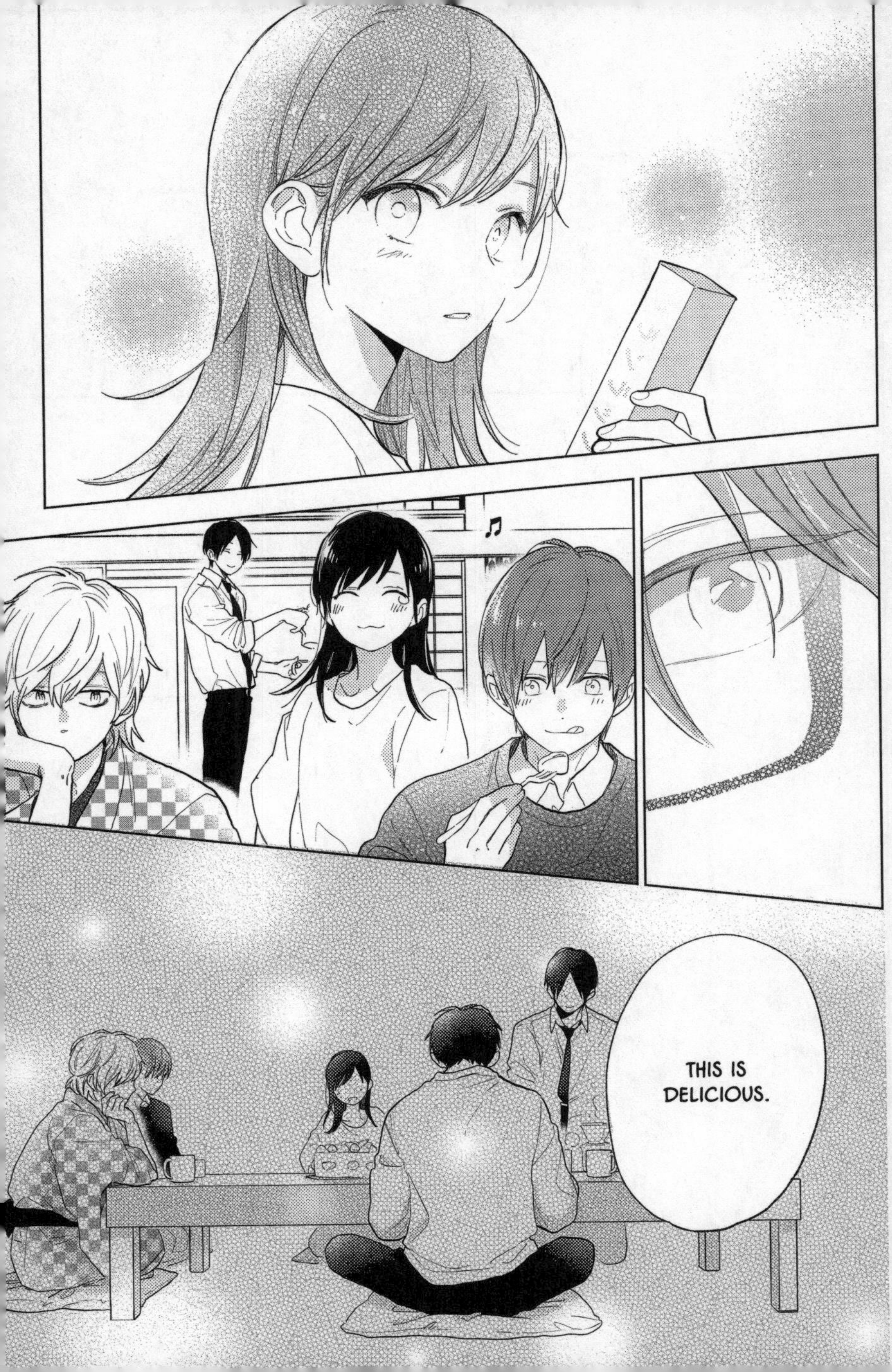
THIS IS
DELICIOUS.

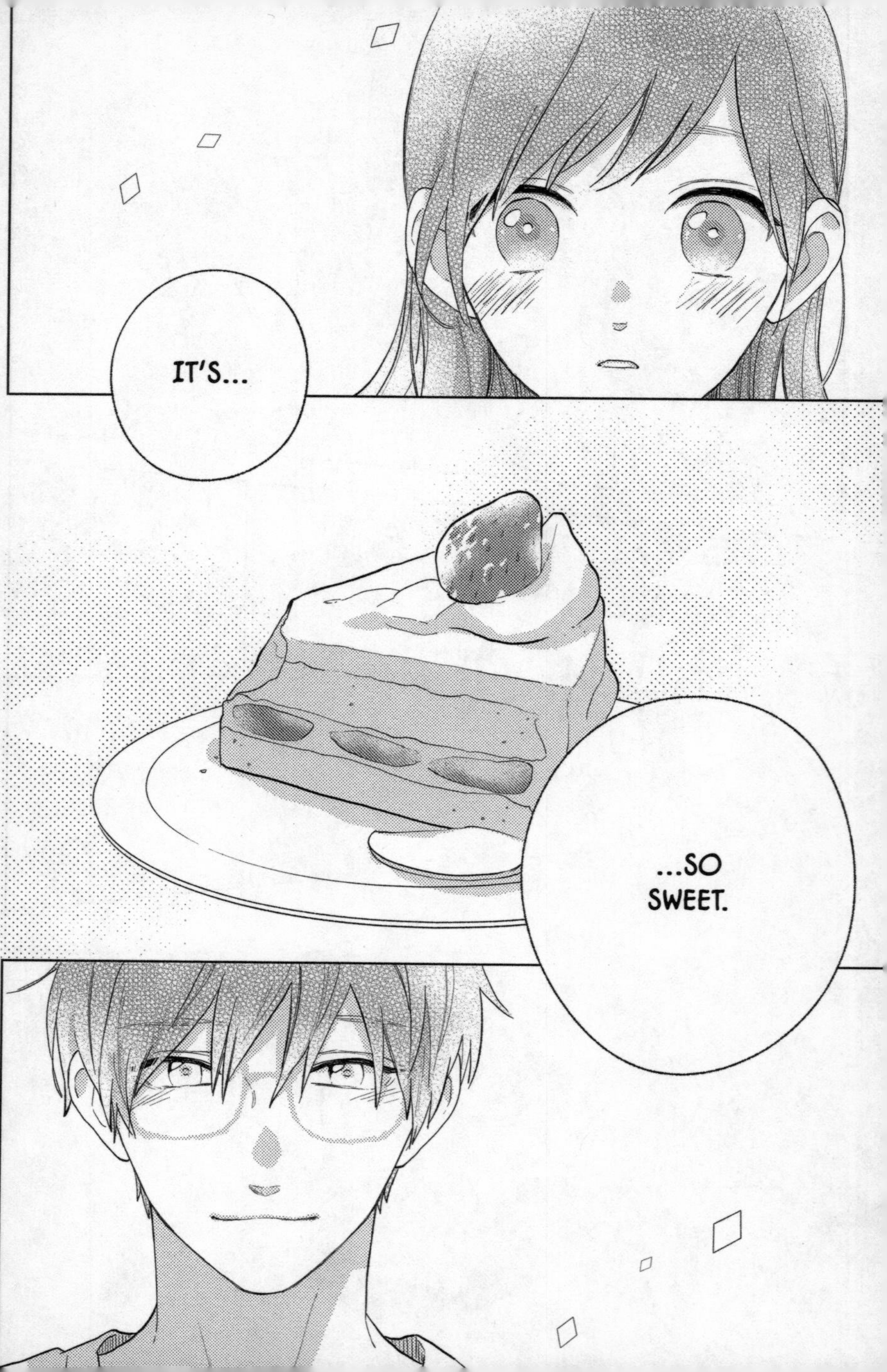
IT'S...
...SO SWEET.

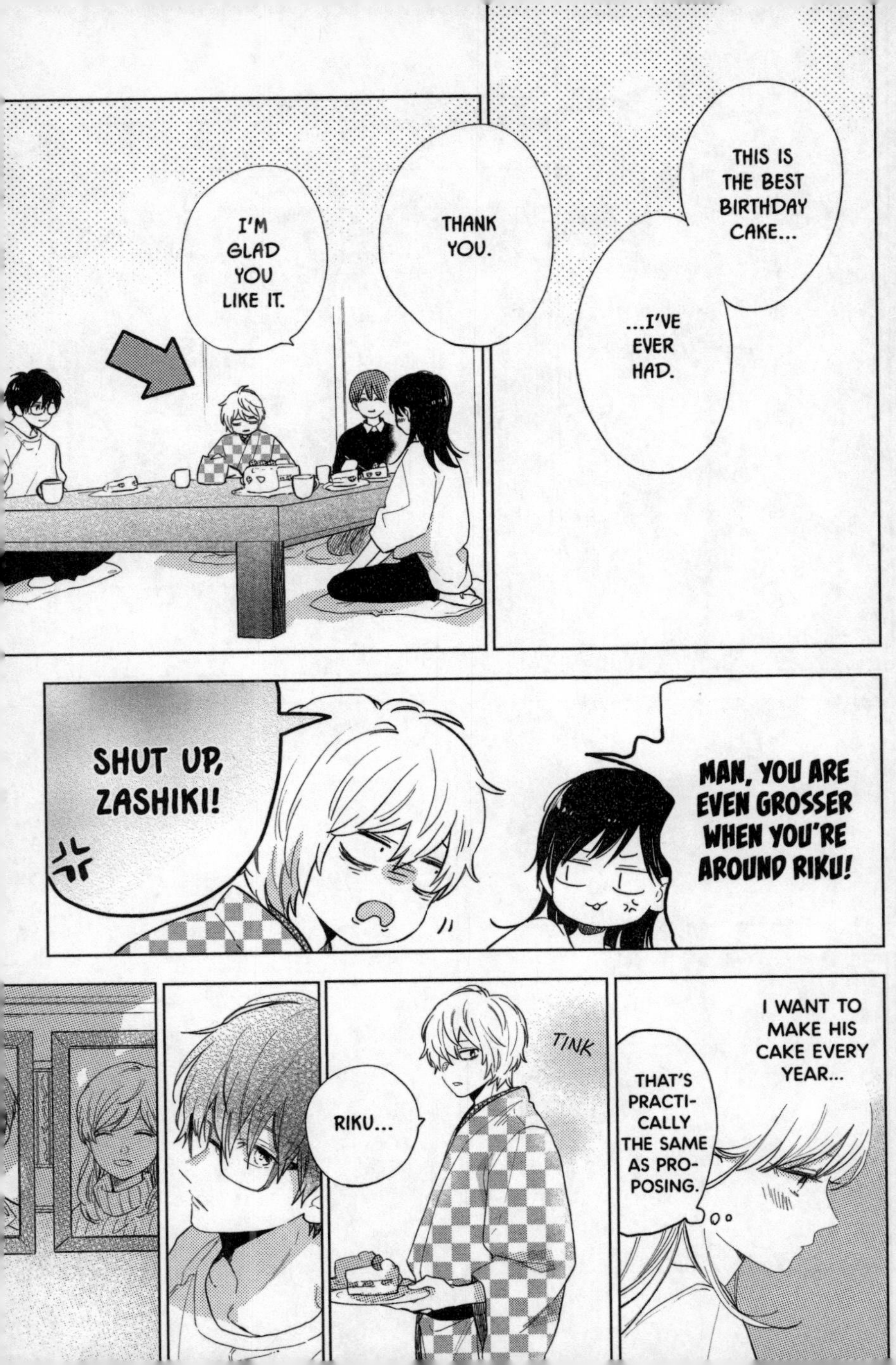
THIS IS THE BEST BIRTHDAY CAKE...
...I'VE EVER HAD.
THANK YOU.
I'M GLAD YOU LIKE IT.
MAN, YOU ARE EVEN GROSSER WHEN YOU'RE AROUND RIKU!
SHUT UP, ZASHIKI!
I WANT TO MAKE HIS CAKE EVERY YEAR...
THAT'S PRACTI-CALLY THE SAME AS PRO-POSING.
TINK
RIKU...

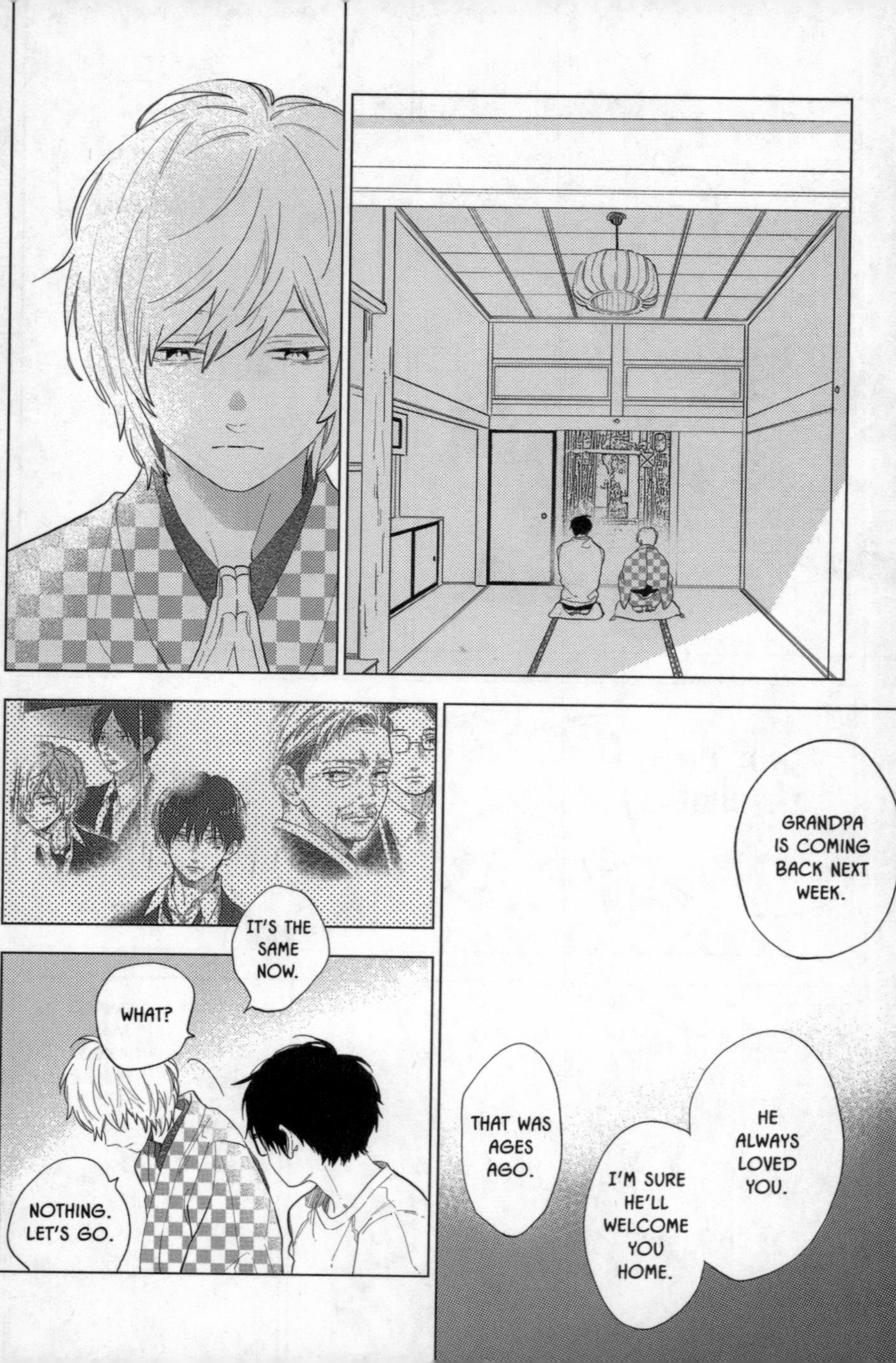
GRANDPA IS COMING BACK NEXT WEEK.
HE ALWAYS LOVED YOU.
I'M SURE HE'LL WELCOME YOU HOME.
THAT WAS AGES AGO.
IT'S THE SAME NOW.
WHAT?
NOTHING. LET'S GO.

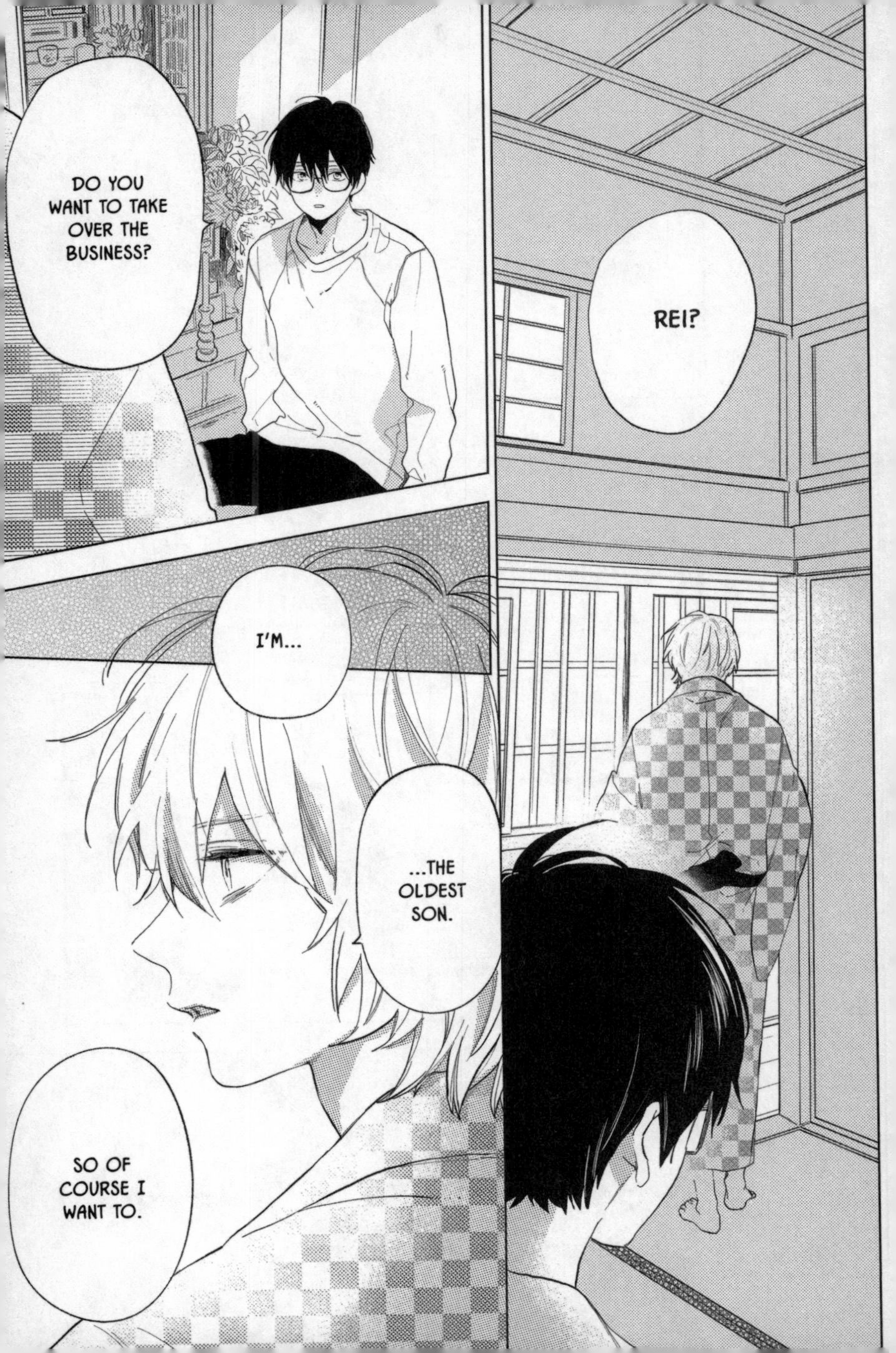
REI?
DO YOU WANT TO TAKE OVER THE BUSINESS?
I'M...
...THE OLDEST SON.
SO OF COURSE I WANT TO.

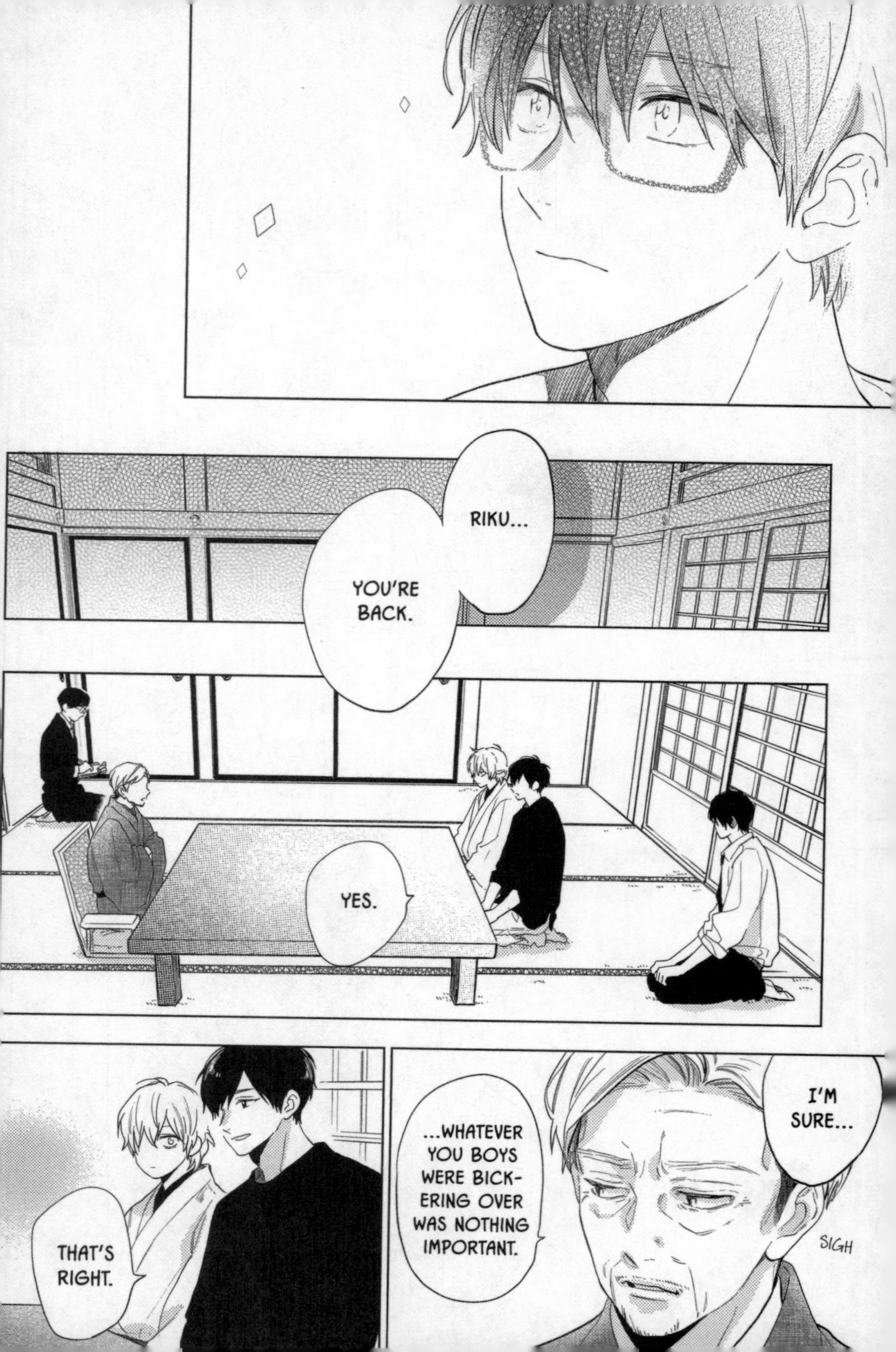
RIKU...
YOU'RE BACK.
YES.
I'M SURE...
...WHATEVER YOU BOYS WERE BICK- ERING OVER WAS NOTHING IMPORTANT.
SIGH
THAT'S RIGHT.

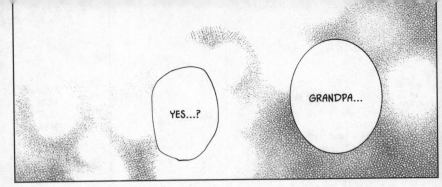

GRANDPA...

YES...?

REI...

...IS REALLY THINKING SERIOUSLY ABOUT THIS HOUSEHOLD.

HE'S PRACTICALLY OBSESSED.

!

RIKU...

WHEN I WAS YOUNG, ALL I COULD THINK ABOUT WAS MYSELF.

I WASN'T PREPARED TO SUPPORT REI.

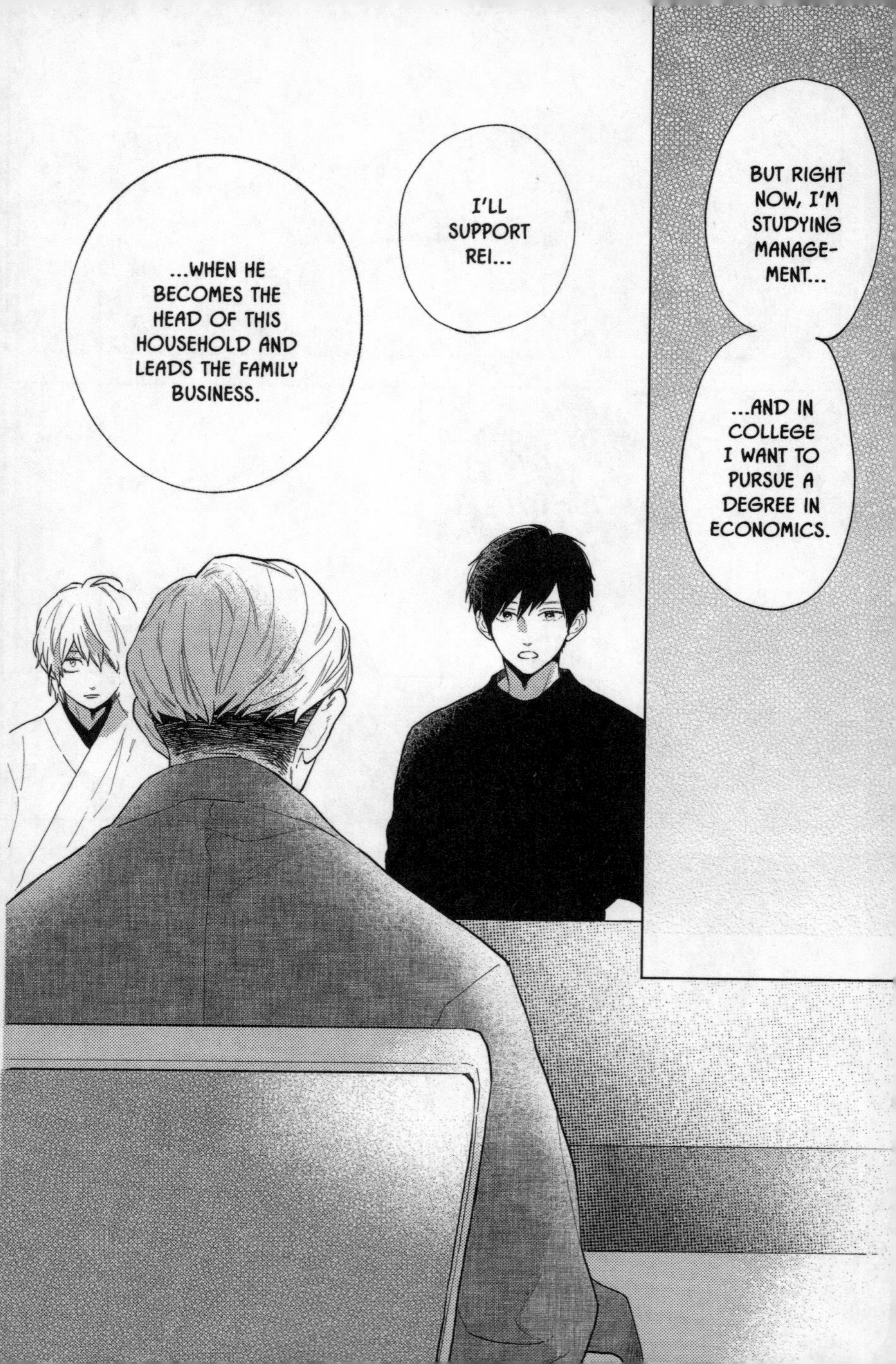
BUT RIGHT NOW, I'M STUDYING MANAGE-MENT...
...AND IN COLLEGE I WANT TO PURSUE A DEGREE IN ECONOMICS.
I'LL SUPPORT REI...
...WHEN HE BECOMES THE HEAD OF THIS HOUSEHOLD AND LEADS THE FAMILY BUSINESS.

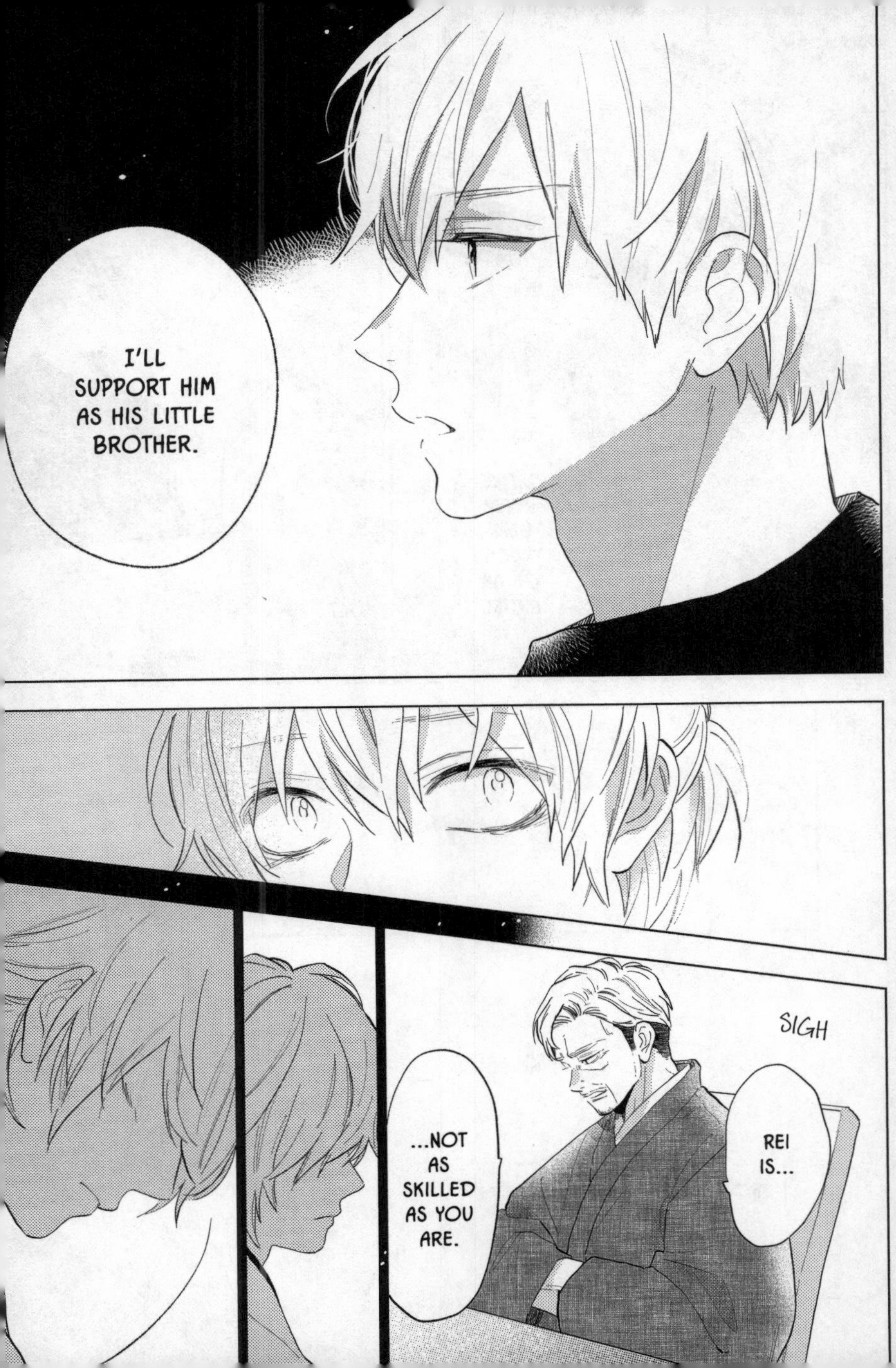
I'LL SUPPORT HIM AS HIS LITTLE BROTHER.
SIGH
REI IS...
...NOT AS SKILLED AS YOU ARE.

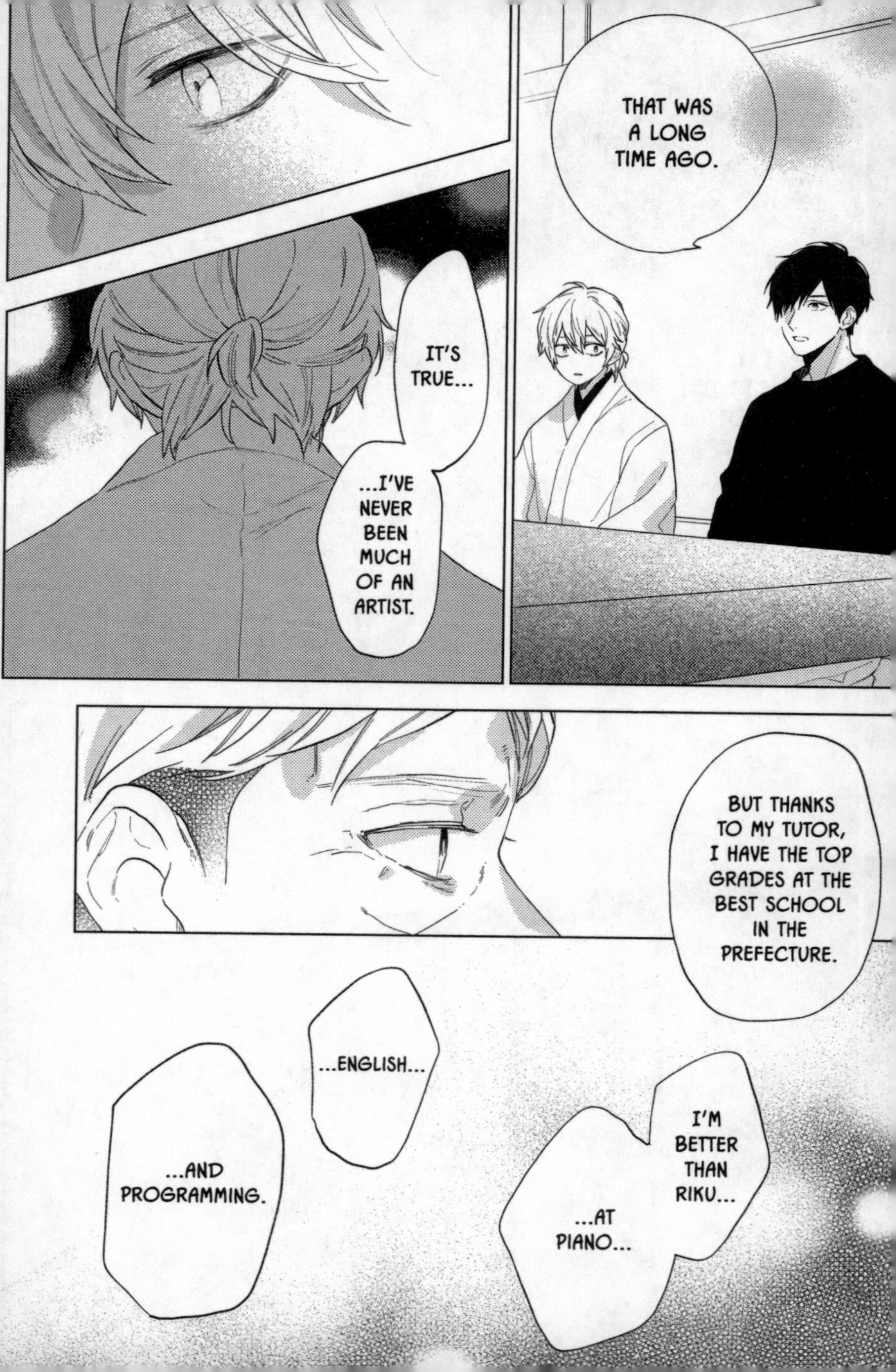
THAT WAS A LONG TIME AGO.
IT'S TRUE...
...I'VE NEVER BEEN MUCH OF AN ARTIST.
BUT THANKS TO MY TUTOR, I HAVE THE TOP GRADES AT THE BEST SCHOOL IN THE PREFECTURE.
I'M BETTER THAN RIKU...
...AT PIANO...
...ENGLISH...
...AND PROGRAMMING.

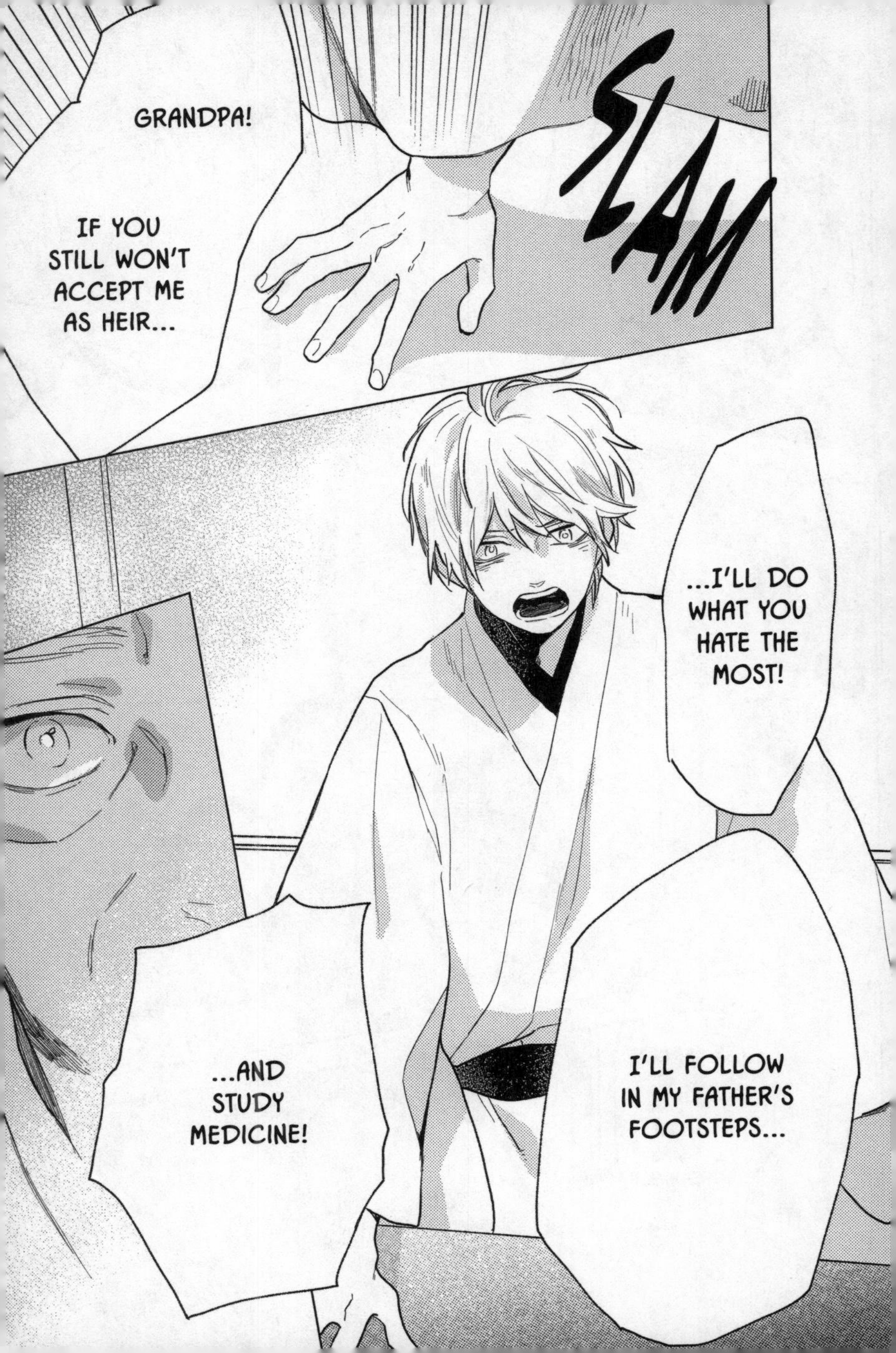
SLAM
GRANDPA!
IF YOU STILL WON'T ACCEPT ME AS HEIR...
...I'LL DO WHAT YOU HATE THE MOST!
I'LL FOLLOW IN MY FATHER'S FOOTSTEPS...
...AND STUDY MEDICINE!

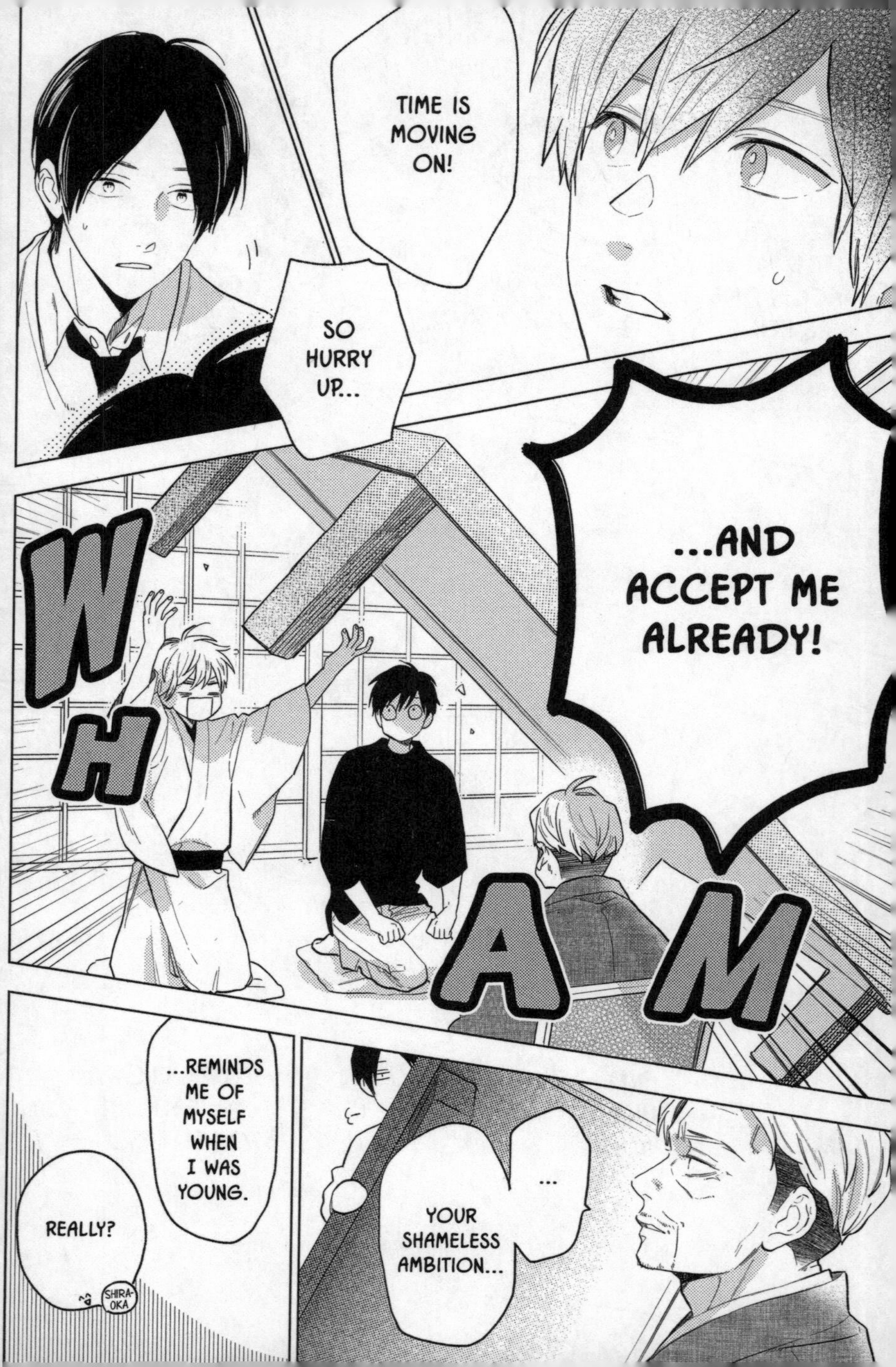
TIME IS MOVING ON!
SO HURRY UP...
...AND ACCEPT ME ALREADY!
WHAM
...
YOUR SHAMELESS AMBITION...
...REMINDS ME OF MYSELF WHEN I WAS YOUNG.
REALLY?
SHIRA-OKA

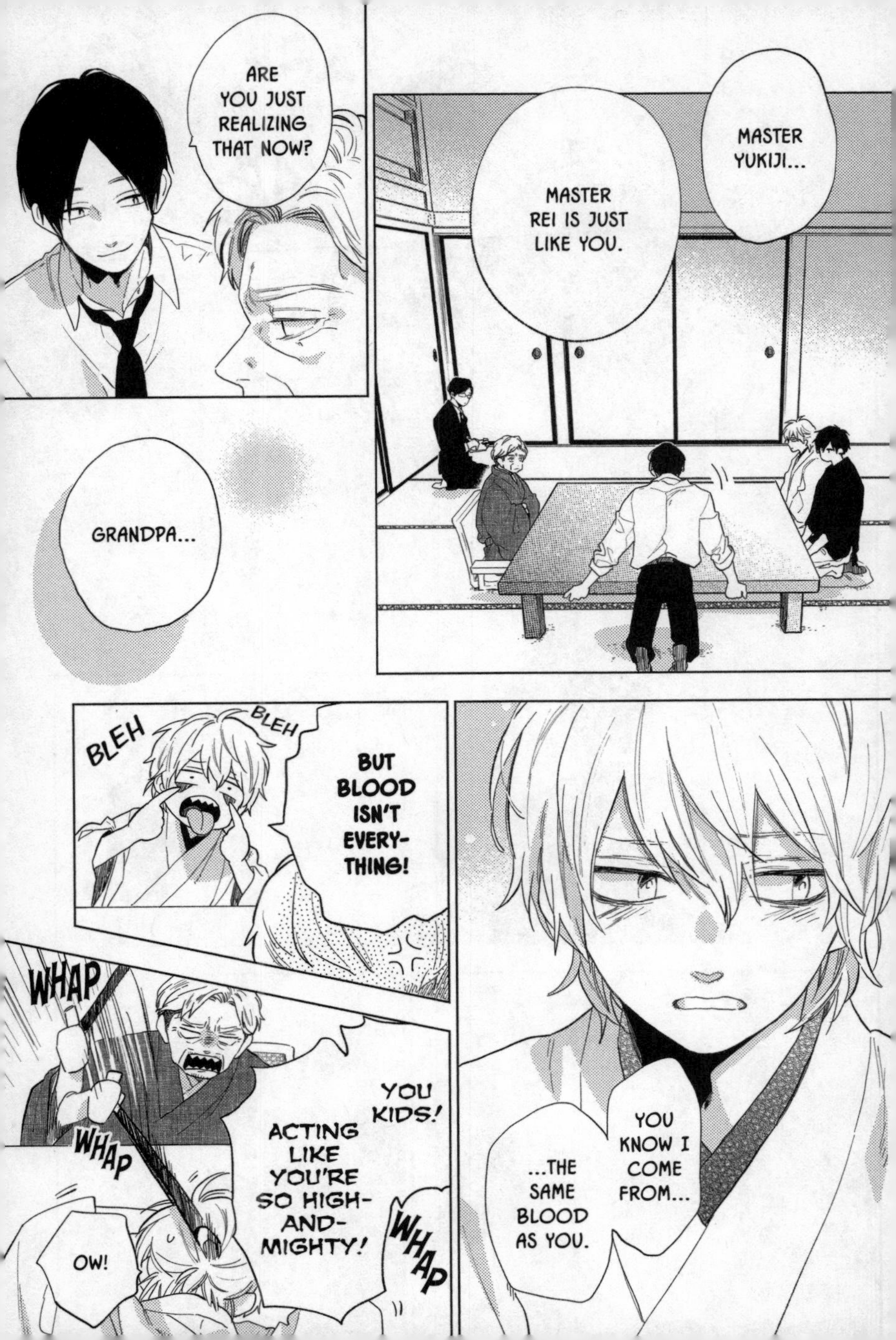
MASTER YUKIJI...
MASTER REI IS JUST LIKE YOU.
ARE YOU JUST REALIZING THAT NOW?
GRANDPA...
YOU KNOW I COME FROM...
...THE SAME BLOOD AS YOU.
BLEH
BLEH
BUT BLOOD ISN'T EVERYTHING!
WHAP
WHAP
YOU KIDS!
ACTING LIKE YOU'RE SO HIGH-AND-MIGHTY!
WHAP
OW!

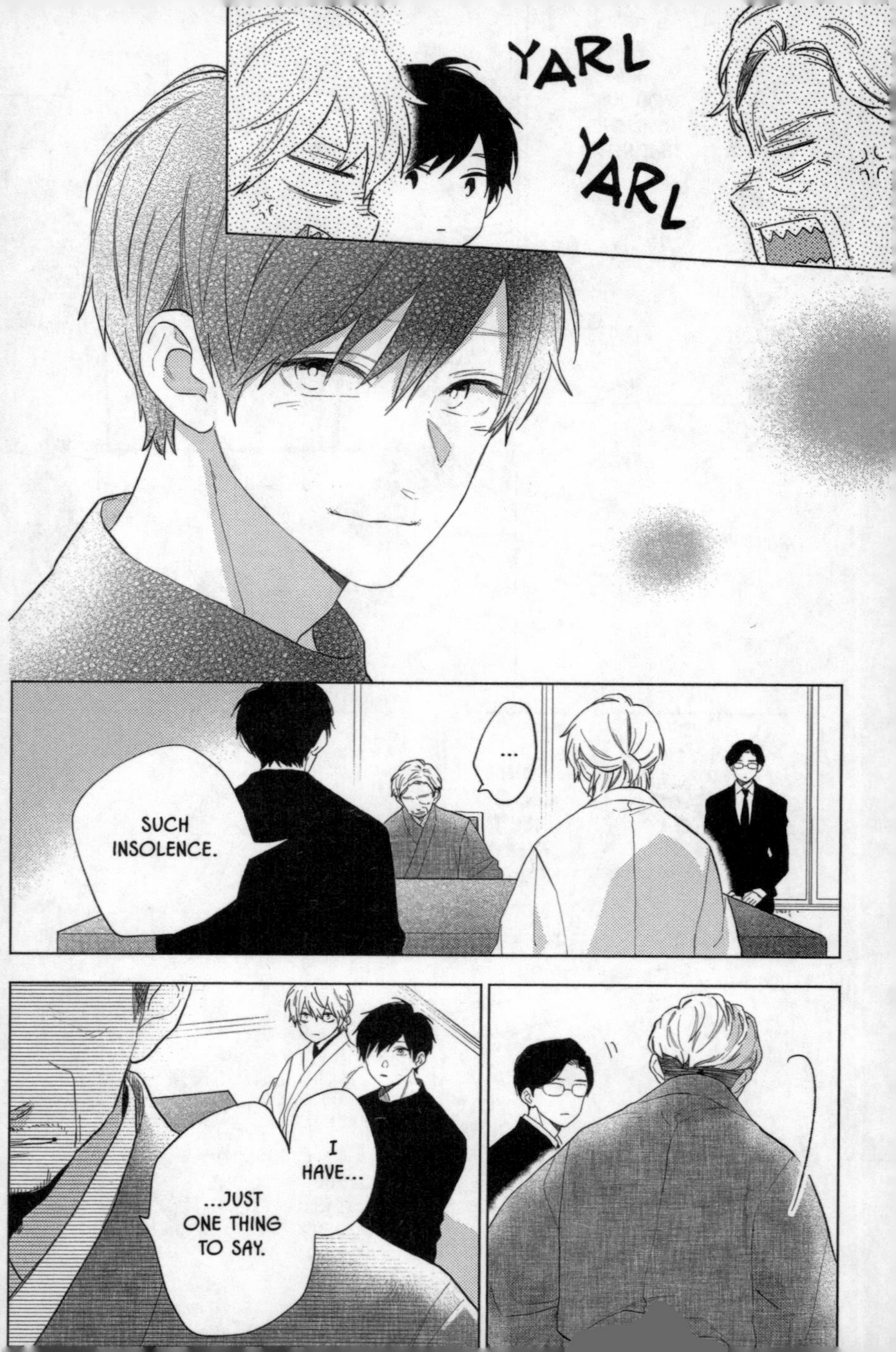
YARL
YARL
...
SUCH INSOLENCE.
I HAVE...
...JUST ONE THING TO SAY.

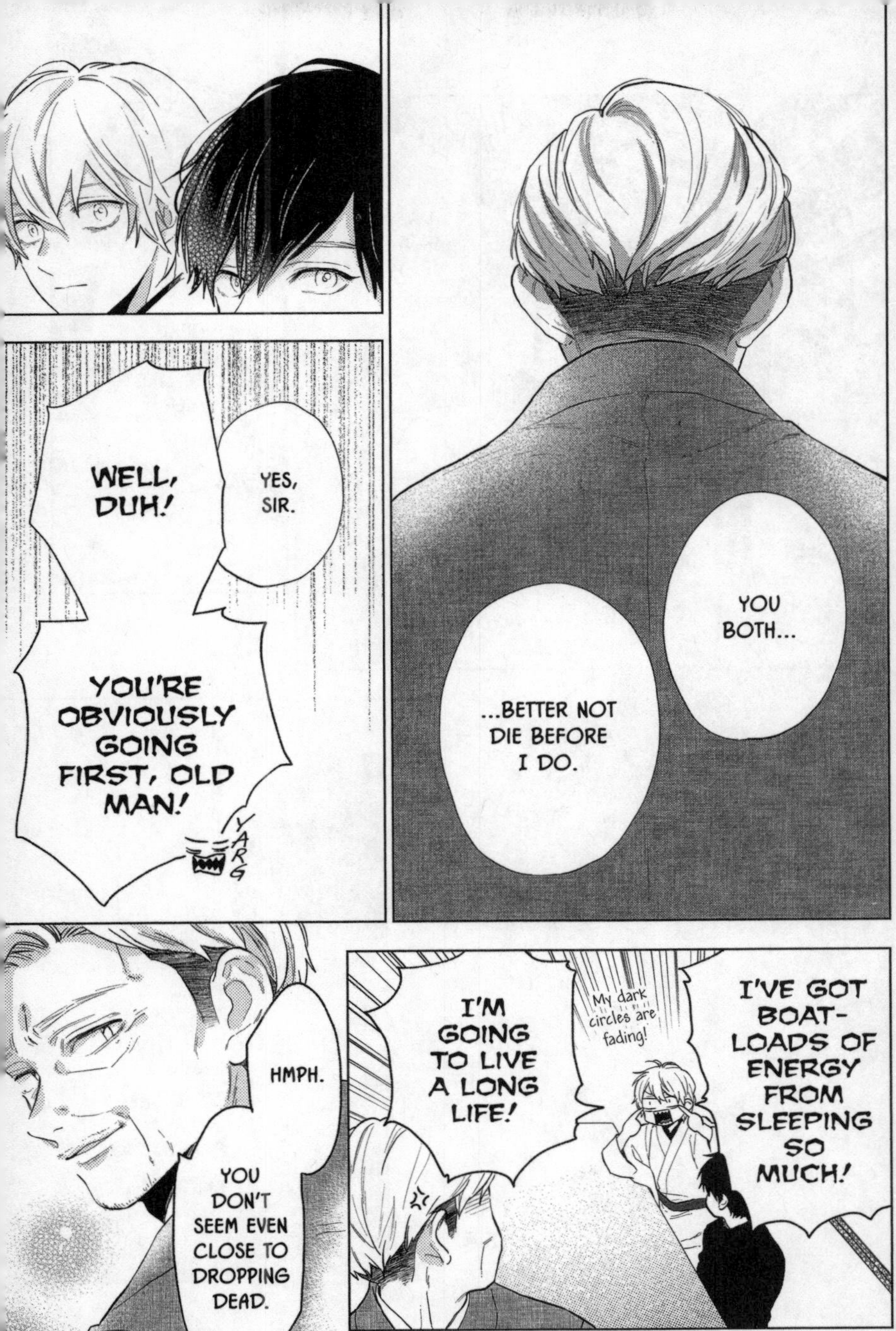
YOU BOTH...
...BETTER NOT DIE BEFORE I DO.
YES, SIR.
WELL, DUH!
YOU'RE OBVIOUSLY GOING FIRST, OLD MAN!
YARG
I'VE GOT BOAT-LOADS OF ENERGY FROM SLEEPING SO MUCH!
My dark circles are fading!
I'M GOING TO LIVE A LONG LIFE!
HMPH.
YOU DON'T SEEM EVEN CLOSE TO DROPPING DEAD.

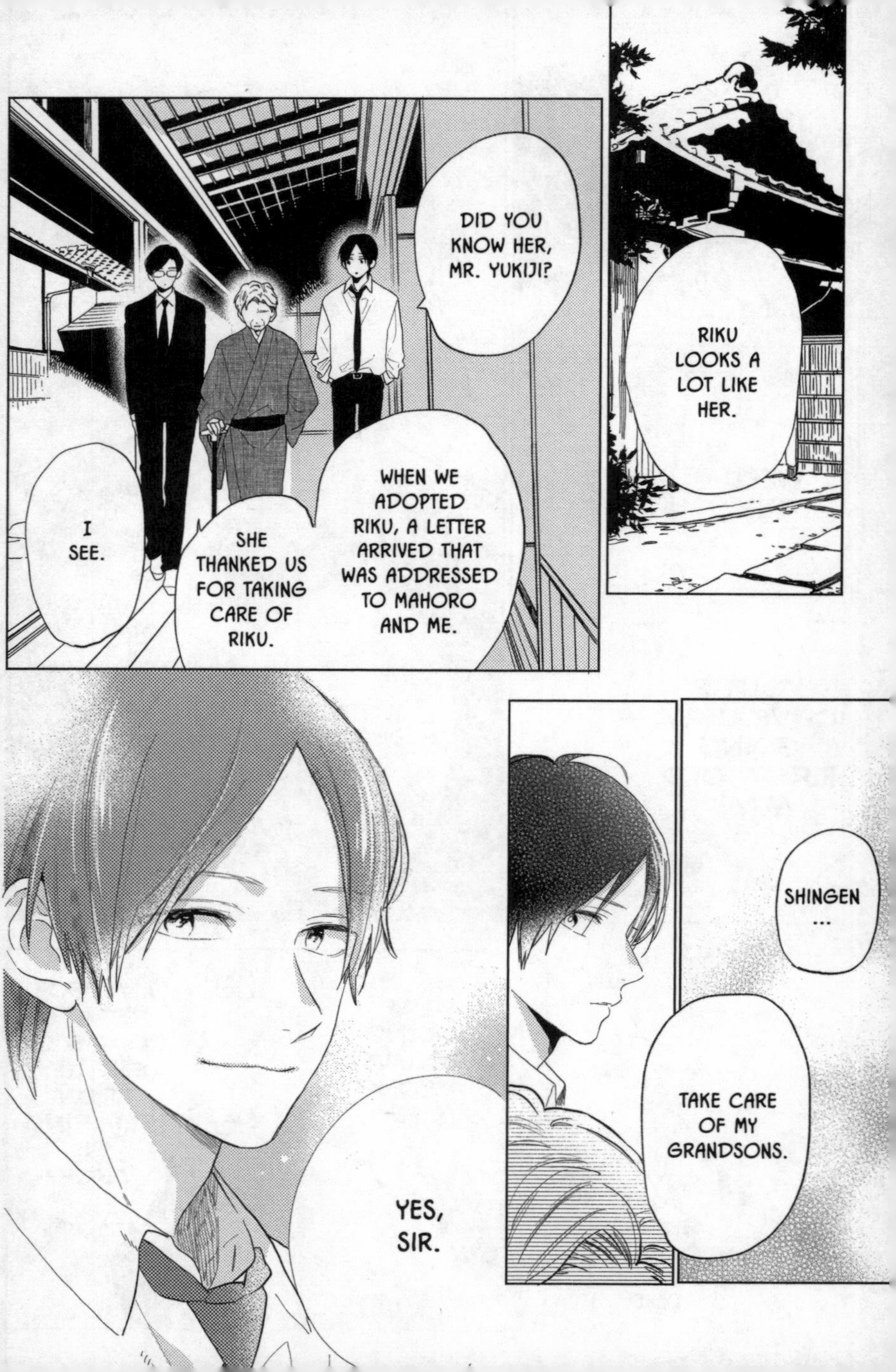
RIKU LOOKS A LOT LIKE HER.
DID YOU KNOW HER, MR. YUKIJI?
WHEN WE ADOPTED RIKU, A LETTER ARRIVED THAT WAS ADDRESSED TO MAHORO AND ME.
SHE THANKED US FOR TAKING CARE OF RIKU.
I SEE.
SHINGEN ...
TAKE CARE OF MY GRANDSONS.
YES, SIR.

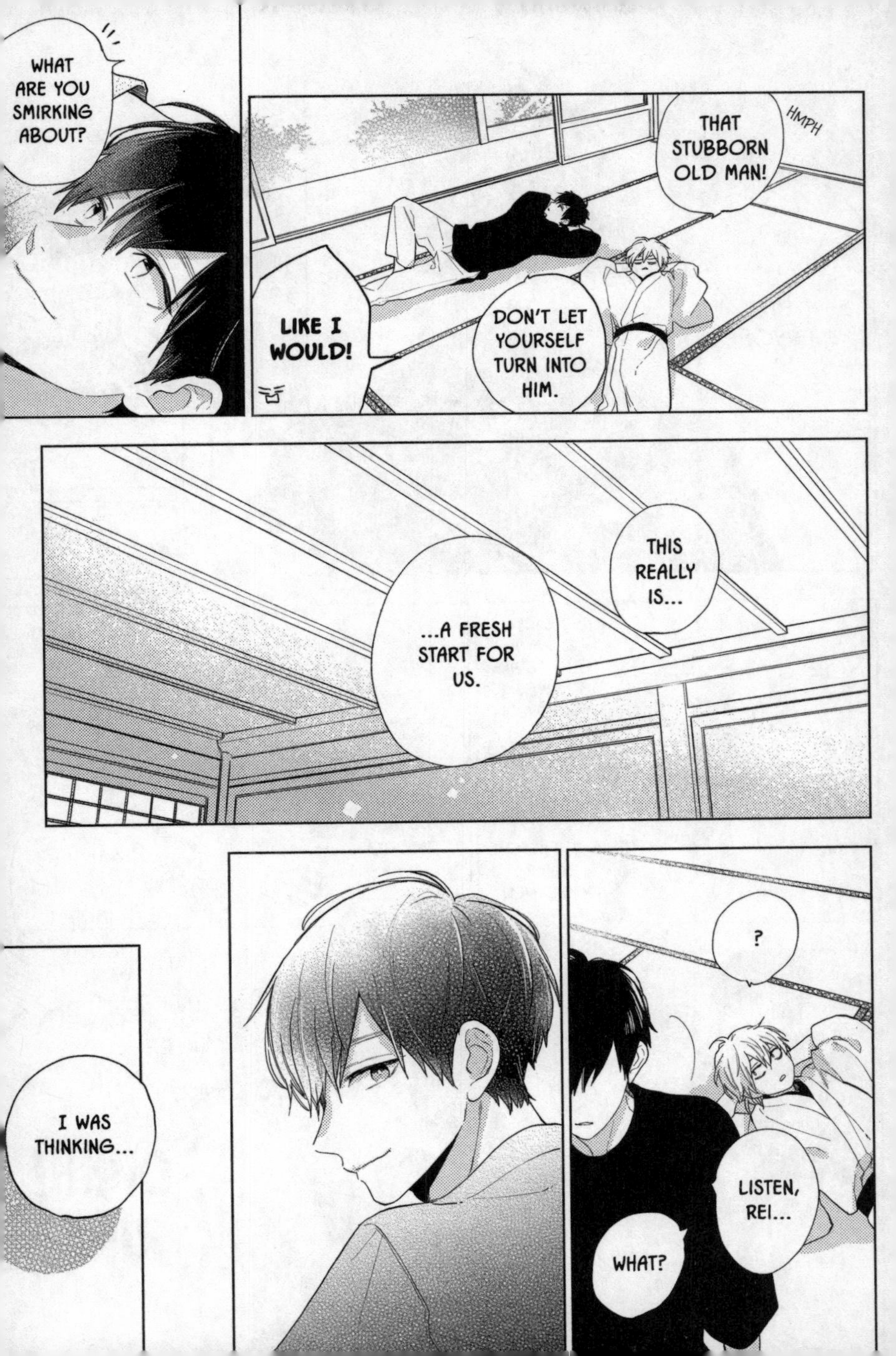
THAT STUBBORN OLD MAN!
HMPH
DON'T LET YOURSELF TURN INTO HIM.
LIKE I WOULD!
WHAT ARE YOU SMIRKING ABOUT?
THIS REALLY IS...
...A FRESH START FOR US.
?
LISTEN, REI...
WHAT?
I WAS THINKING...

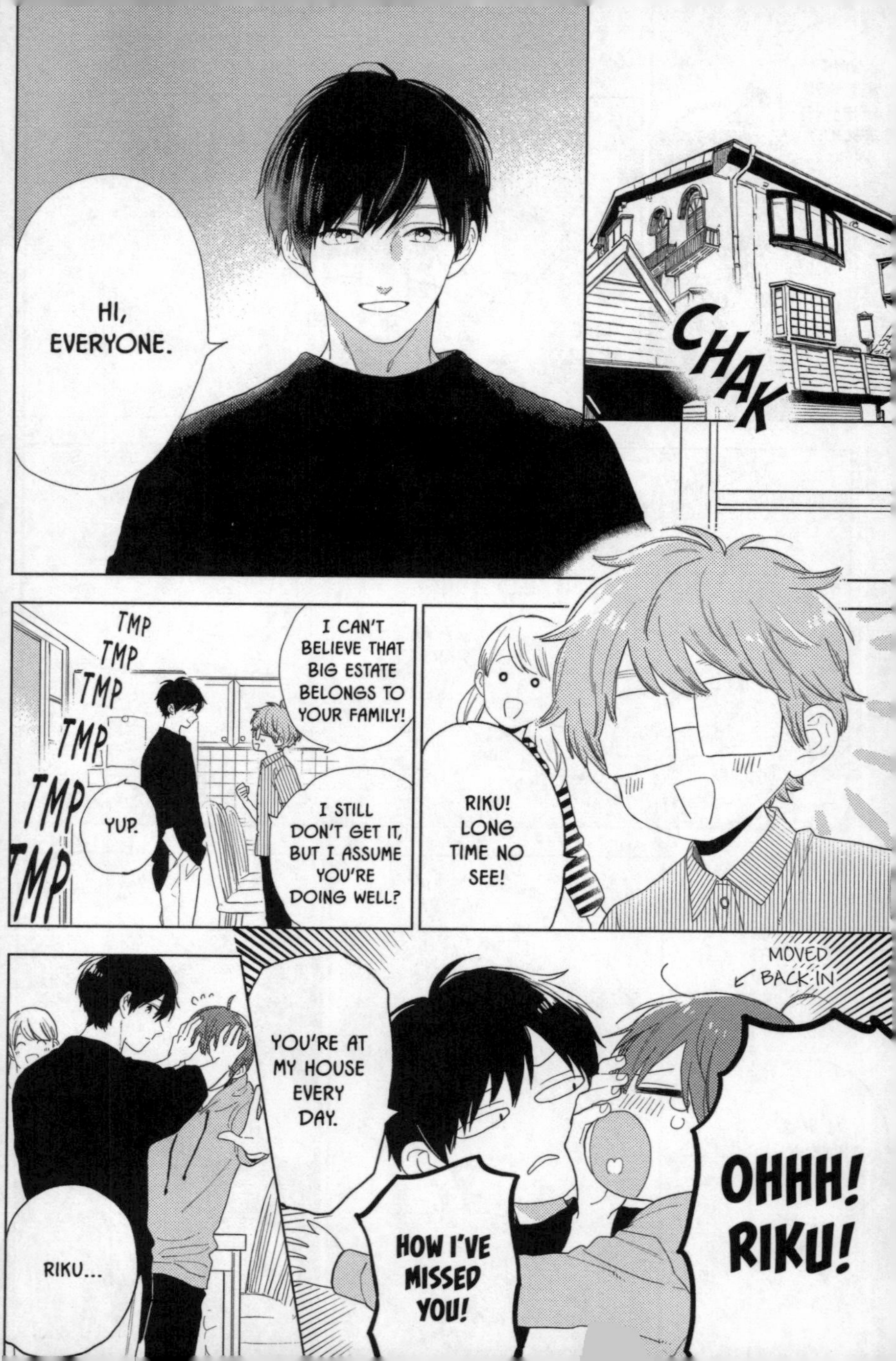
CHAK
HI, EVERYONE.
RIKU! LONG TIME NO SEE!
I CAN'T BELIEVE THAT BIG ESTATE BELONGS TO YOUR FAMILY!
TMP TMP TMP TMP TMP TMP
I STILL DON'T GET IT, BUT I ASSUME YOU'RE DOING WELL?
YUP.
MOVED BACK IN
OHHH! RIKU!
HOW I'VE MISSED YOU!
YOU'RE AT MY HOUSE EVERY DAY.
RIKU...

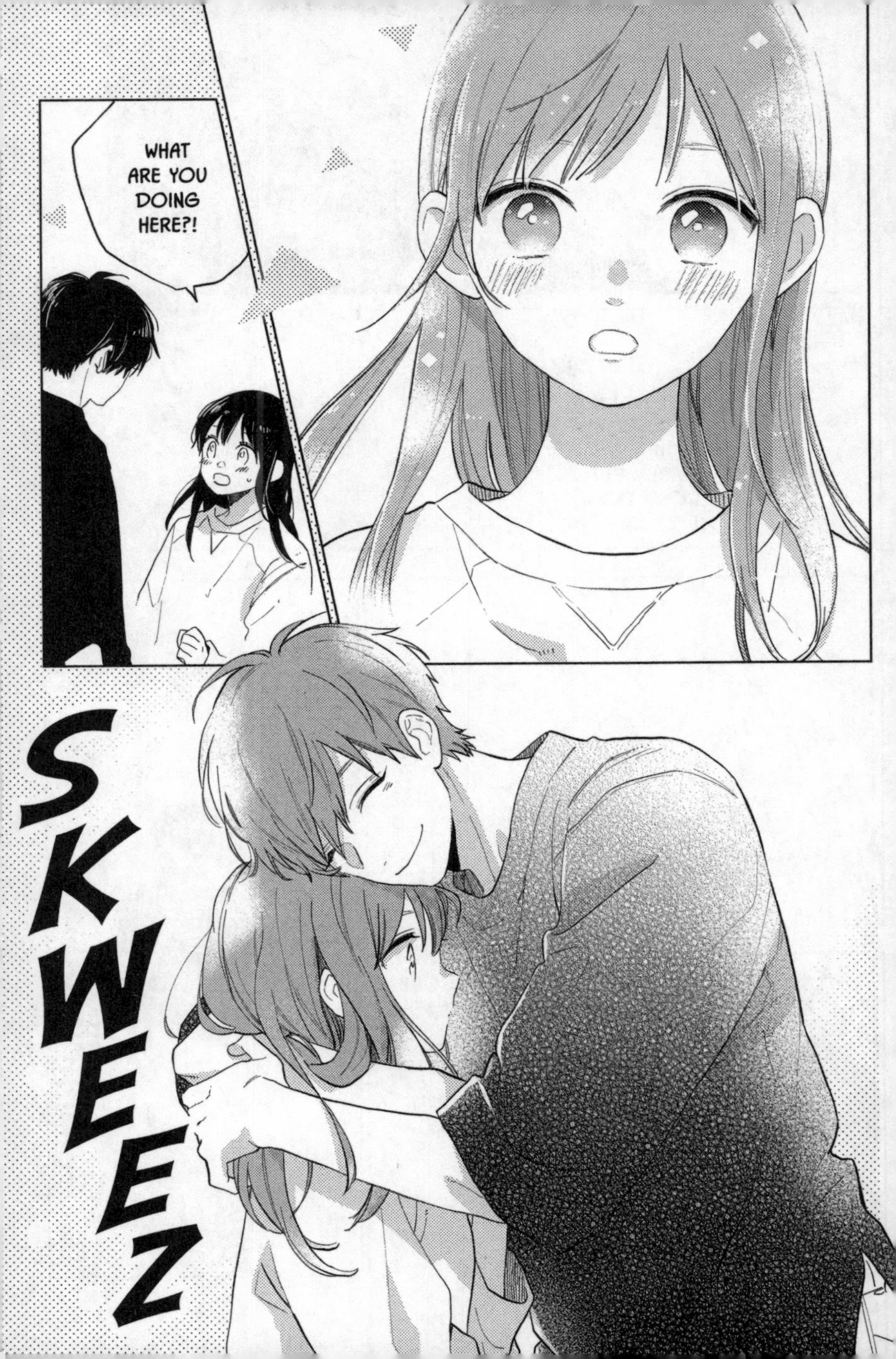
WHAT ARE YOU DOING HERE?!
SKWEEZ

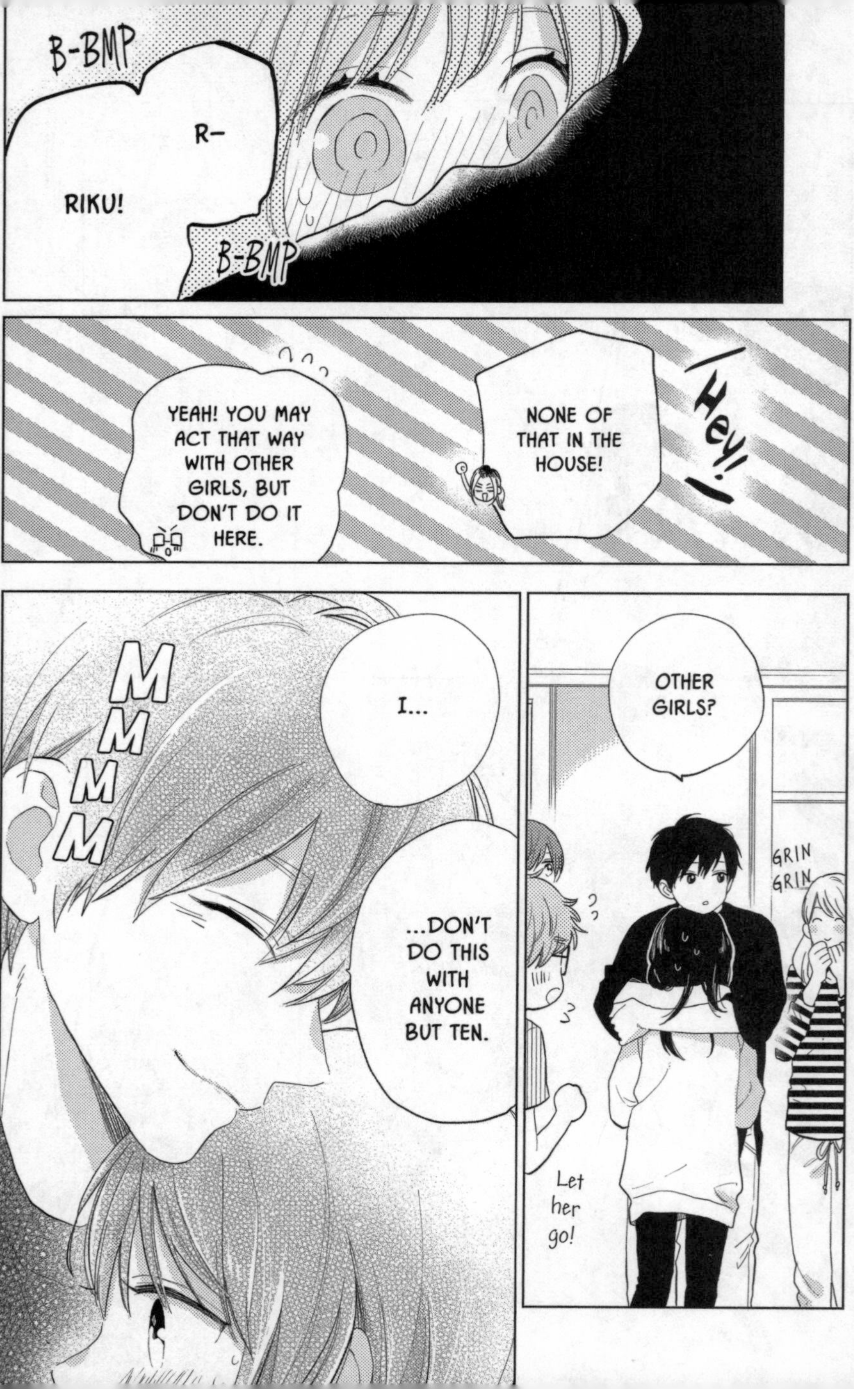
B-BMP
R–
RIKU!
B-BMP
Hey!!
NONE OF THAT IN THE HOUSE!
YEAH! YOU MAY ACT THAT WAY WITH OTHER GIRLS, BUT DON'T DO IT HERE.
OTHER GIRLS?
GRIN GRIN
Let her go!
MMMM
I...
...DON'T DO THIS WITH ANYONE BUT TEN.

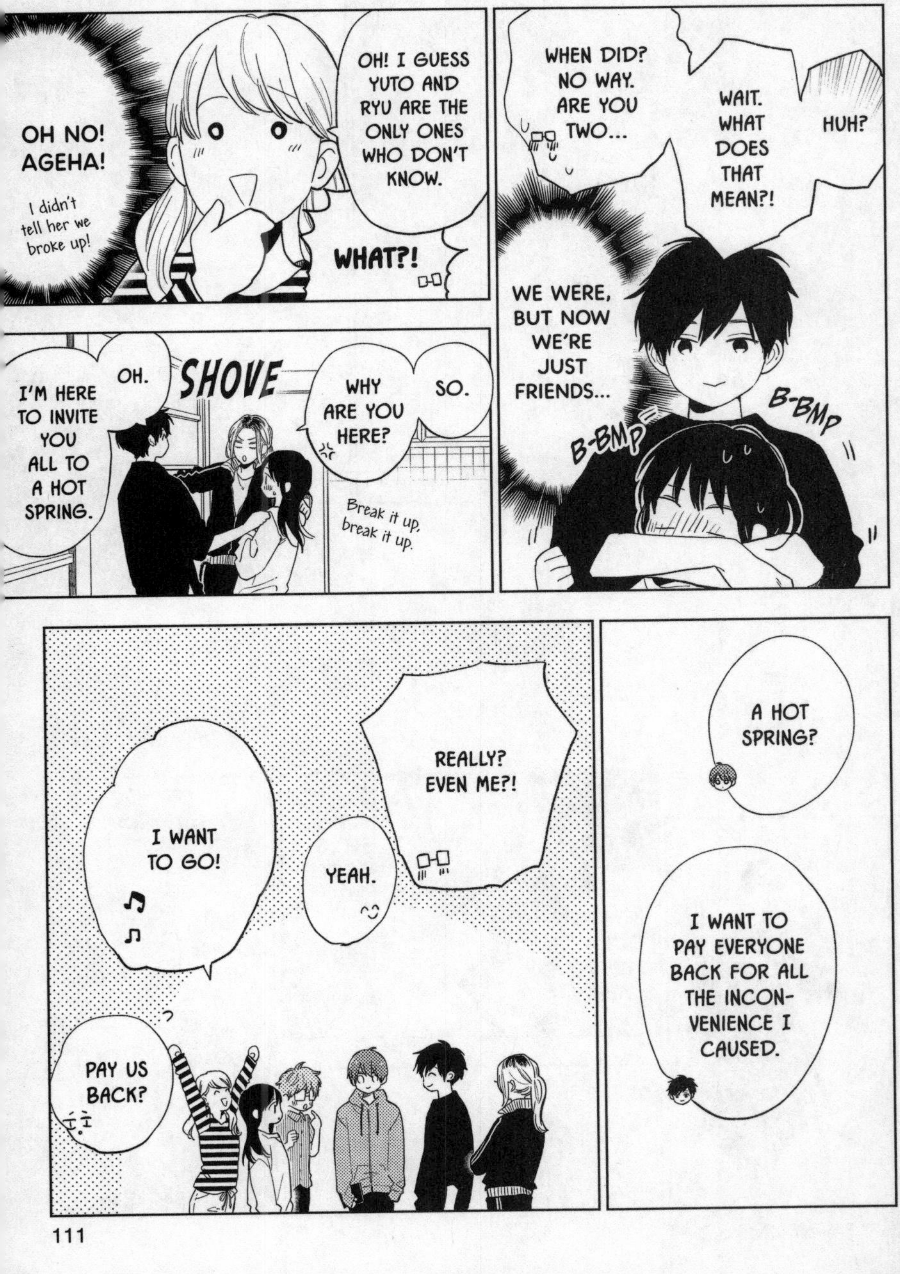
HUH?
WAIT. WHAT DOES THAT MEAN?!
WHEN DID? NO WAY. ARE YOU TWO...
WE WERE, BUT NOW WE'RE JUST FRIENDS...
B-BMP
B-BMP
OH! I GUESS YUTO AND RYU ARE THE ONLY ONES WHO DON'T KNOW.
WHAT?!
OH NO! AGEHA!
I didn't tell her we broke up!
SO.
WHY ARE YOU HERE?
Break it up, break it up.
SHOVE
OH.
I'M HERE TO INVITE YOU ALL TO A HOT SPRING.
A HOT SPRING?
I WANT TO PAY EVERYONE BACK FOR ALL THE INCON-VENIENCE I CAUSED.
REALLY? EVEN ME?!
YEAH.
I WANT TO GO!
PAY US BACK?

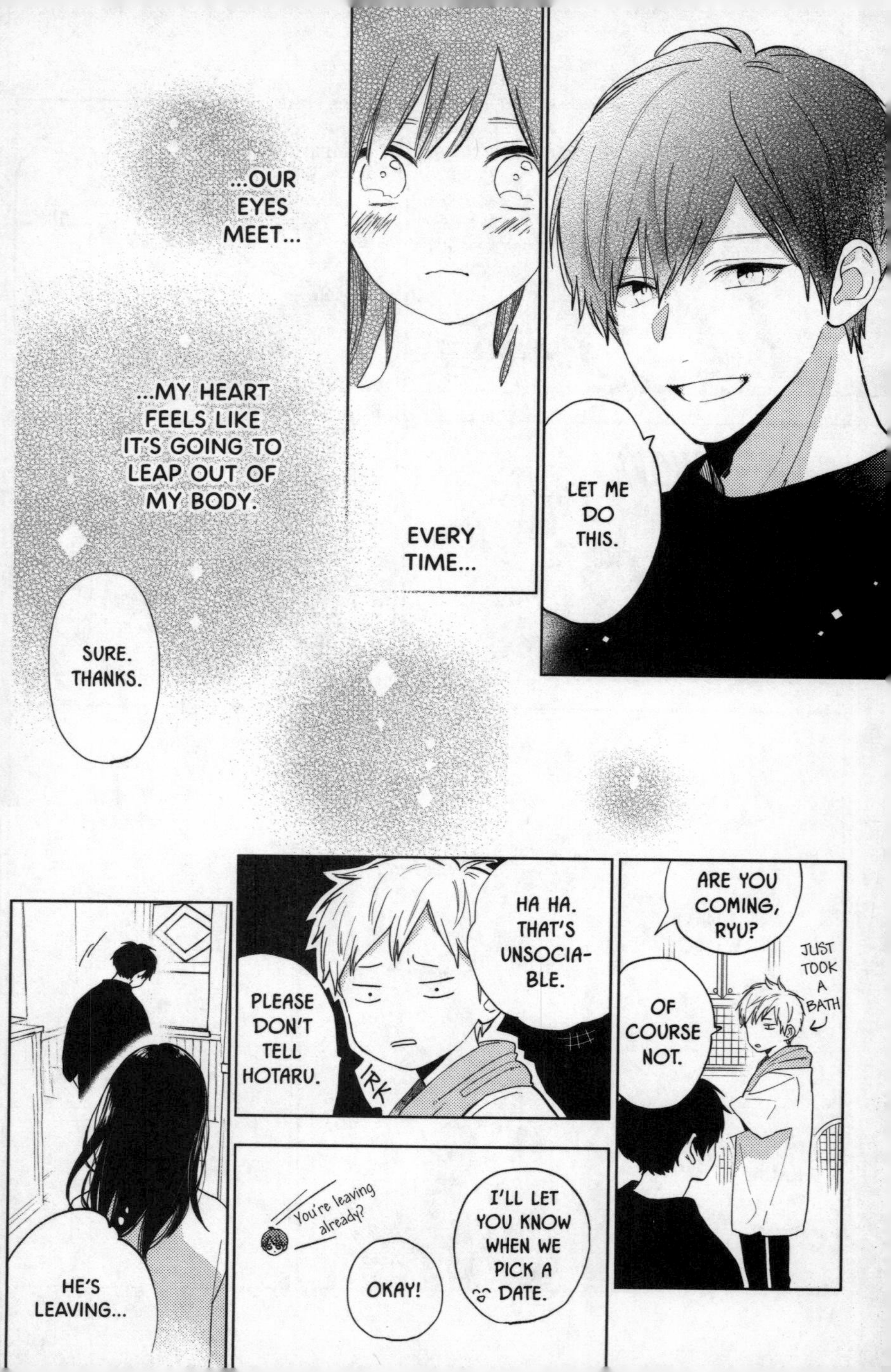
LET ME DO THIS.
EVERY TIME...
...OUR EYES MEET...
...MY HEART FEELS LIKE IT'S GOING TO LEAP OUT OF MY BODY.
SURE. THANKS.
ARE YOU COMING, RYU?
JUST TOOK A BATH
OF COURSE NOT.
HA HA. THAT'S UNSOCIABLE.
PLEASE DON'T TELL HOTARU.
IRK
I'LL LET YOU KNOW WHEN WE PICK A DATE.
OKAY!
You're leaving already?
HE'S LEAVING...

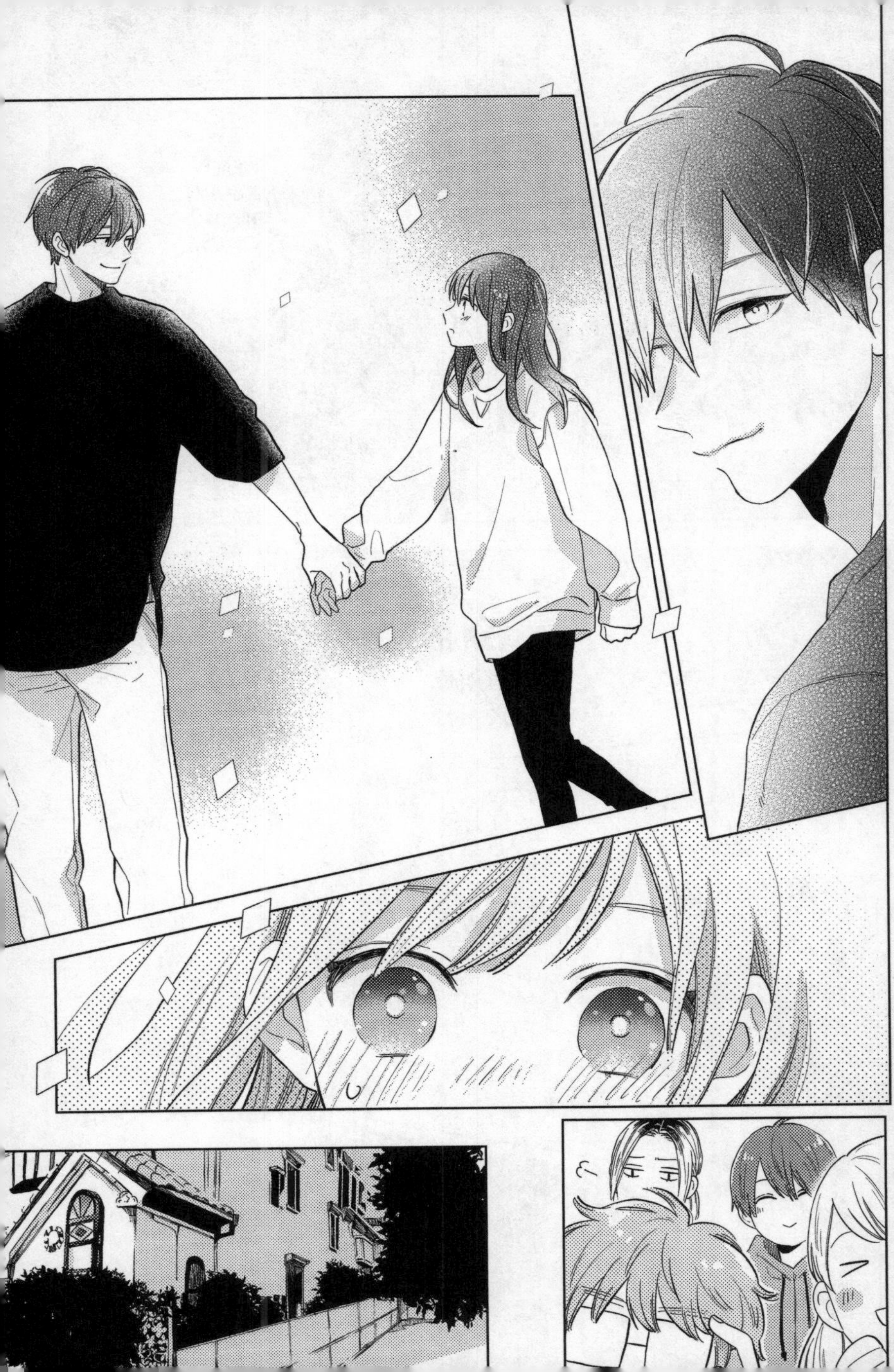

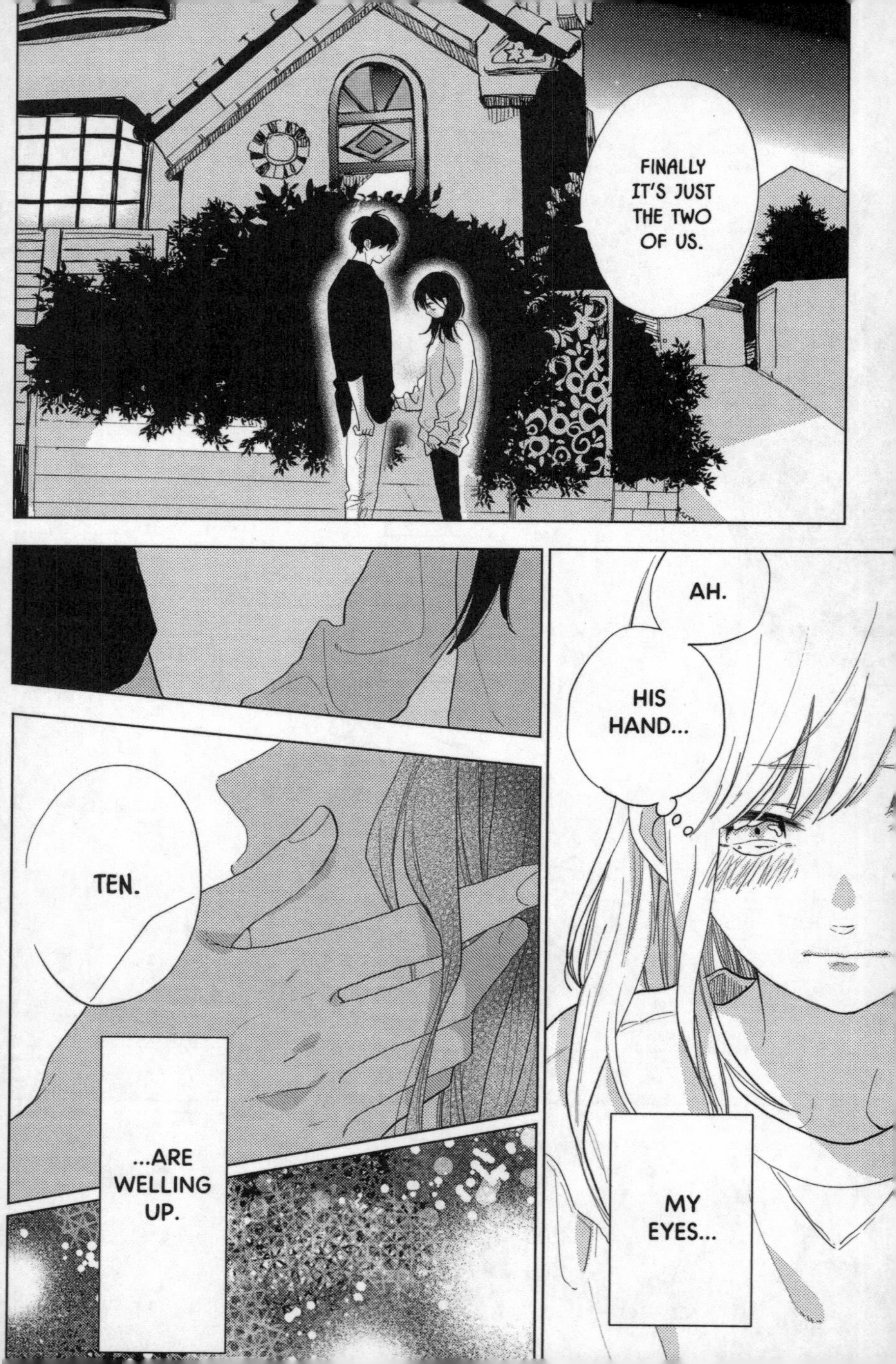
FINALLY IT'S JUST THE TWO OF US.
AH.
HIS HAND...
MY EYES...
TEN.
...ARE WELLING UP.

HUH?

OH...

TEN.

I'M SORRY I YELLED AT YOU OVER THERE.

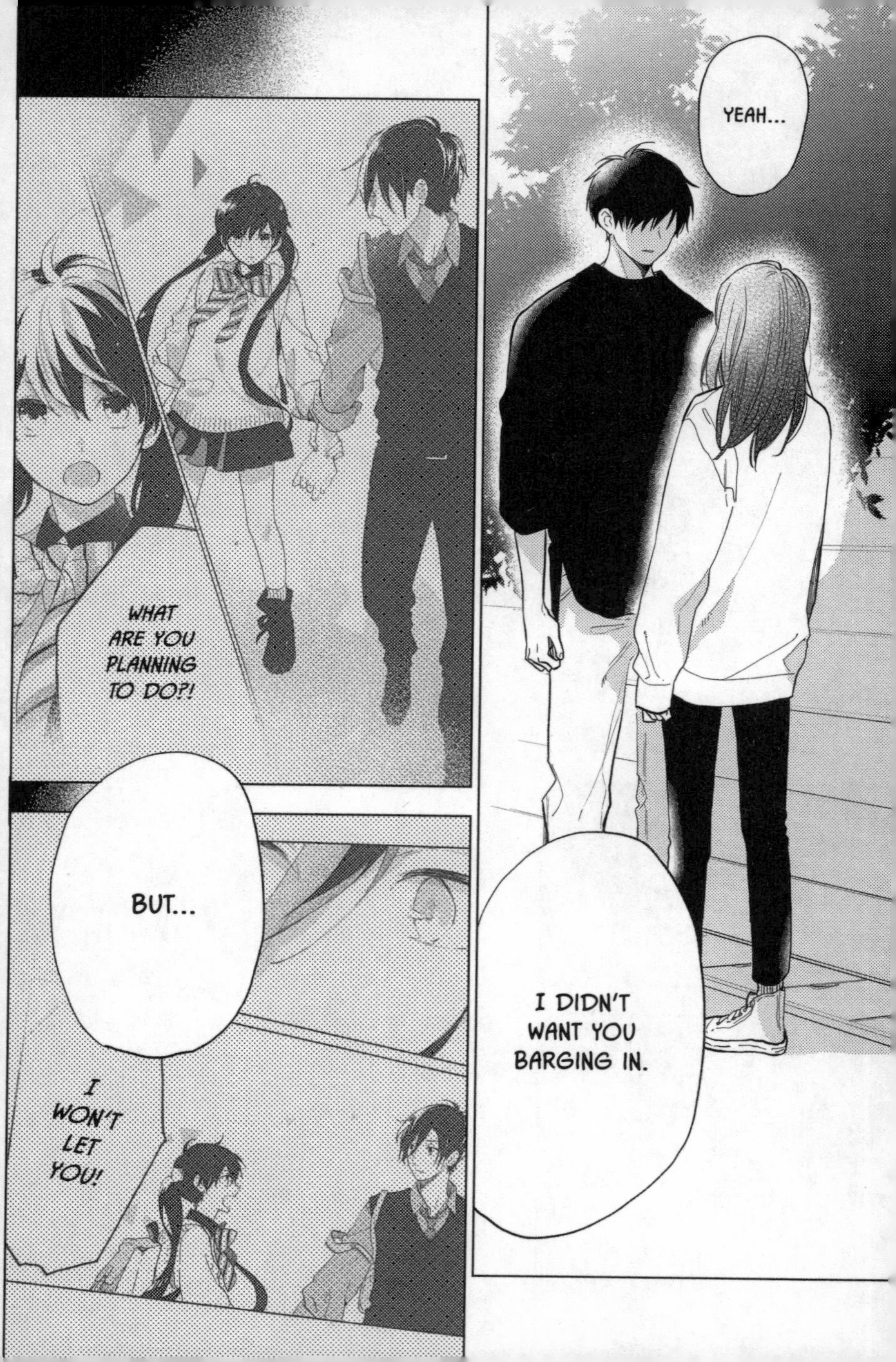
YEAH...
I DIDN'T WANT YOU BARGING IN.
WHAT ARE YOU PLANNING TO DO?!
BUT...
I WON'T LET YOU!

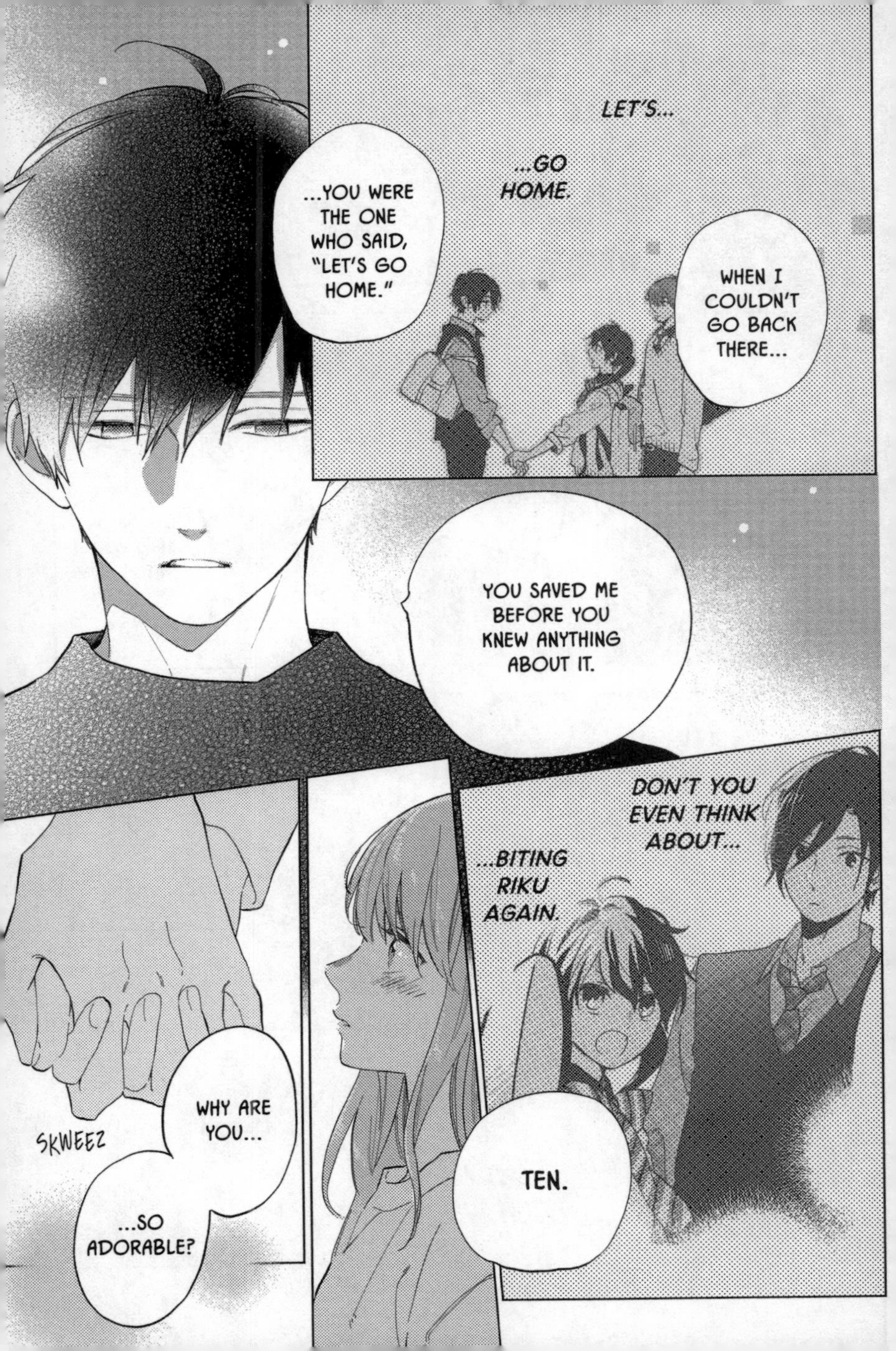
LET'S...
...GO HOME.
WHEN I COULDN'T GO BACK THERE...
...YOU WERE THE ONE WHO SAID, "LET'S GO HOME."
YOU SAVED ME BEFORE YOU KNEW ANYTHING ABOUT IT.
DON'T YOU EVEN THINK ABOUT...
...BITING RIKU AGAIN.
TEN.
SKWEEZ
WHY ARE YOU...
...SO ADORABLE?

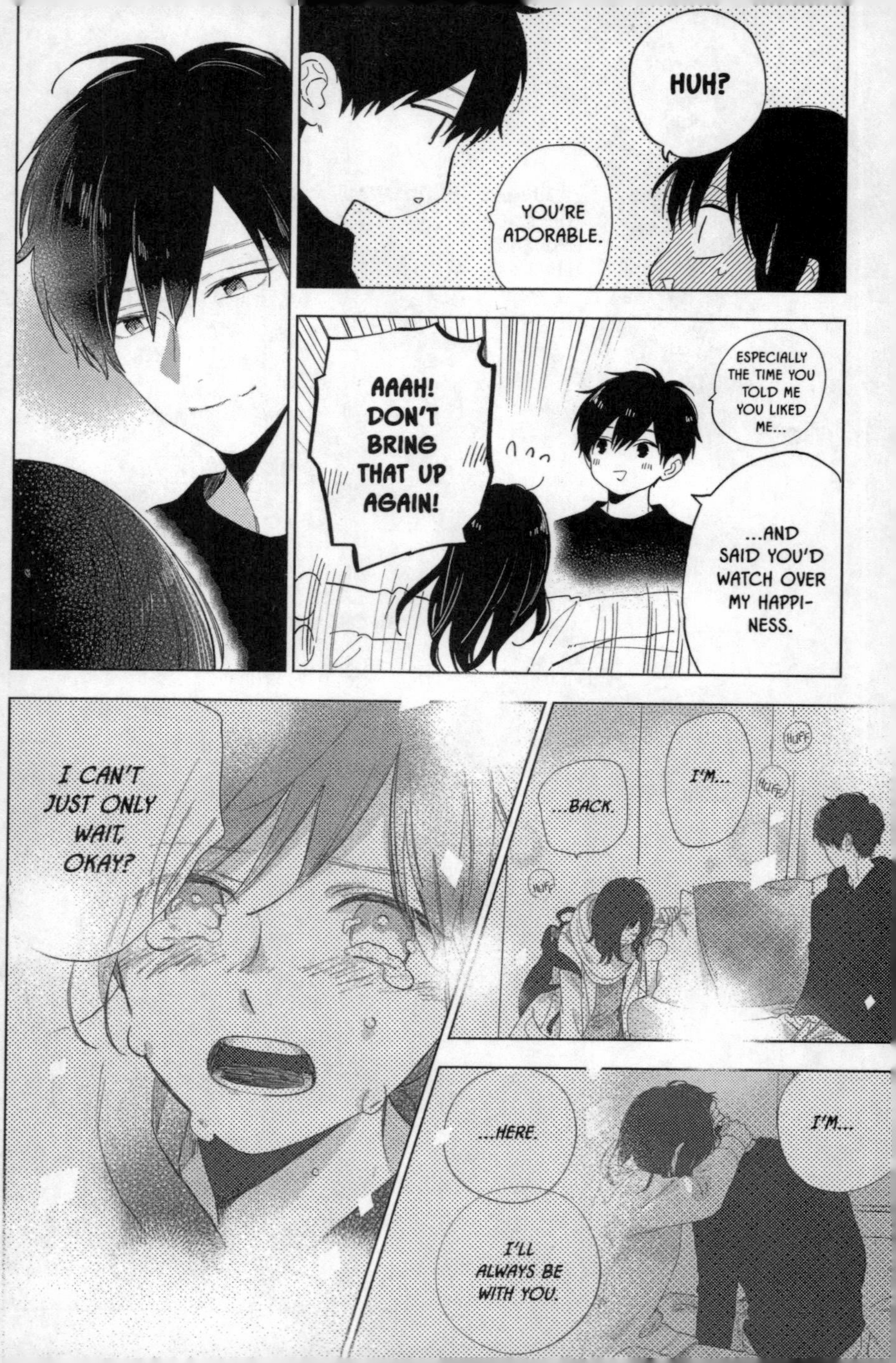
HUH?
YOU'RE ADORABLE.
ESPECIALLY THE TIME YOU TOLD ME YOU LIKED ME...
...AND SAID YOU'D WATCH OVER MY HAPPINESS.
AAAH! DON'T BRING THAT UP AGAIN!
HUFF
I'M...
HUFF
...BACK.
HUFF
I'M...
...HERE.
I'LL ALWAYS BE WITH YOU.
I CAN'T JUST ONLY WAIT, OKAY?

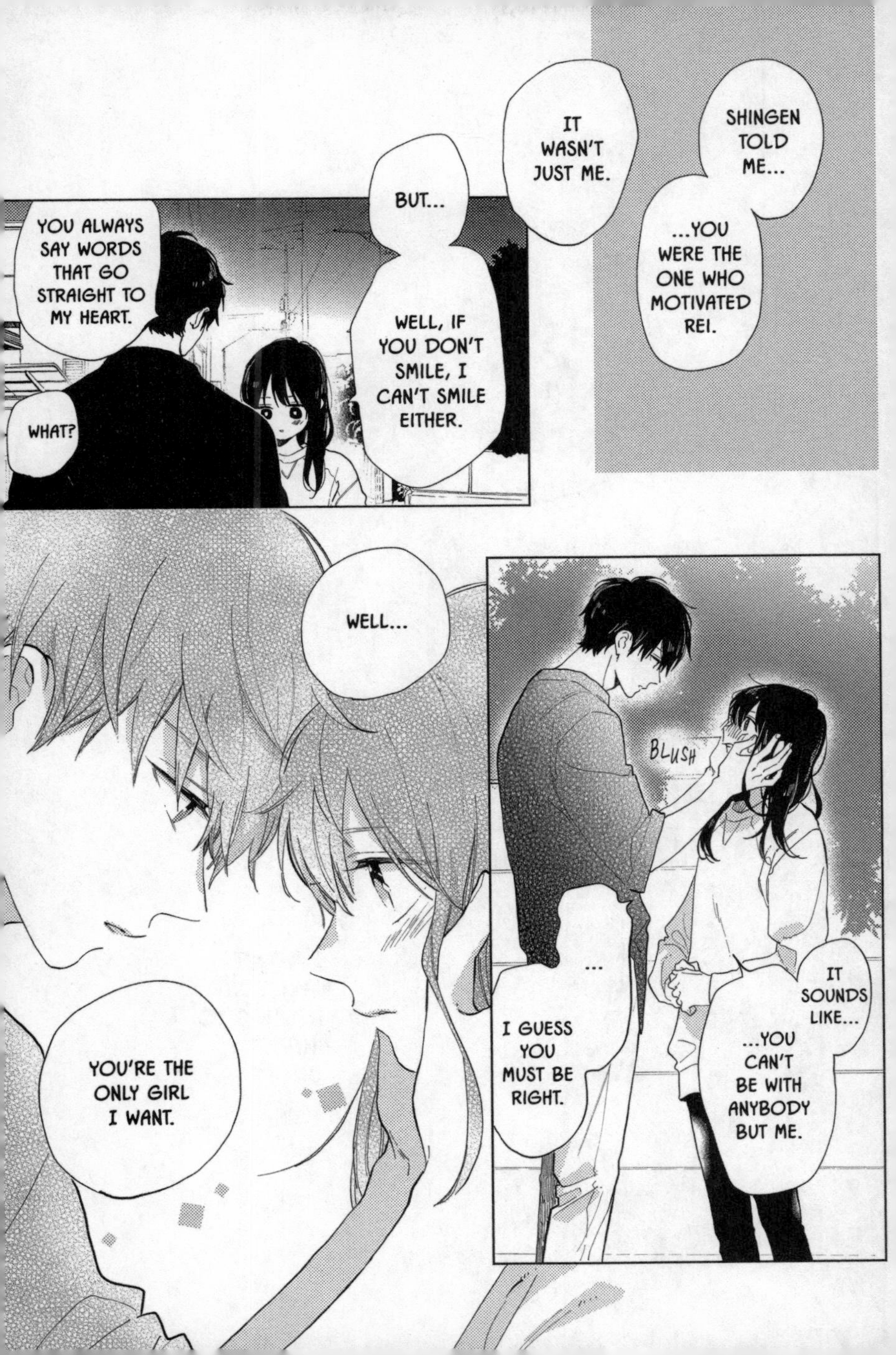
SHINGEN TOLD ME...
...YOU WERE THE ONE WHO MOTIVATED REI.
IT WASN'T JUST ME.
BUT...
WELL, IF YOU DON'T SMILE, I CAN'T SMILE EITHER.
YOU ALWAYS SAY WORDS THAT GO STRAIGHT TO MY HEART.
WHAT?
BLUSH
IT SOUNDS LIKE...
...YOU CAN'T BE WITH ANYBODY BUT ME.
...
I GUESS YOU MUST BE RIGHT.
WELL...
YOU'RE THE ONLY GIRL I WANT.

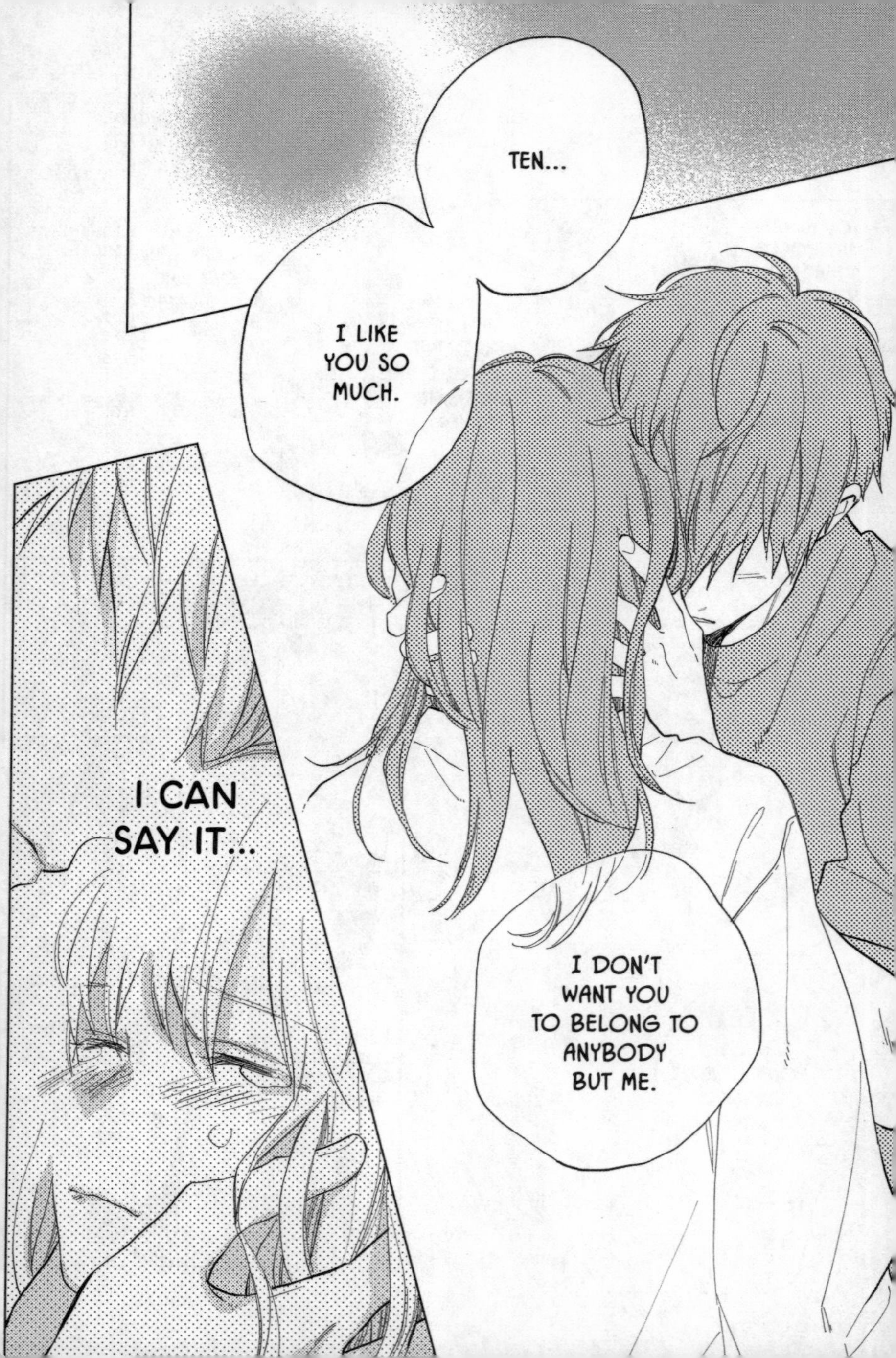
TEN...
I LIKE YOU SO MUCH.
I DON'T WANT YOU TO BELONG TO ANYBODY BUT ME.
I CAN SAY IT...

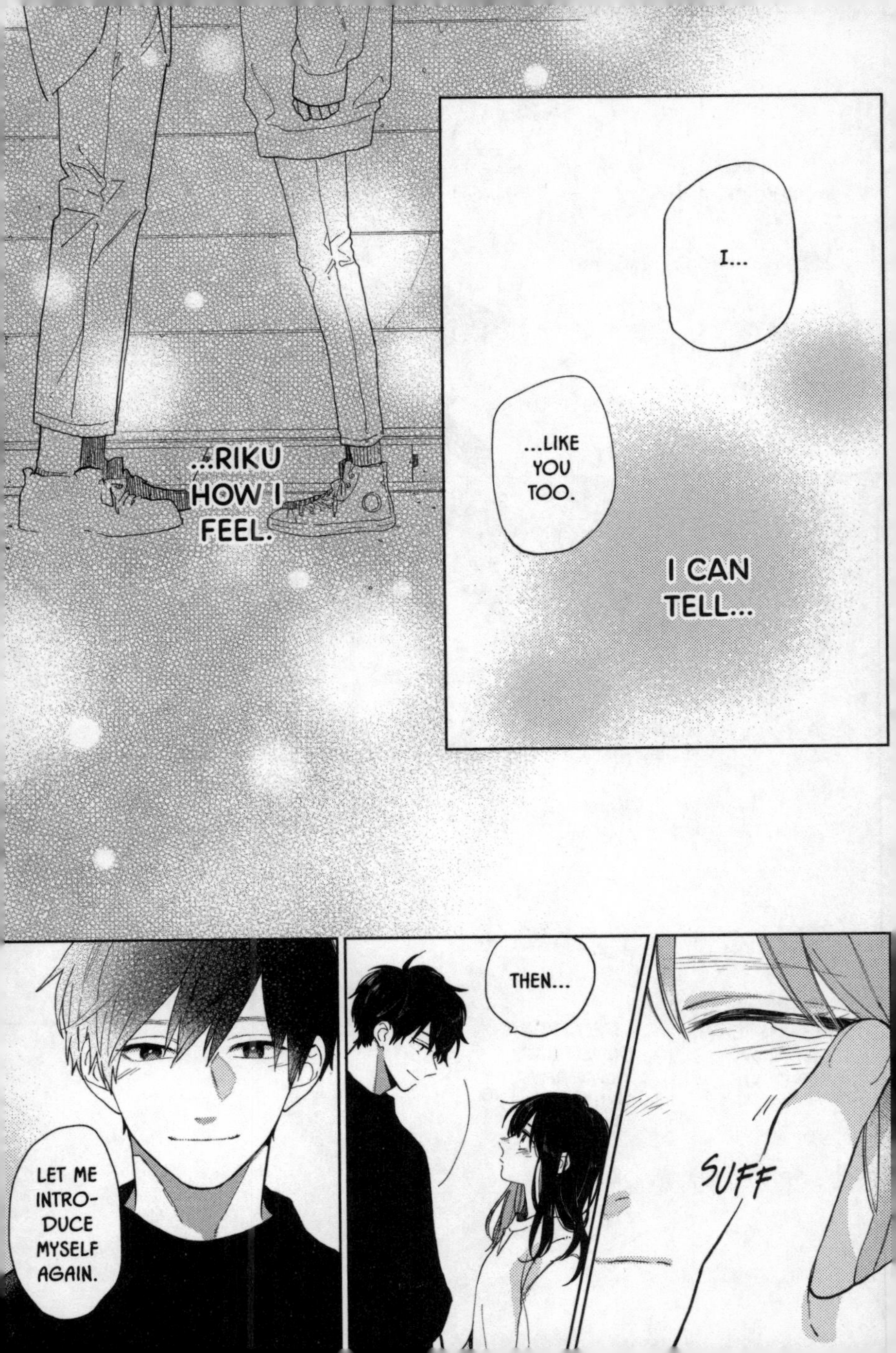

I...
...LIKE YOU TOO.
I CAN TELL...
...RIKU HOW I FEEL.
SUFF
THEN...
LET ME INTRO-DUCE MYSELF AGAIN.

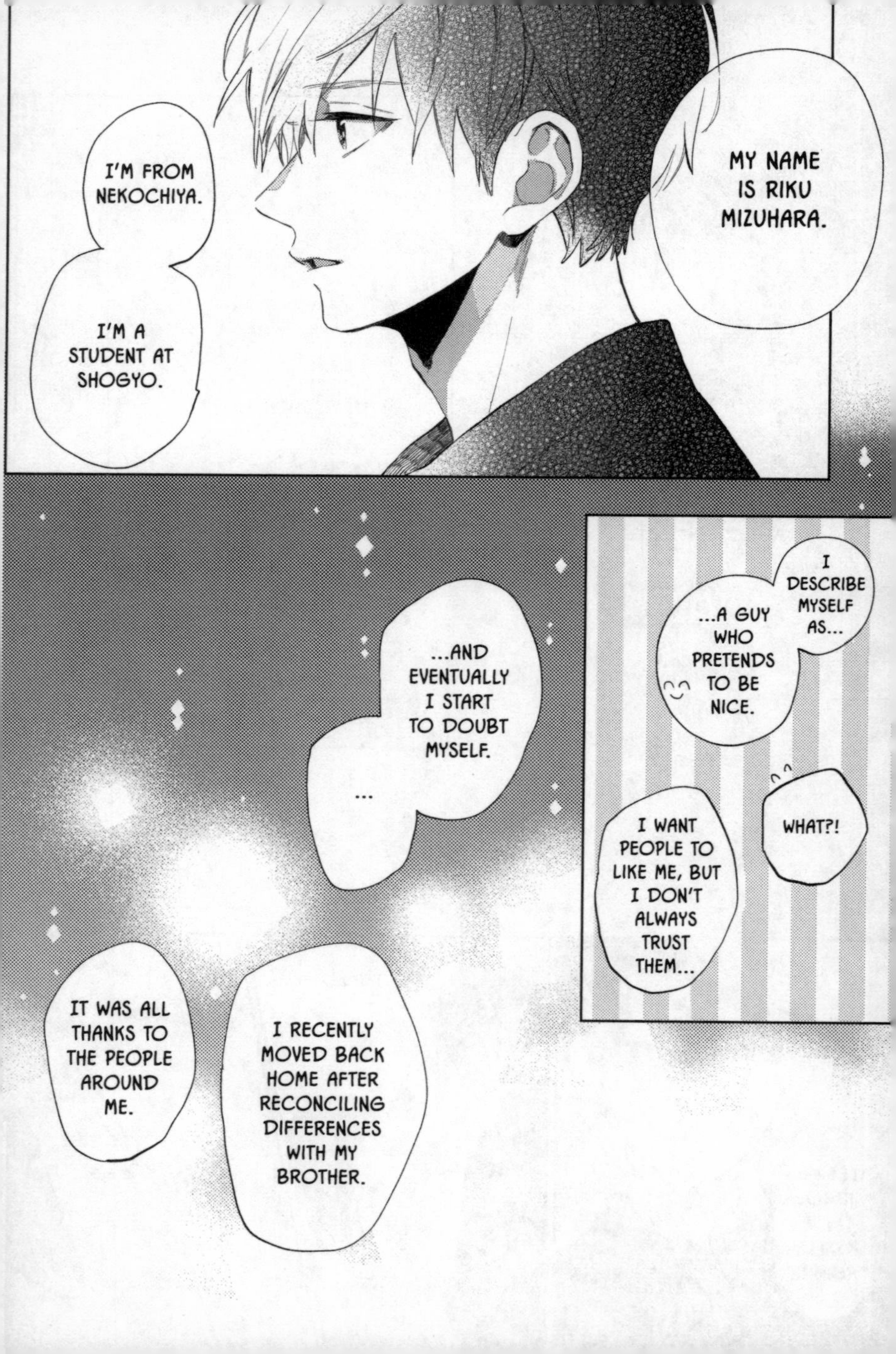
MY NAME IS RIKU MIZUHARA.
I'M FROM NEKOCHIYA.
I'M A STUDENT AT SHOGYO.
I DESCRIBE MYSELF AS...
...A GUY WHO PRETENDS TO BE NICE.
WHAT?!
I WANT PEOPLE TO LIKE ME, BUT I DON'T ALWAYS TRUST THEM...
...AND EVENTUALLY I START TO DOUBT MYSELF.
...
I RECENTLY MOVED BACK HOME AFTER RECONCILING DIFFERENCES WITH MY BROTHER.
IT WAS ALL THANKS TO THE PEOPLE AROUND ME.

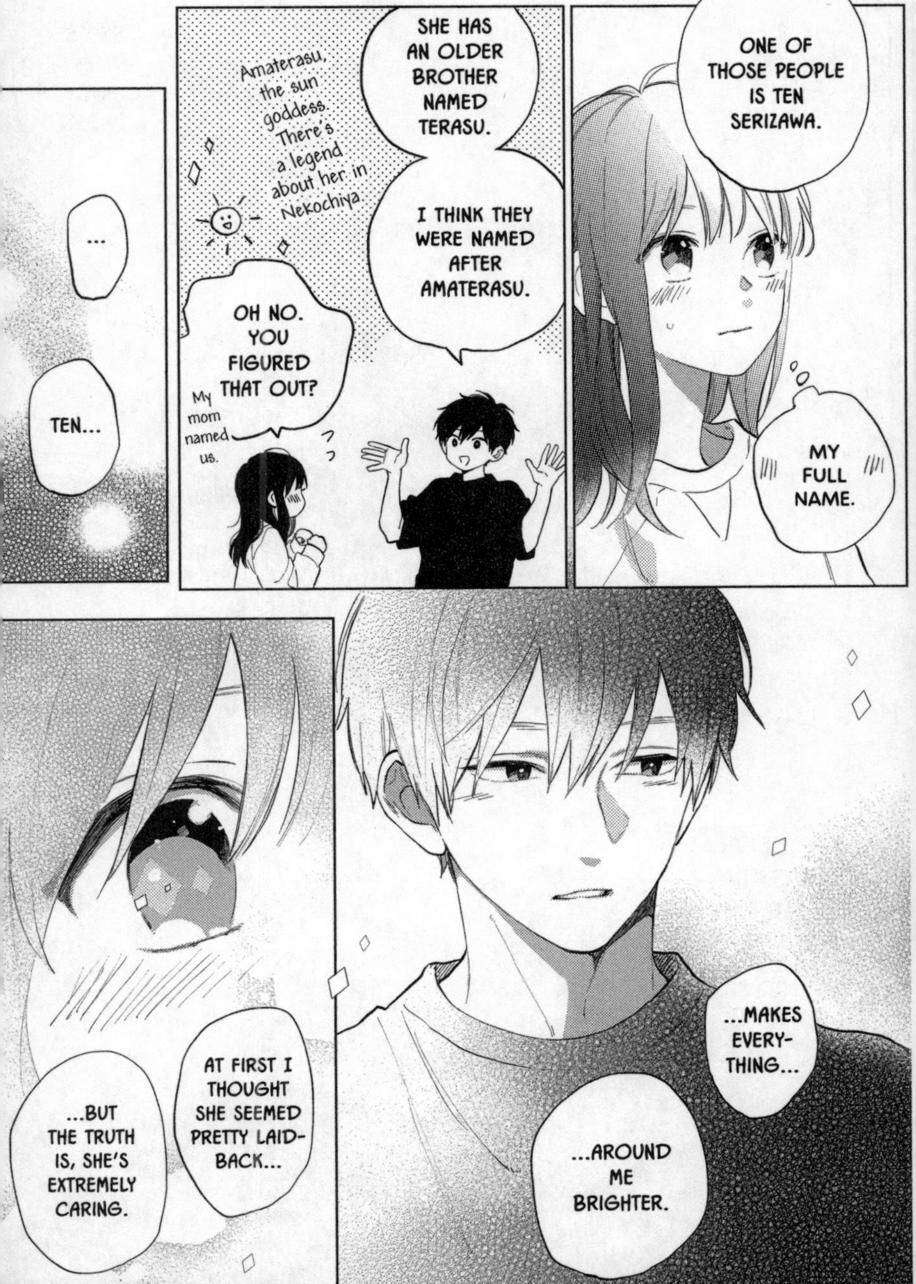
ONE OF THOSE PEOPLE IS TEN SERIZAWA.
MY FULL NAME.
SHE HAS AN OLDER BROTHER NAMED TERASU.
I THINK THEY WERE NAMED AFTER AMATERASU.
Amaterasu, the sun goddess. There's a legend about her in Nekochiya.
OH NO. YOU FIGURED THAT OUT?
My mom named us.
...
TEN...
...MAKES EVERY-THING...
...AROUND ME BRIGHTER.
AT FIRST I THOUGHT SHE SEEMED PRETTY LAID-BACK...
...BUT THE TRUTH IS, SHE'S EXTREMELY CARING.

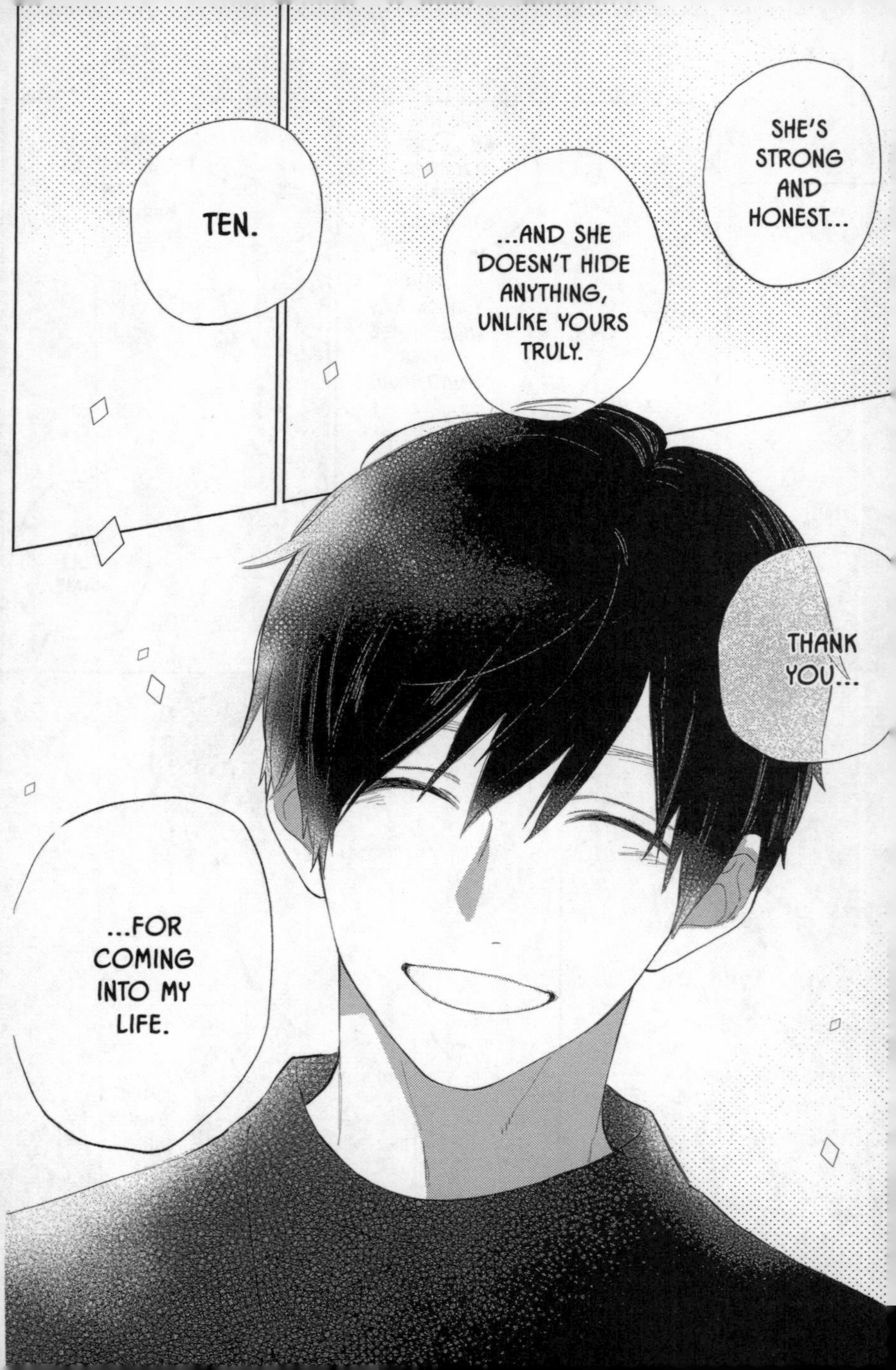
SHE'S STRONG AND HONEST...
...AND SHE DOESN'T HIDE ANYTHING, UNLIKE YOURS TRULY.
TEN.
THANK YOU...
...FOR COMING INTO MY LIFE.

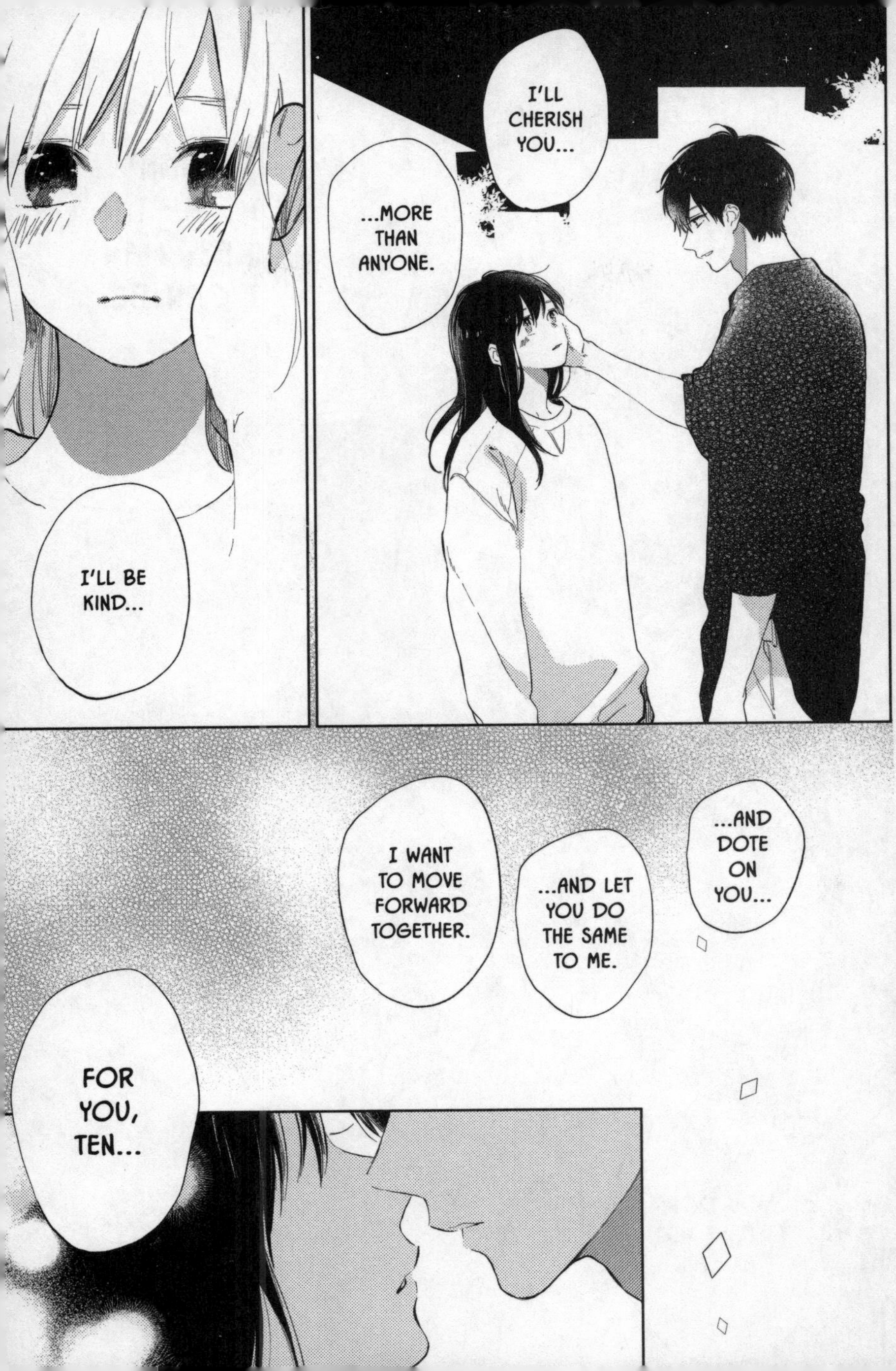
I'LL CHERISH YOU...
...MORE THAN ANYONE.
I'LL BE KIND...
...AND DOTE ON YOU...
...AND LET YOU DO THE SAME TO ME.
I WANT TO MOVE FORWARD TOGETHER.
FOR YOU, TEN...

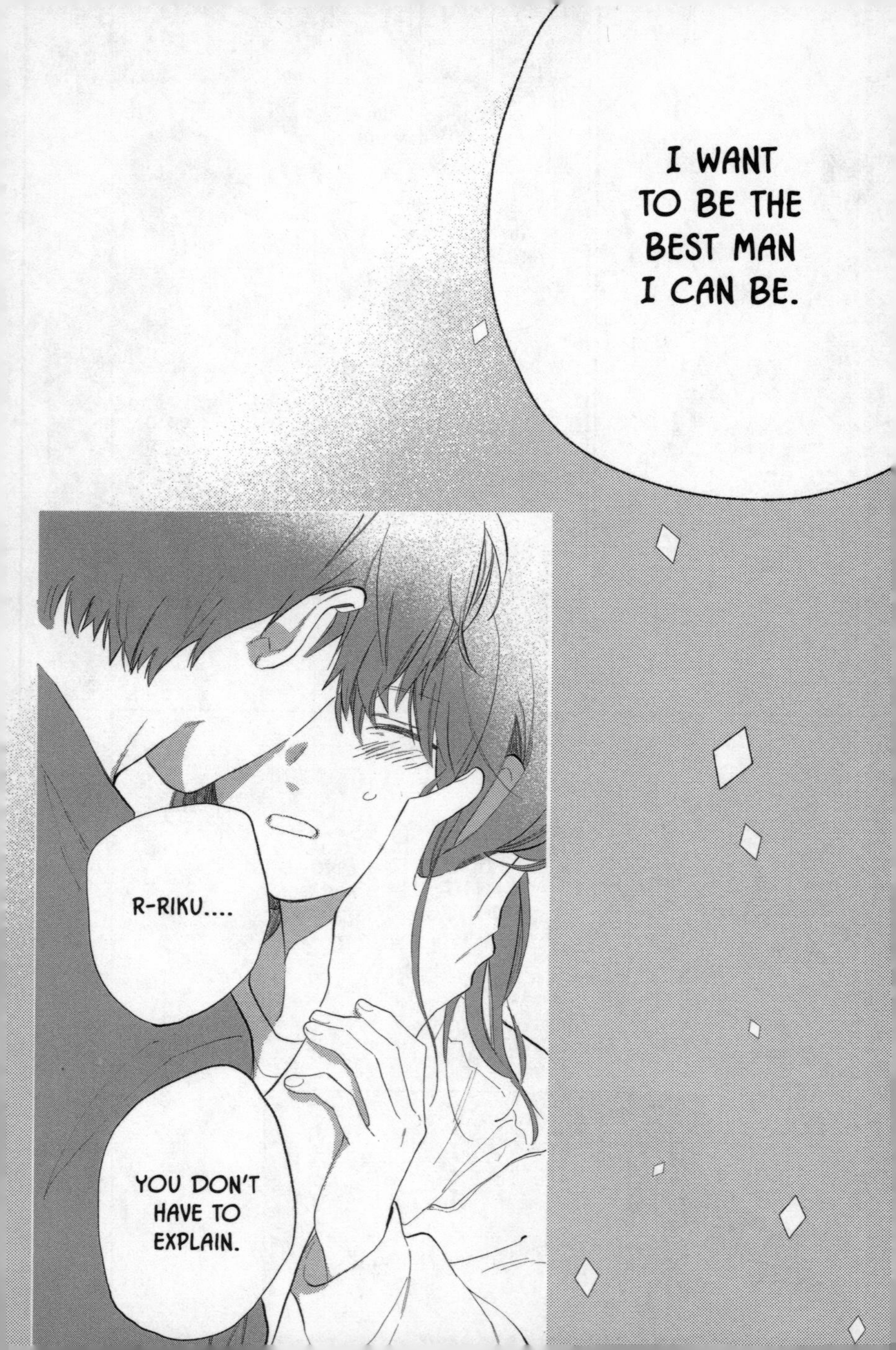
I WANT TO BE THE BEST MAN I CAN BE.
R-RIKU....
YOU DON'T HAVE TO EXPLAIN.

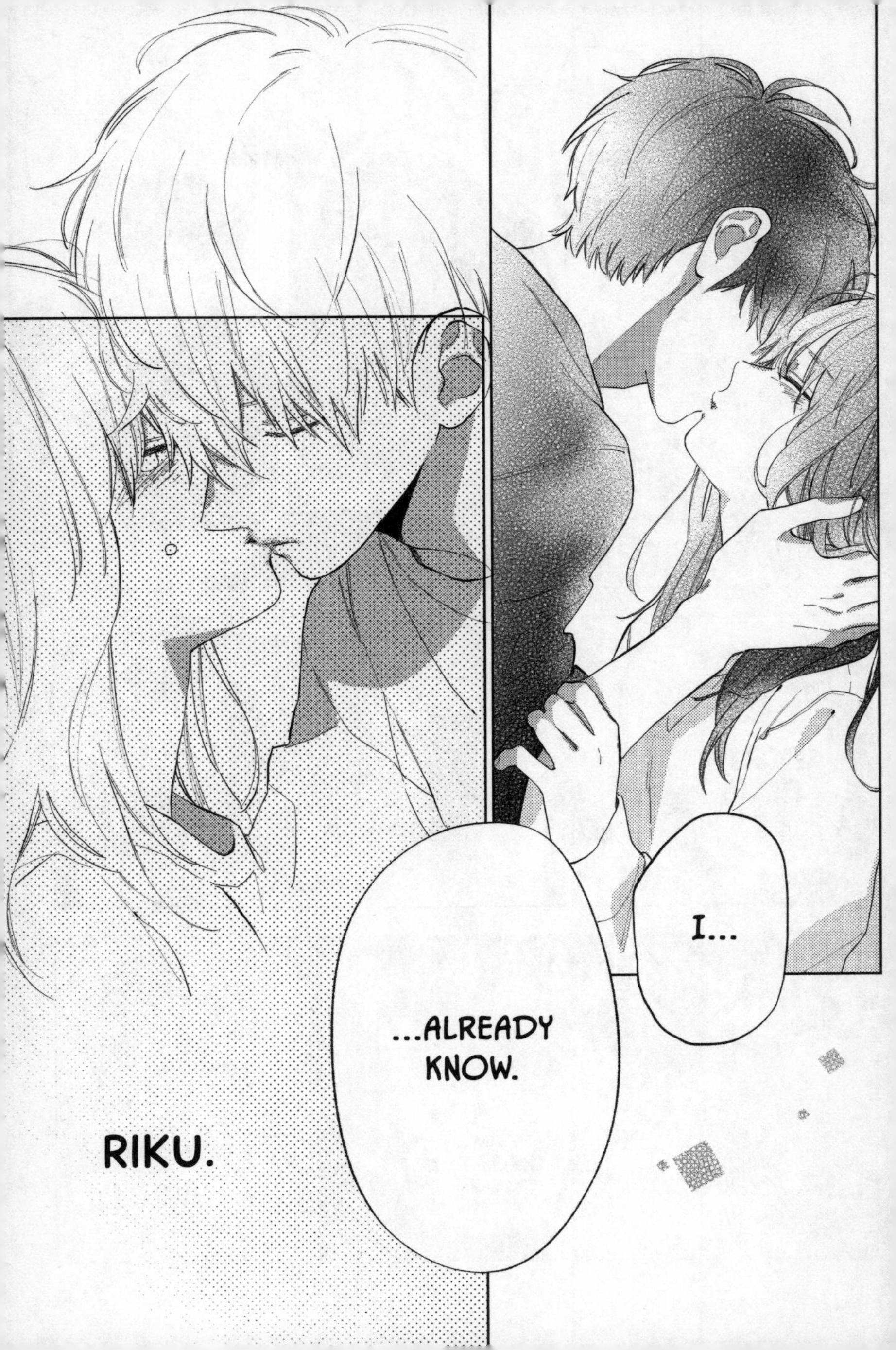
I...
...ALREADY KNOW.
RIKU.

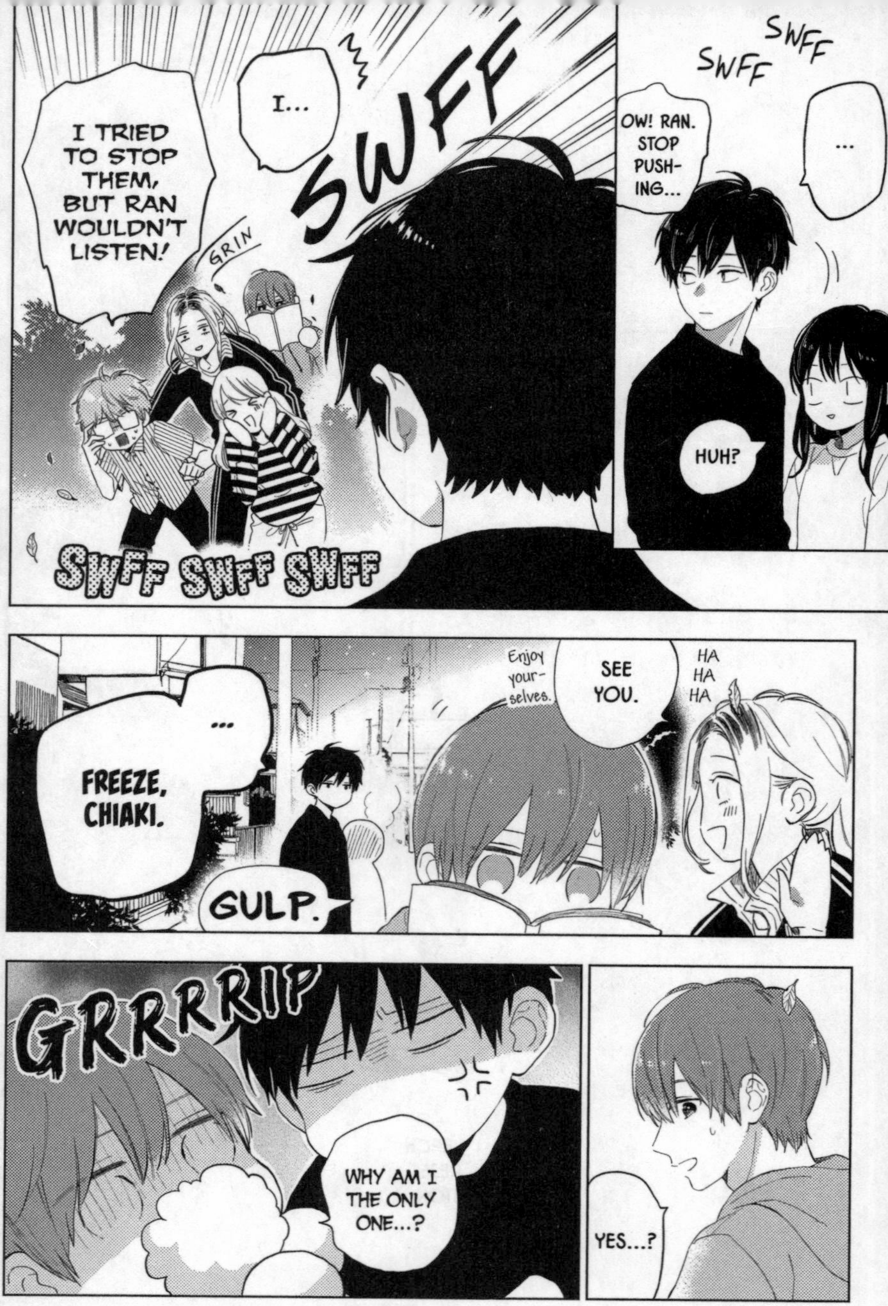
SWFF
SWFF
...
OW! RAN. STOP PUSH-ING...
HUH?
SWFF
I...
I TRIED TO STOP THEM, BUT RAN WOULDN'T LISTEN!
GRIN
SWFF SWFF SWFF
HA HA HA
SEE YOU.
Enjoy your-selves.
... FREEZE, CHIAKI.
GULP.
YES...?
GRRRRIP
WHY AM I THE ONLY ONE...?

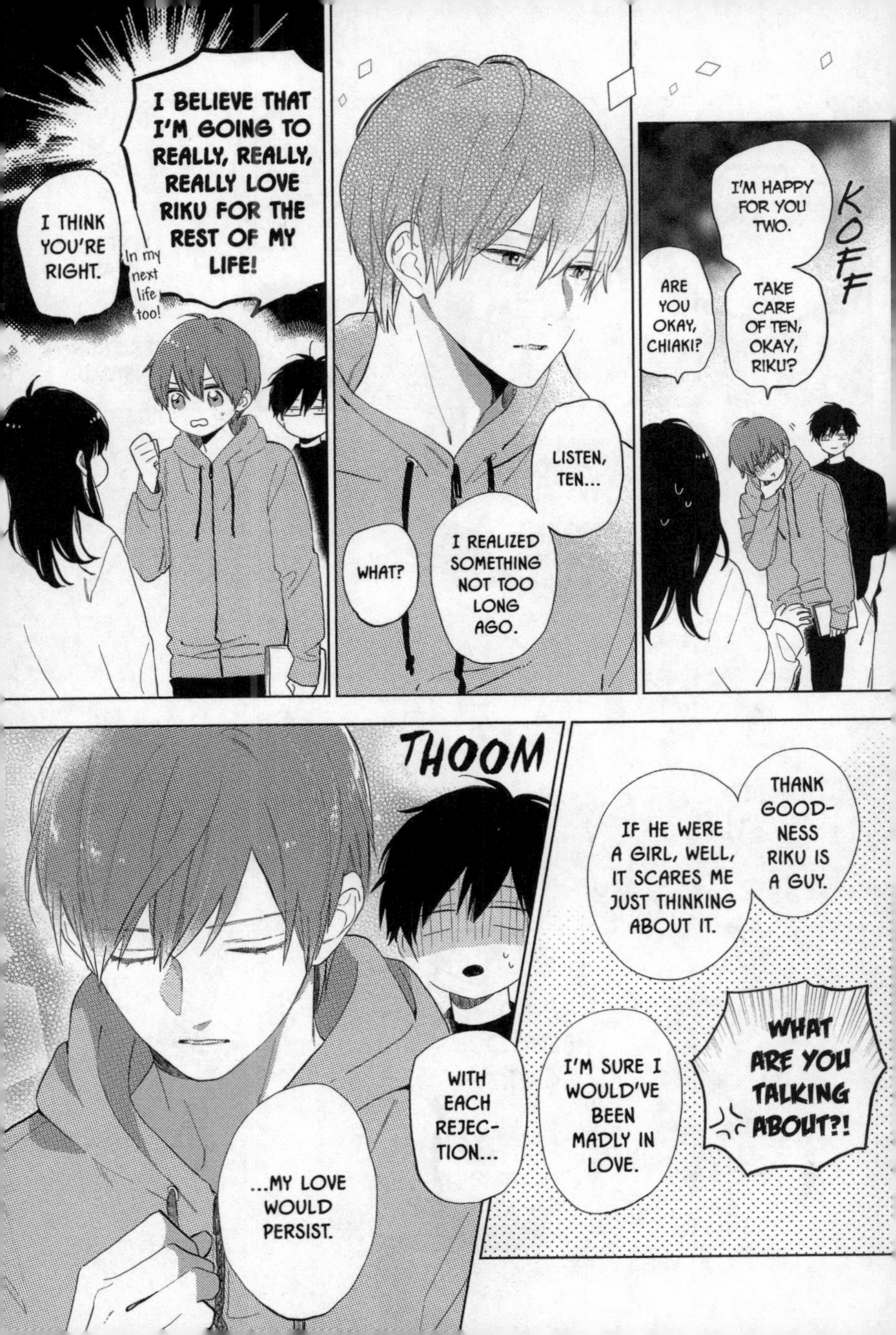
I'M HAPPY FOR YOU TWO.
KOFF
TAKE CARE OF TEN, OKAY, RIKU?
ARE YOU OKAY, CHIAKI?
LISTEN, TEN...
I REALIZED SOMETHING NOT TOO LONG AGO.
WHAT?
I BELIEVE THAT I'M GOING TO REALLY, REALLY, REALLY LOVE RIKU FOR THE REST OF MY LIFE!
In my next life too!
I THINK YOU'RE RIGHT.
THANK GOOD-NESS RIKU IS A GUY.
IF HE WERE A GIRL, WELL, IT SCARES ME JUST THINKING ABOUT IT.
I'M SURE I WOULD'VE BEEN MADLY IN LOVE.
WHAT ARE YOU TALKING ABOUT?!
THOOM
WITH EACH REJEC-TION...
...MY LOVE WOULD PERSIST.

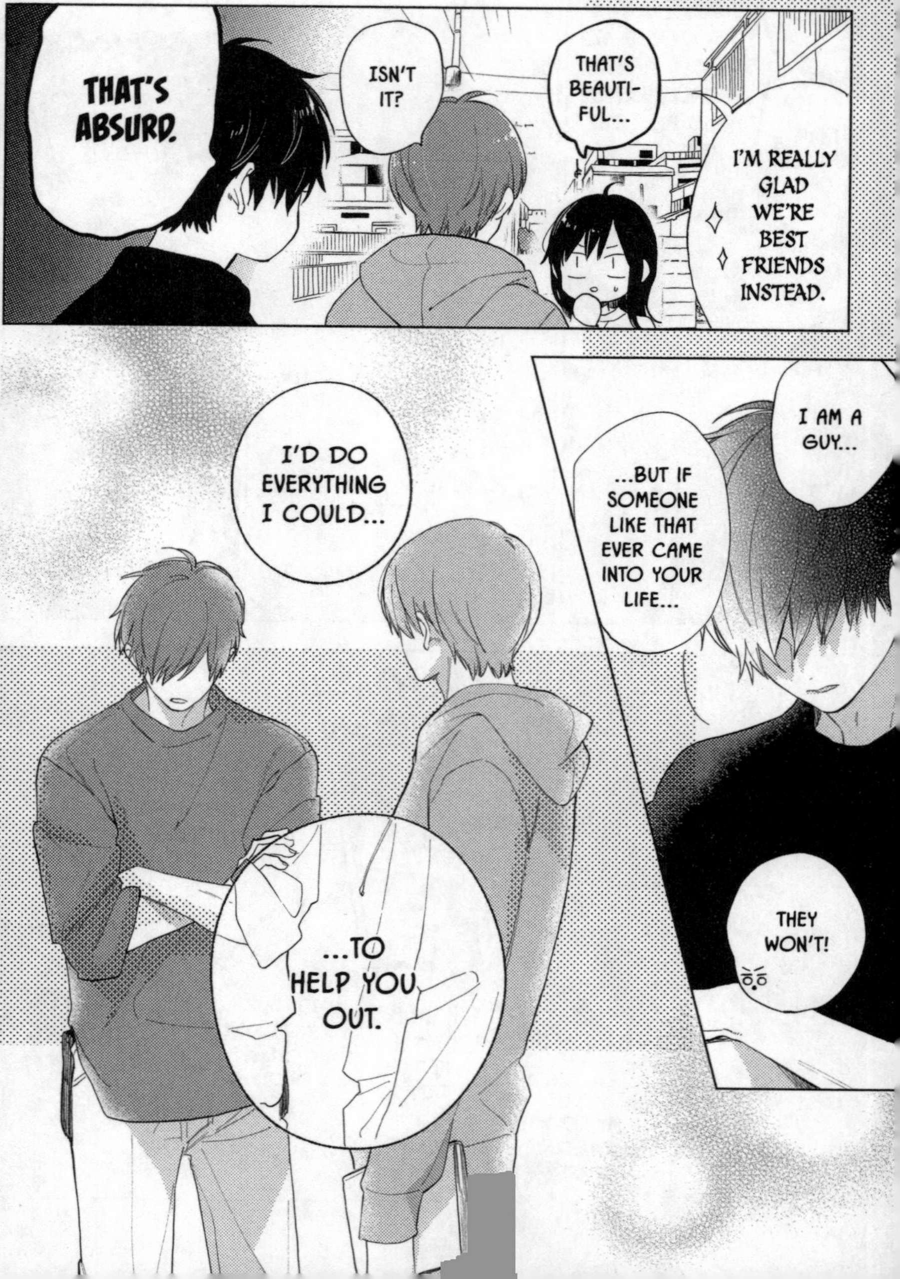
I'M REALLY GLAD WE'RE BEST FRIENDS INSTEAD.
THAT'S BEAUTIFUL...
ISN'T IT?
THAT'S ABSURD.
I AM A GUY...
...BUT IF SOMEONE LIKE THAT EVER CAME INTO YOUR LIFE...
I'D DO EVERYTHING I COULD...
...TO HELP YOU OUT.
THEY WON'T!

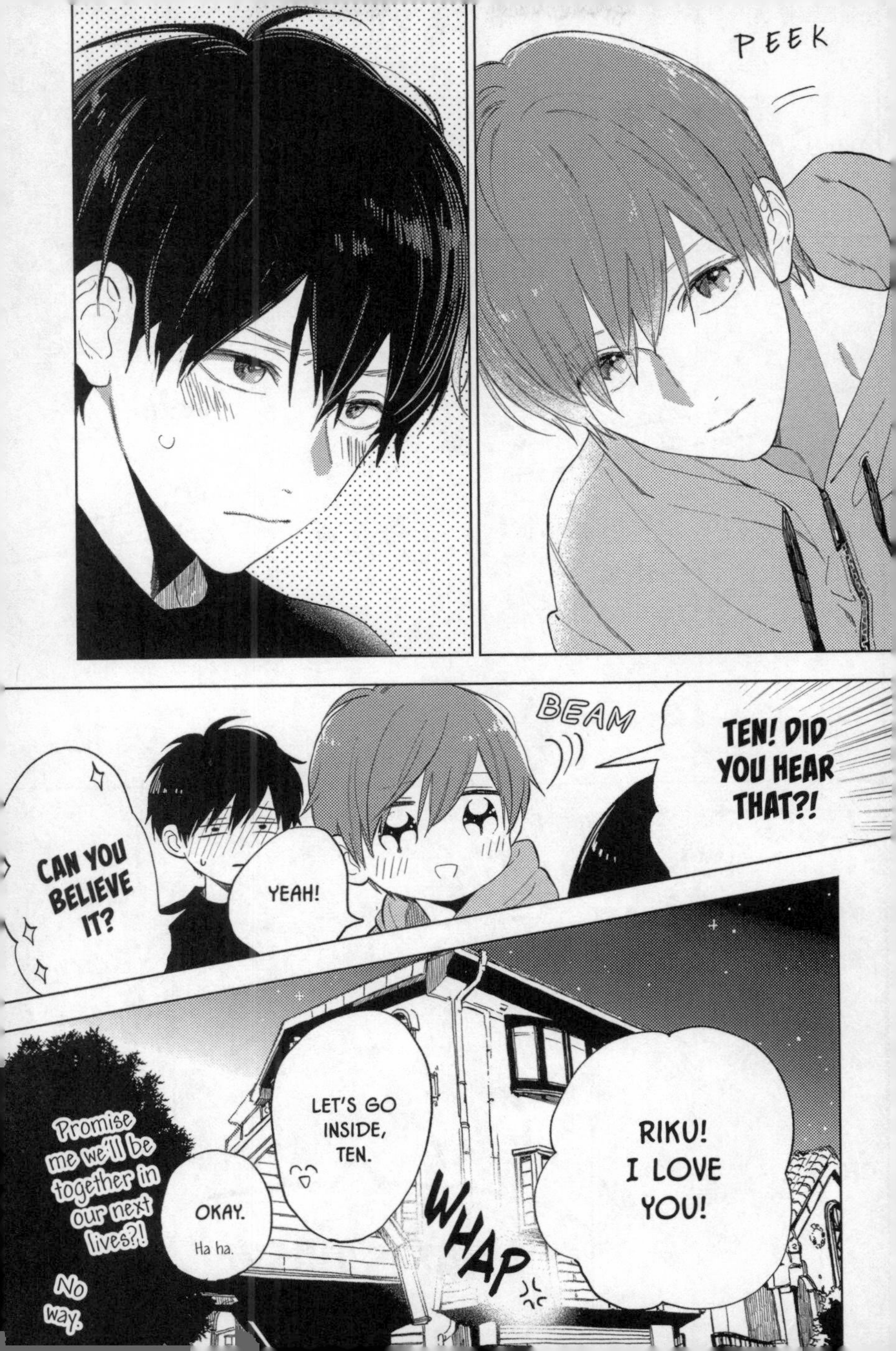
PEEK
TEN! DID YOU HEAR THAT?!
BEAM
YEAH!
CAN YOU BELIEVE IT?
RIKU! I LOVE YOU!
WHAP
LET'S GO INSIDE, TEN.
OKAY.
Ha ha.
Promise me we'll be together in our next lives?!
No way.

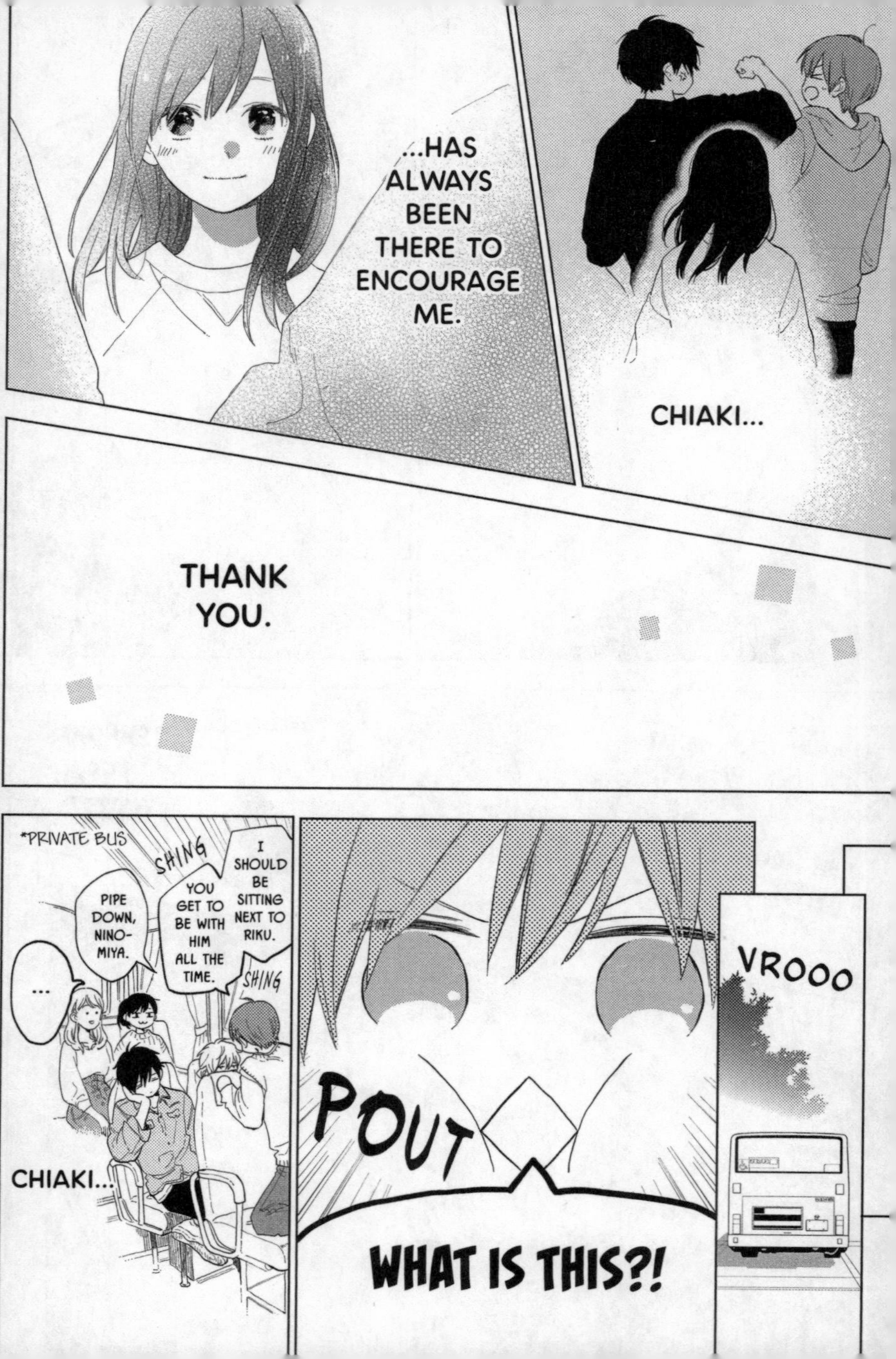
CHIAKI...
...HAS ALWAYS BEEN THERE TO ENCOURAGE ME.
THANK YOU.
VROOO
POUT
WHAT IS THIS?!
*PRIVATE BUS
SHING
I SHOULD BE SITTING NEXT TO RIKU.
SHING
YOU GET TO BE WITH HIM ALL THE TIME.
PIPE DOWN, NINO-MIYA.
...
CHIAKI...

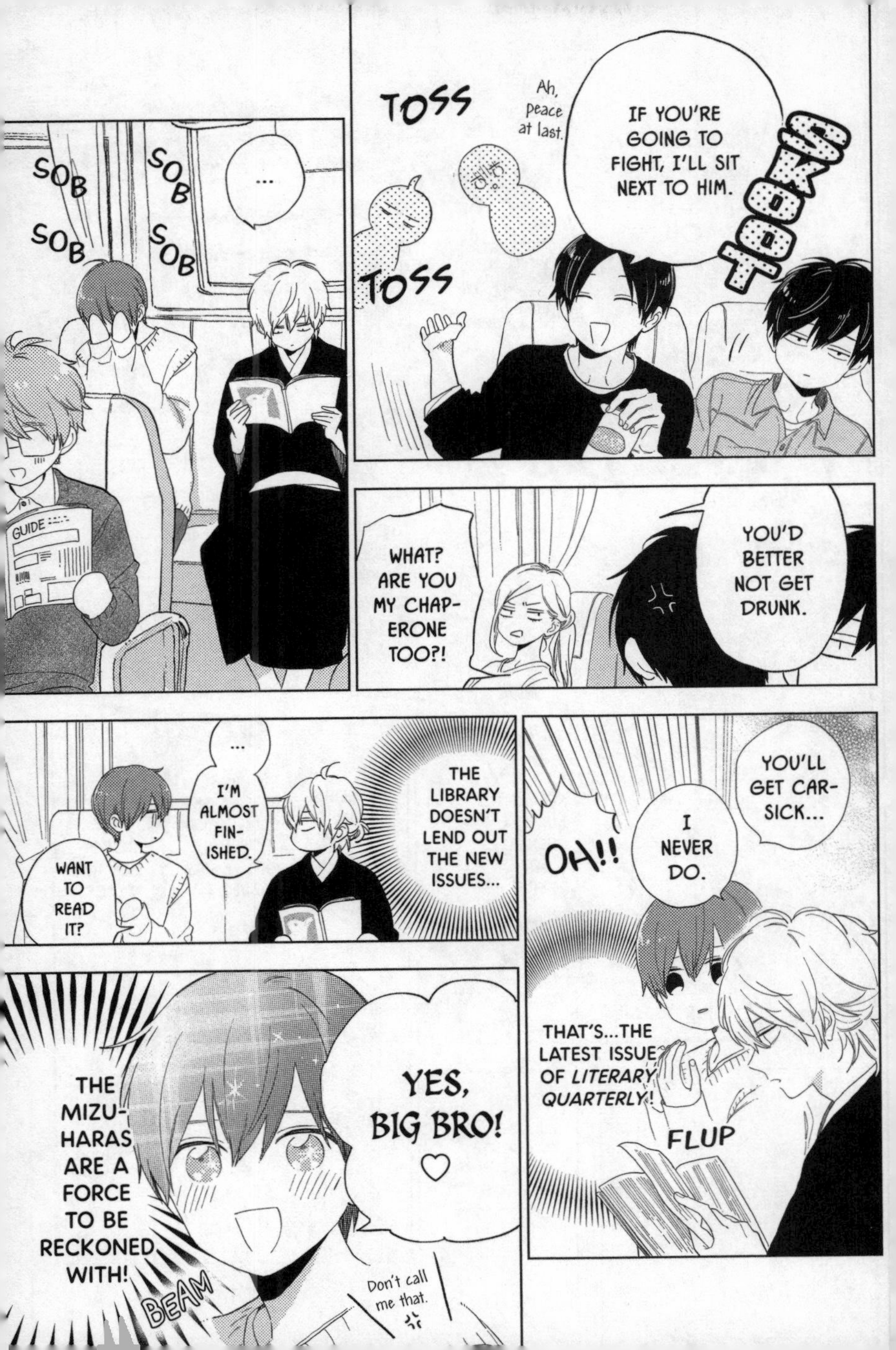
IF YOU'RE GOING TO FIGHT, I'LL SIT NEXT TO HIM.
SKOOT
Ah, peace at last.
TOSS
TOSS
YOU'D BETTER NOT GET DRUNK.
WHAT? ARE YOU MY CHAP-ERONE TOO?!
...
SOB
SOB
SOB
SOB
GUIDE
YOU'LL GET CAR-SICK...
I NEVER DO.
OH!!
THAT'S...THE LATEST ISSUE OF *LITERARY QUARTERLY*!
FLUP
THE LIBRARY DOESN'T LEND OUT THE NEW ISSUES...
...
I'M ALMOST FIN-ISHED.
WANT TO READ IT?
YES, BIG BRO! ♡
THE MIZU-HARAS ARE A FORCE TO BE RECKONED WITH!
BEAM
Don't call me that.

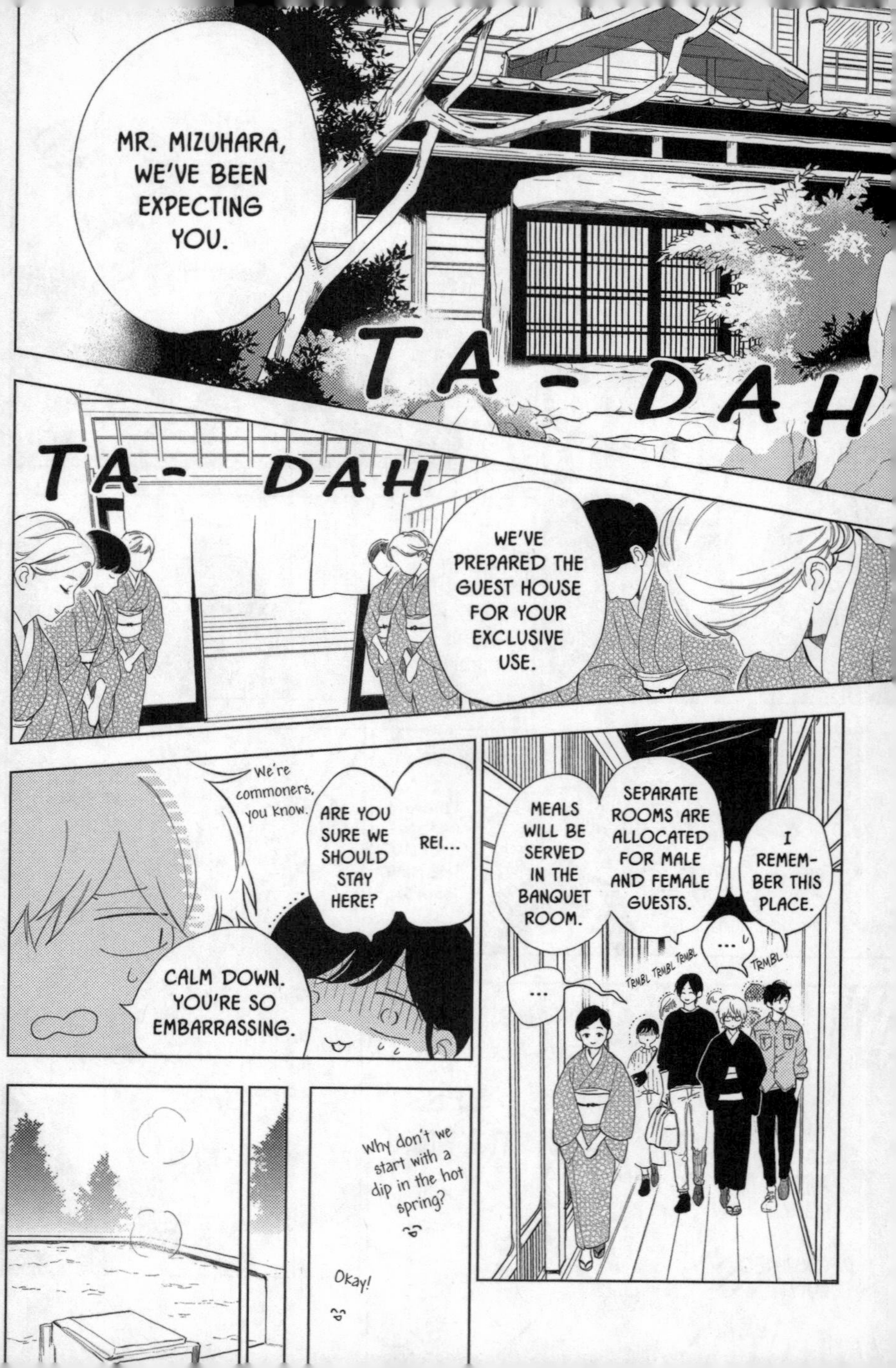
MR. MIZUHARA, WE'VE BEEN EXPECTING YOU.
TA-DAH
TA-DAH
WE'VE PREPARED THE GUEST HOUSE FOR YOUR EXCLUSIVE USE.
I REMEMBER THIS PLACE.
SEPARATE ROOMS ARE ALLOCATED FOR MALE AND FEMALE GUESTS.
MEALS WILL BE SERVED IN THE BANQUET ROOM.
...
TRMBL
TRMBL TRMBL TRMBL
...
REI...
ARE YOU SURE WE SHOULD STAY HERE?
We're commoners, you know.
CALM DOWN. YOU'RE SO EMBARRASSING.
Why don't we start with a dip in the hot spring?
Okay!

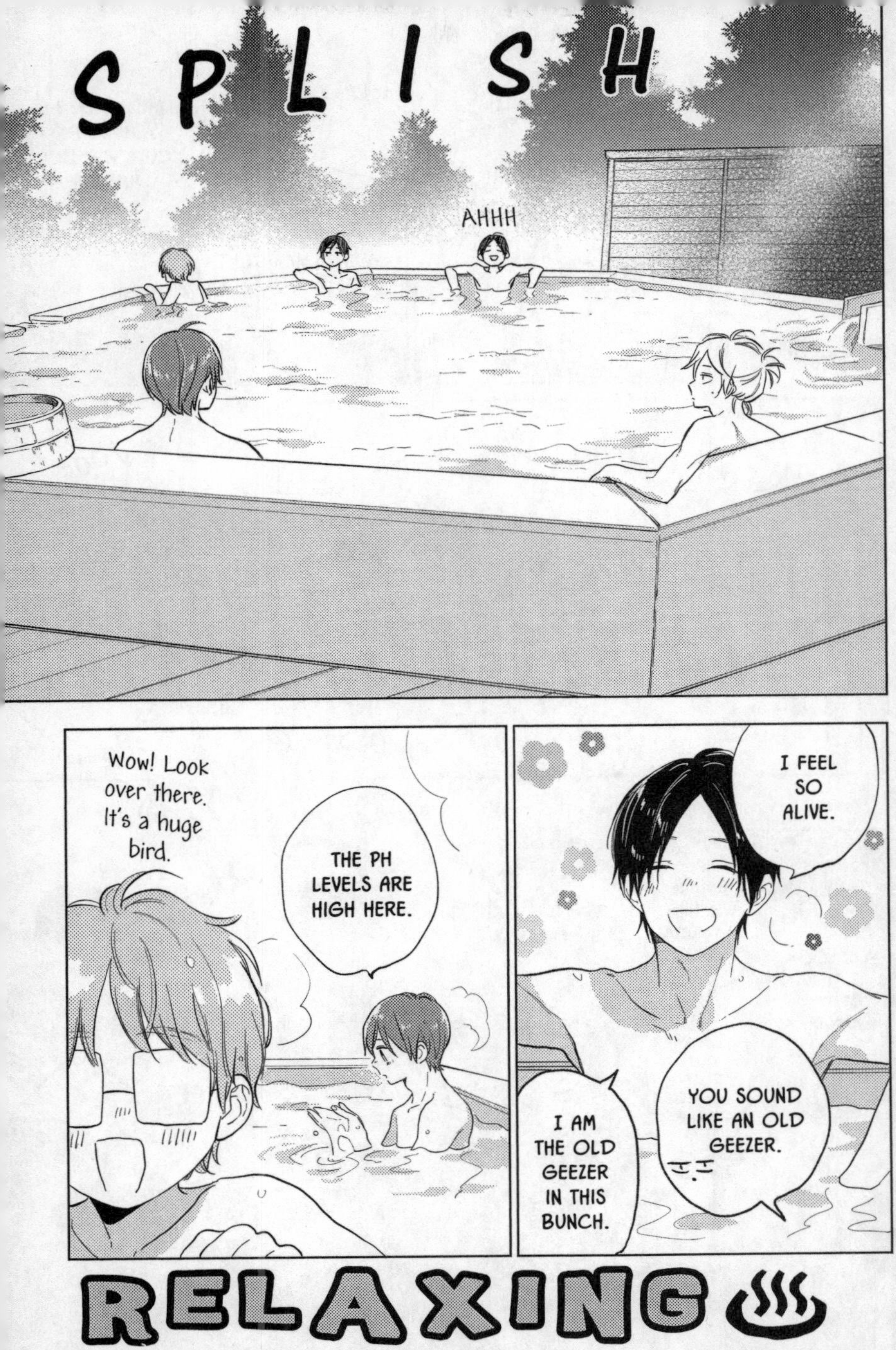
SPLISH
AHHH
I FEEL SO ALIVE.
YOU SOUND LIKE AN OLD GEEZER.
I AM THE OLD GEEZER IN THIS BUNCH.
THE PH LEVELS ARE HIGH HERE.
Wow! Look over there. It's a huge bird.
RELAXING

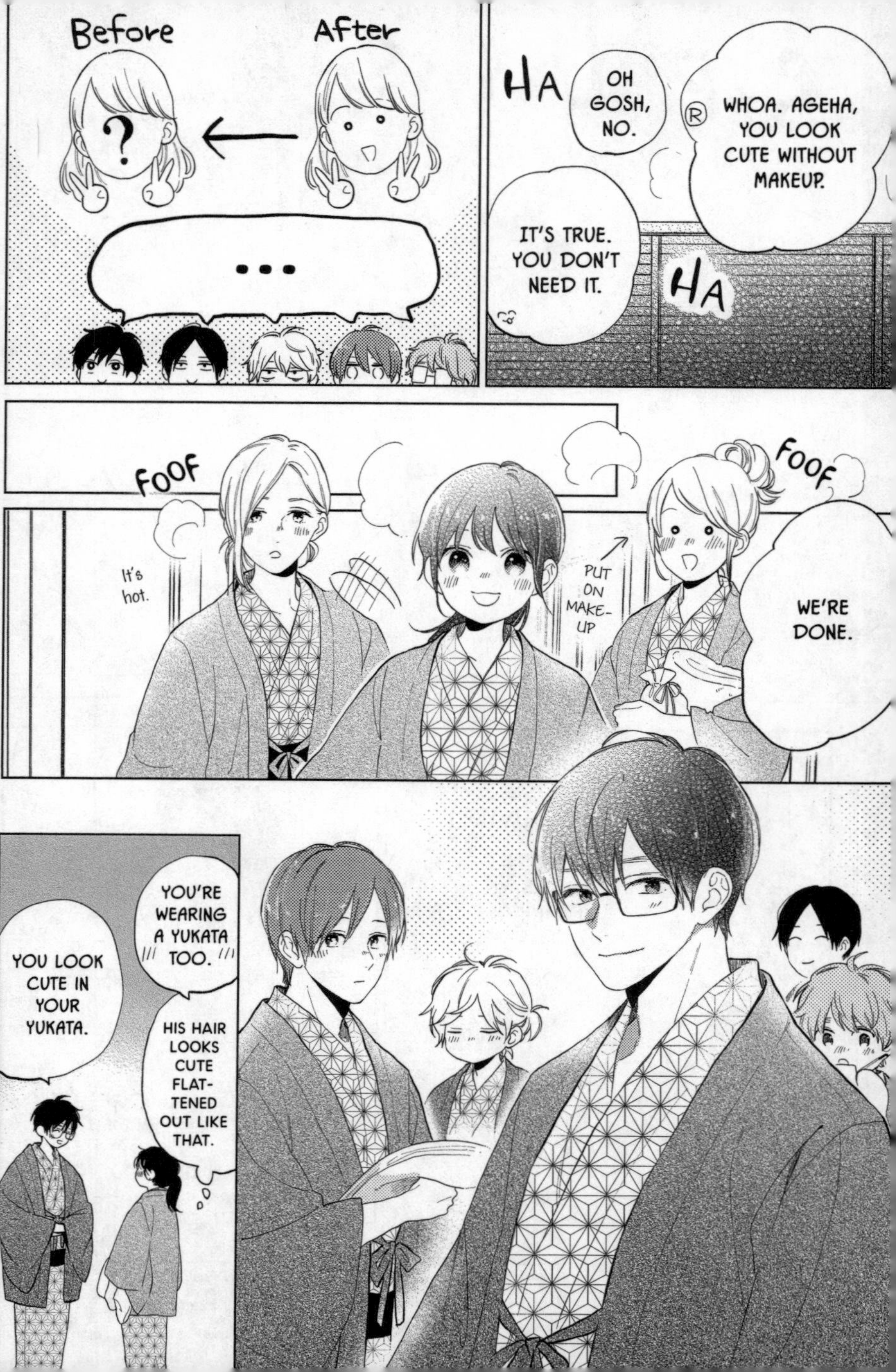
WHOA. AGEHA, YOU LOOK CUTE WITHOUT MAKEUP.
OH GOSH, NO.
HA
IT'S TRUE. YOU DON'T NEED IT.
HA
After
Before
...
FOOF
WE'RE DONE.
PUT ON MAKE-UP
FOOF
It's hot.
YOU'RE WEARING A YUKATA TOO.
HIS HAIR LOOKS CUTE FLAT-TENED OUT LIKE THAT.
YOU LOOK CUTE IN YOUR YUKATA.

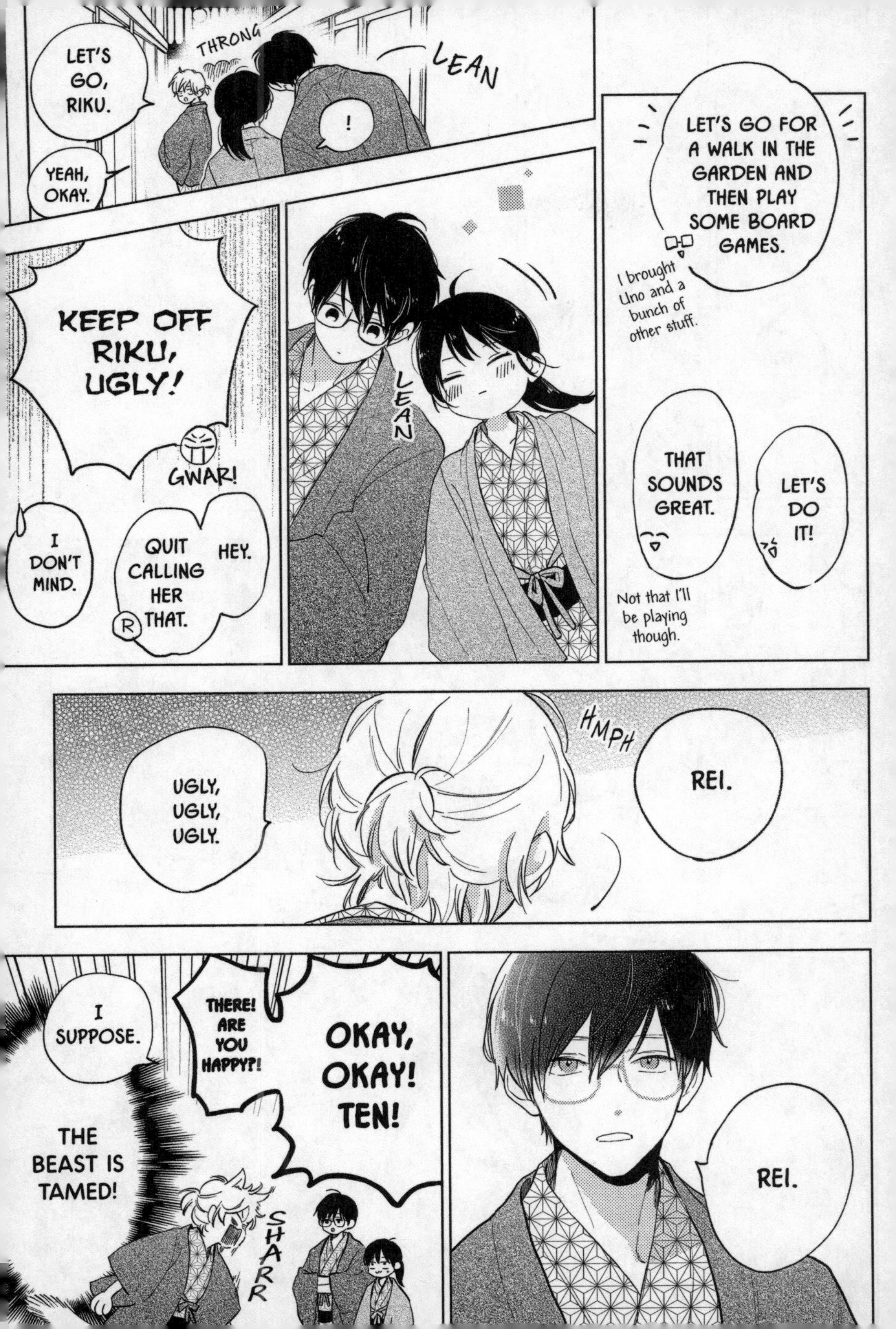
LET'S GO, RIKU.
YEAH, OKAY.
THRONG
LEAN
!
LET'S GO FOR A WALK IN THE GARDEN AND THEN PLAY SOME BOARD GAMES.
I brought Uno and a bunch of other stuff.
LET'S DO IT!
THAT SOUNDS GREAT.
Not that I'll be playing though.
LEAN
KEEP OFF RIKU, UGLY!
GWAR!
HEY.
QUIT CALLING HER THAT.
R
I DON'T MIND.
REI.
HMPH
UGLY, UGLY, UGLY.
REI.
OKAY, OKAY! TEN!
THERE! ARE YOU HAPPY?!
I SUPPOSE.
SHARR
THE BEAST IS TAMED!

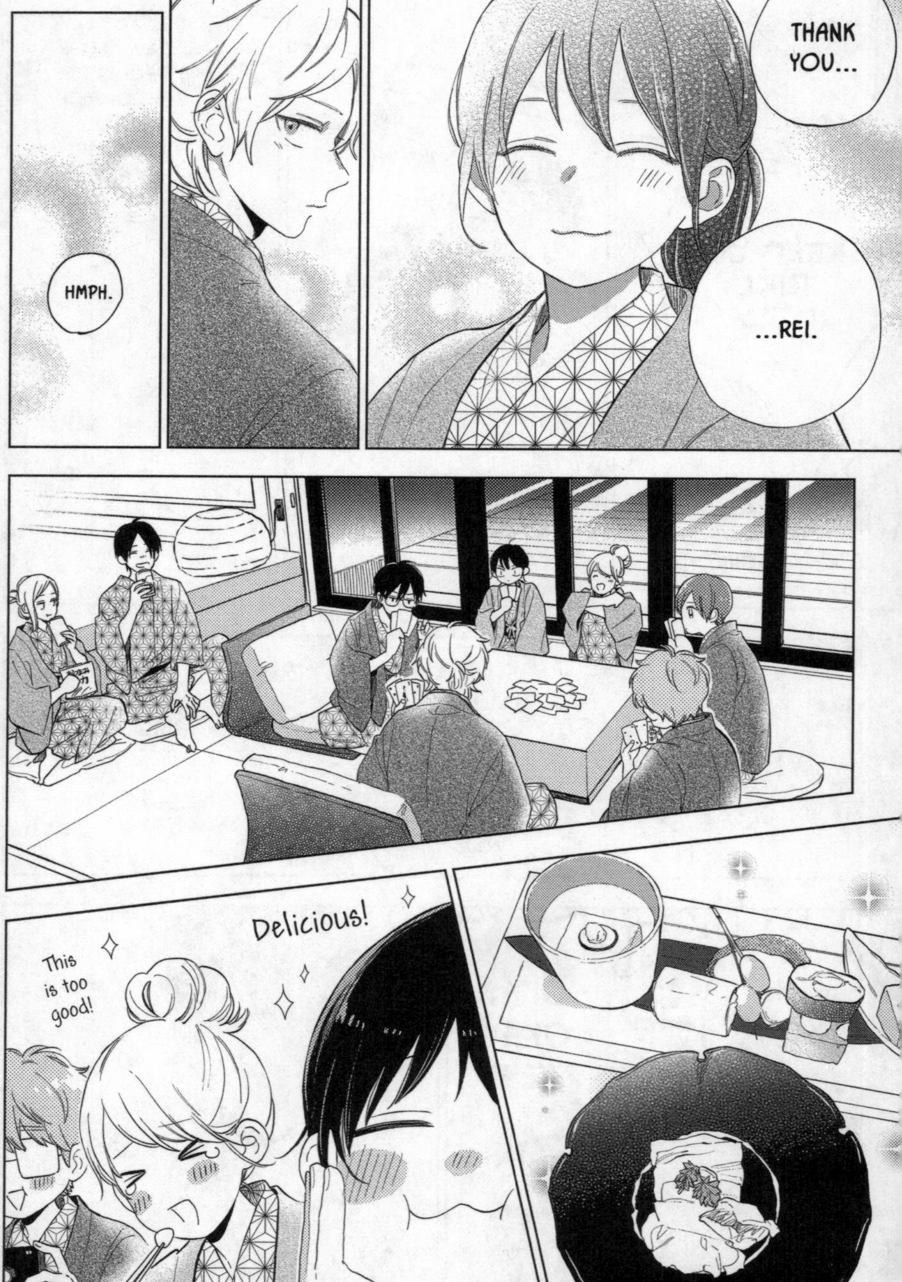
THANK YOU...
...REI.
HMPH.
Delicious!
This is too good!

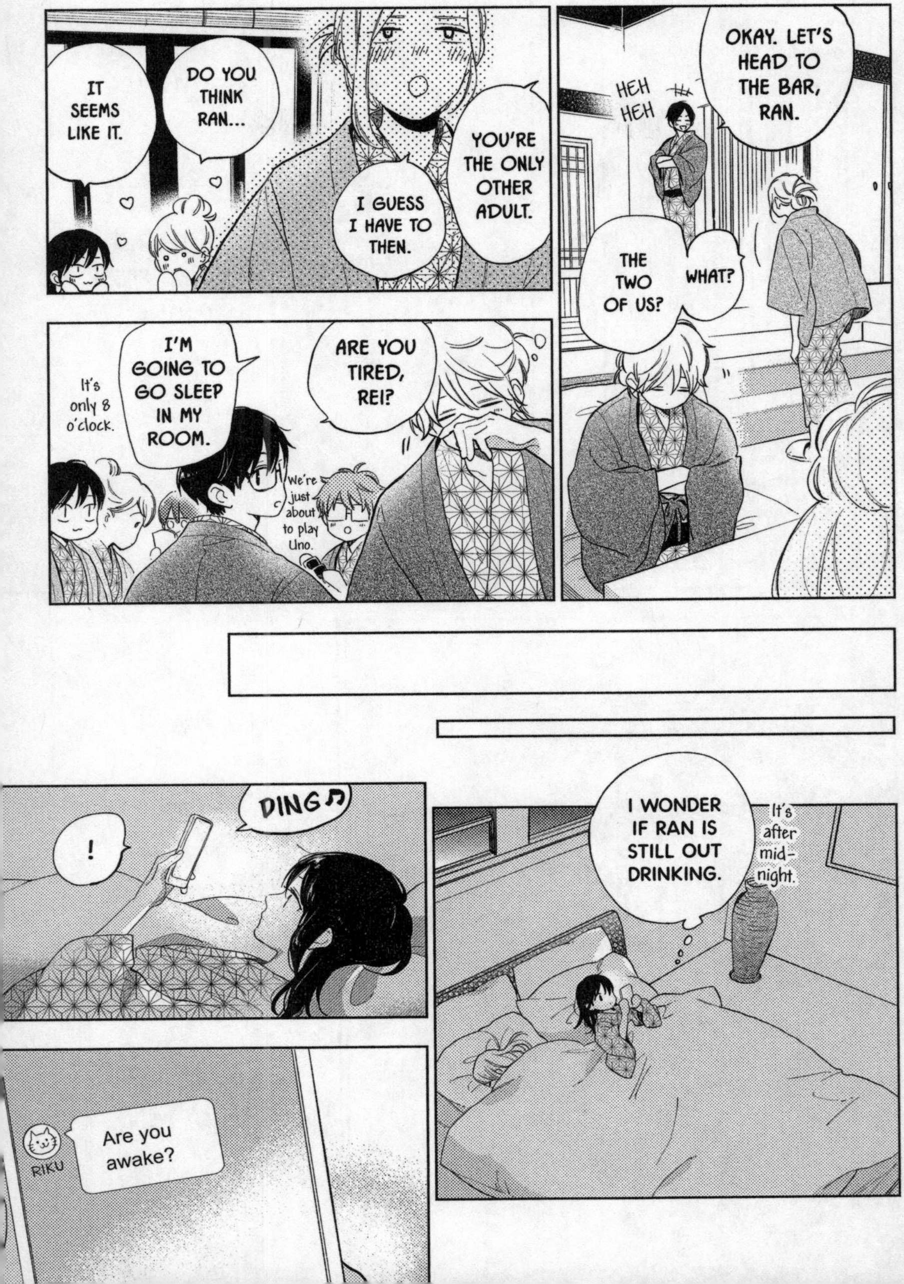
OKAY. LET'S HEAD TO THE BAR, RAN.
HEH HEH
WHAT?
THE TWO OF US?
YOU'RE THE ONLY OTHER ADULT.
I GUESS I HAVE TO THEN.
DO YOU THINK RAN...
IT SEEMS LIKE IT.
ARE YOU TIRED, REI?
We're just about to play Uno.
I'M GOING TO GO SLEEP IN MY ROOM.
It's only 8 o'clock.
I WONDER IF RAN IS STILL OUT DRINKING.
It's after mid-night.
DING♪
!
RIKU
Are you awake?

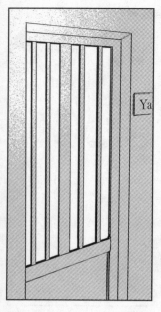

Are you awake?

I'm in the Yamazakura room.

CHAK

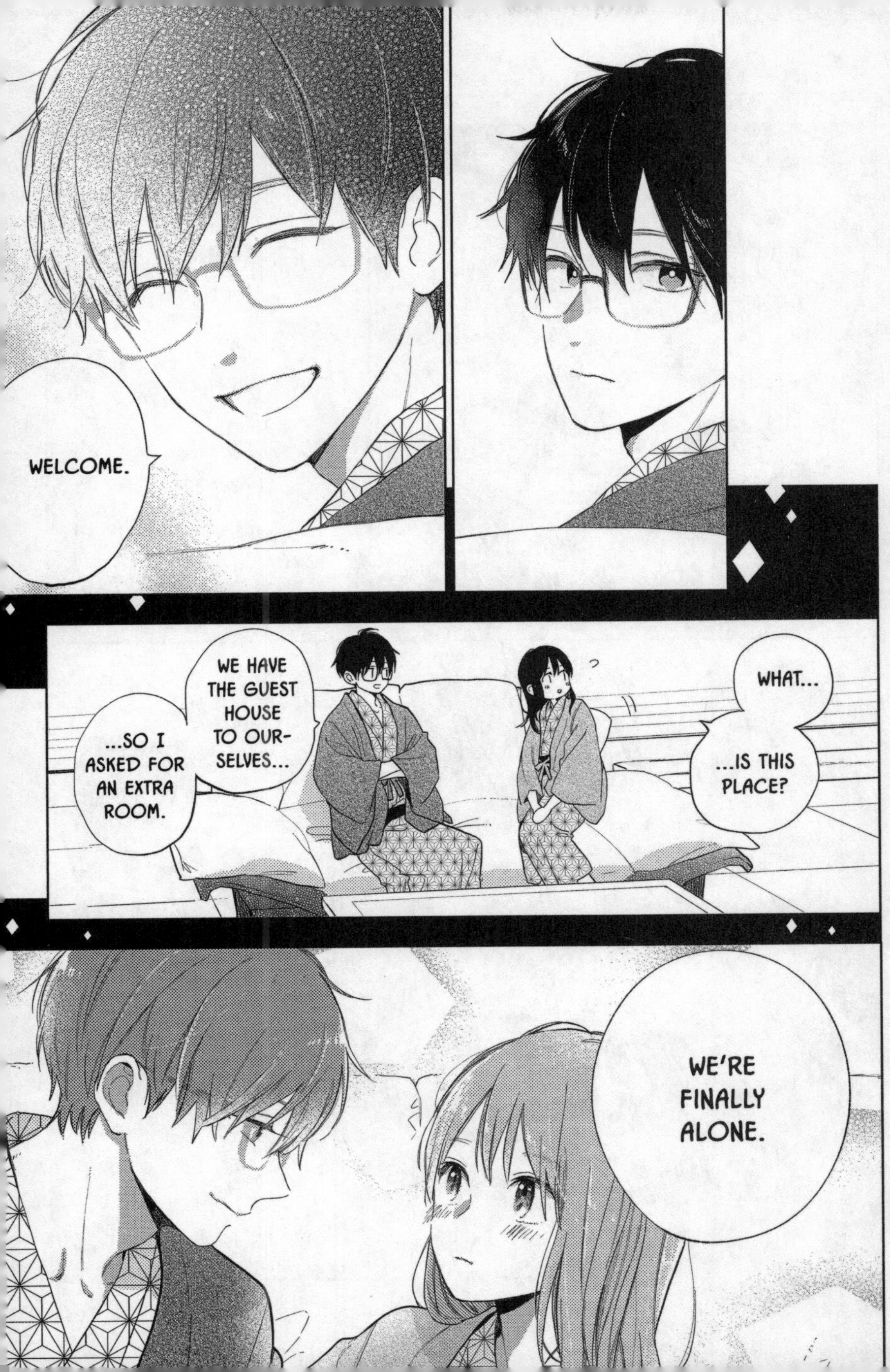
WELCOME.
WHAT... ...IS THIS PLACE?
WE HAVE THE GUEST HOUSE TO OUR-SELVES...
...SO I ASKED FOR AN EXTRA ROOM.
WE'RE FINALLY ALONE.

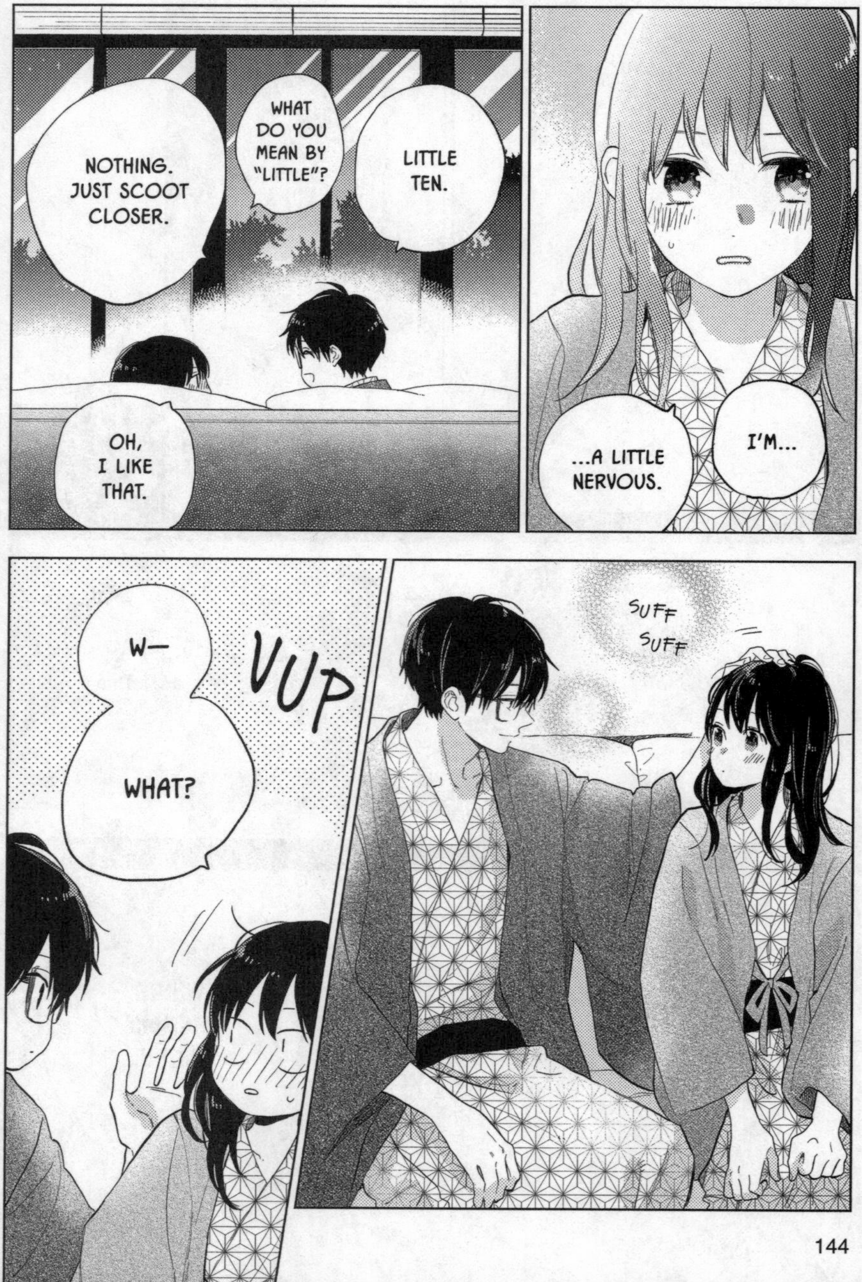
I'M...
...A LITTLE NERVOUS.
LITTLE TEN.
WHAT DO YOU MEAN BY "LITTLE"?
NOTHING. JUST SCOOT CLOSER.
OH, I LIKE THAT.
SUFF SUFF
VUP
W— WHAT?

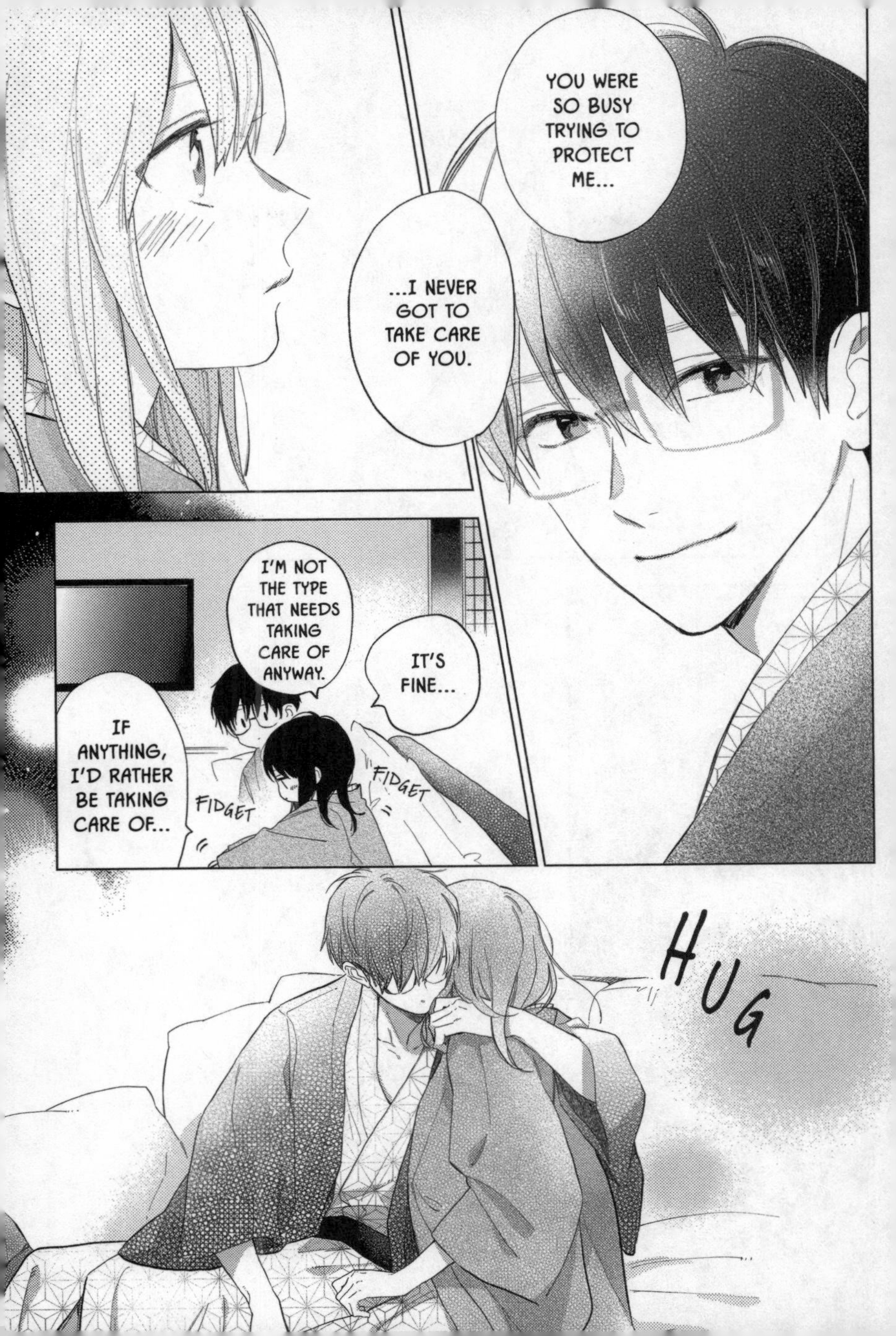
YOU WERE SO BUSY TRYING TO PROTECT ME...
...I NEVER GOT TO TAKE CARE OF YOU.
IT'S FINE...
I'M NOT THE TYPE THAT NEEDS TAKING CARE OF ANYWAY.
FIDGET
FIDGET
IF ANYTHING, I'D RATHER BE TAKING CARE OF...
HUG

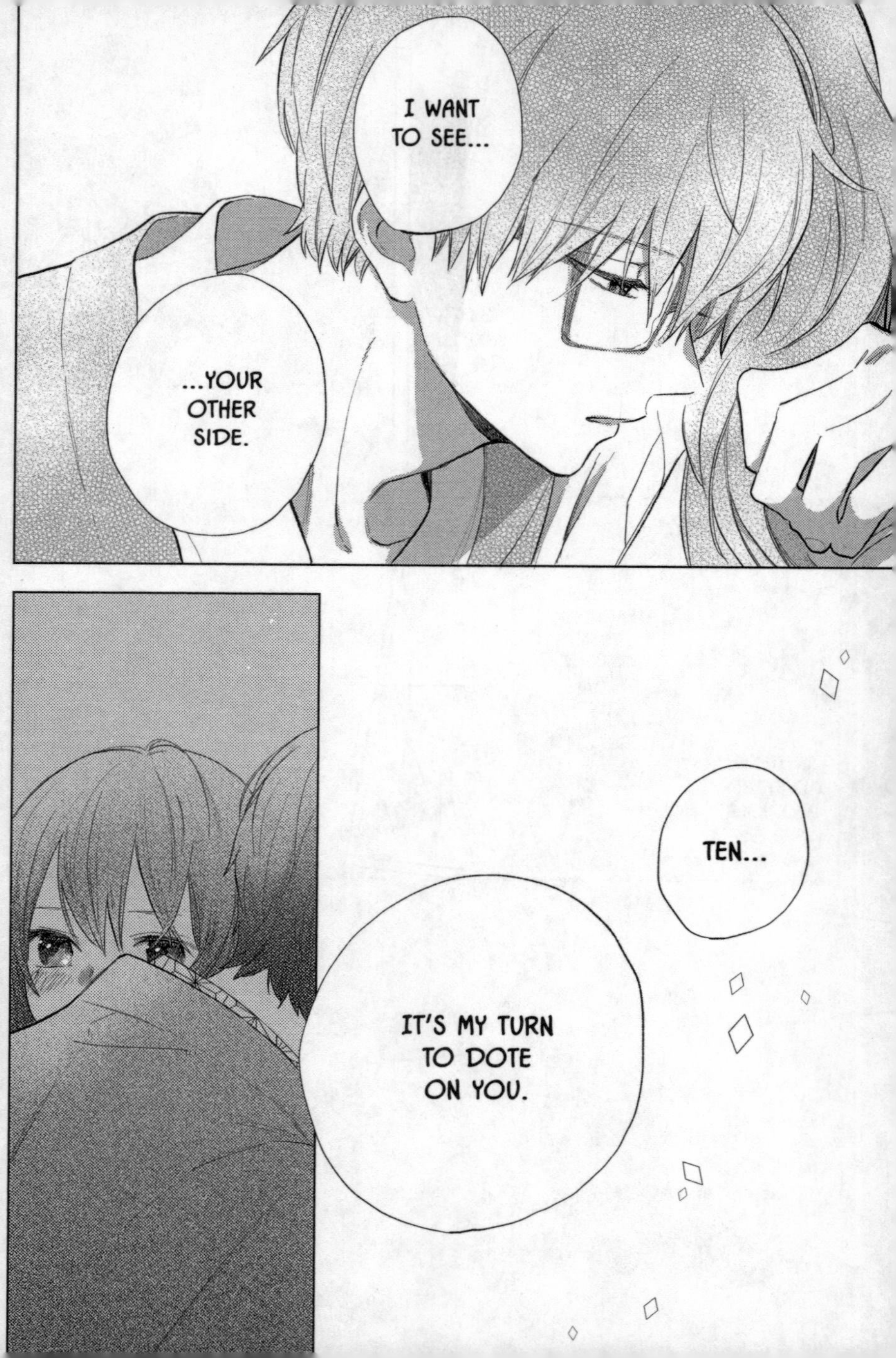
I WANT TO SEE...
...YOUR OTHER SIDE.
TEN...
IT'S MY TURN TO DOTE ON YOU.

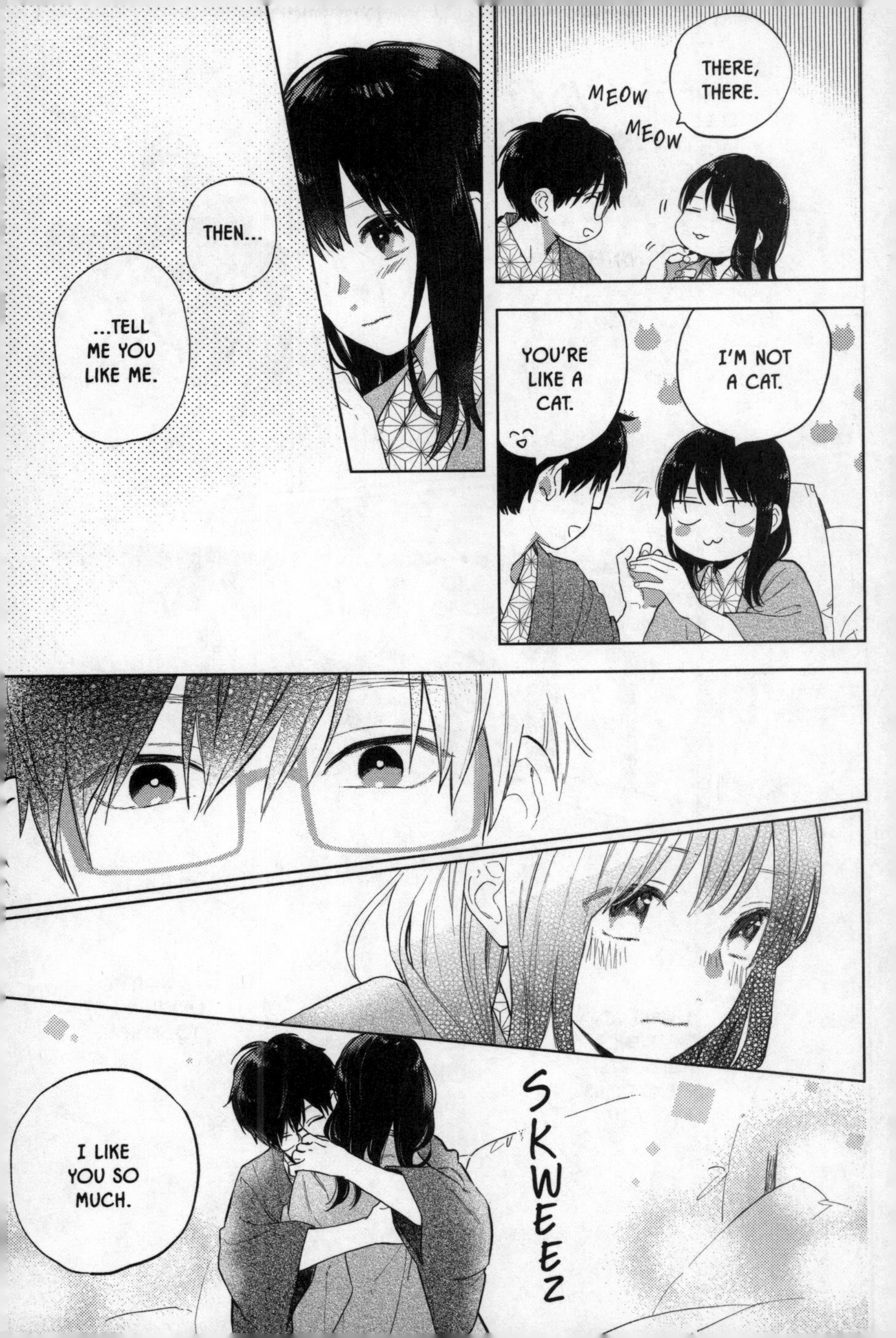
THERE, THERE.
MEOW MEOW
I'M NOT A CAT.
YOU'RE LIKE A CAT.
THEN...
...TELL ME YOU LIKE ME.
SKWEEZ
I LIKE YOU SO MUCH.

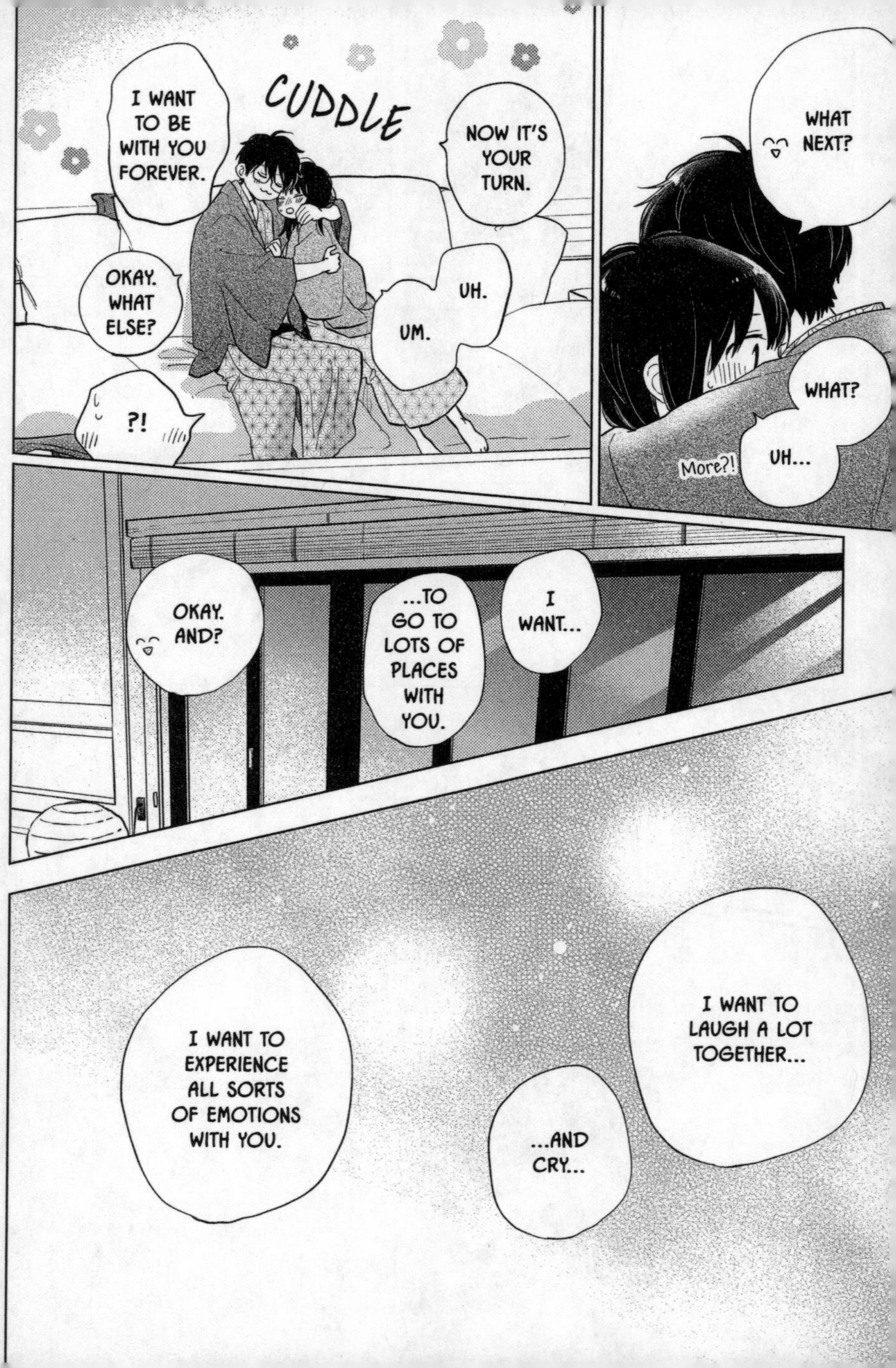
WHAT NEXT?
WHAT?
UH...
More?!
NOW IT'S YOUR TURN.
CUDDLE
I WANT TO BE WITH YOU FOREVER.
UH.
UM.
OKAY. WHAT ELSE?
?!
I WANT...
...TO GO TO LOTS OF PLACES WITH YOU.
OKAY. AND?
I WANT TO LAUGH A LOT TOGETHER...
...AND CRY...
I WANT TO EXPERIENCE ALL SORTS OF EMOTIONS WITH YOU.

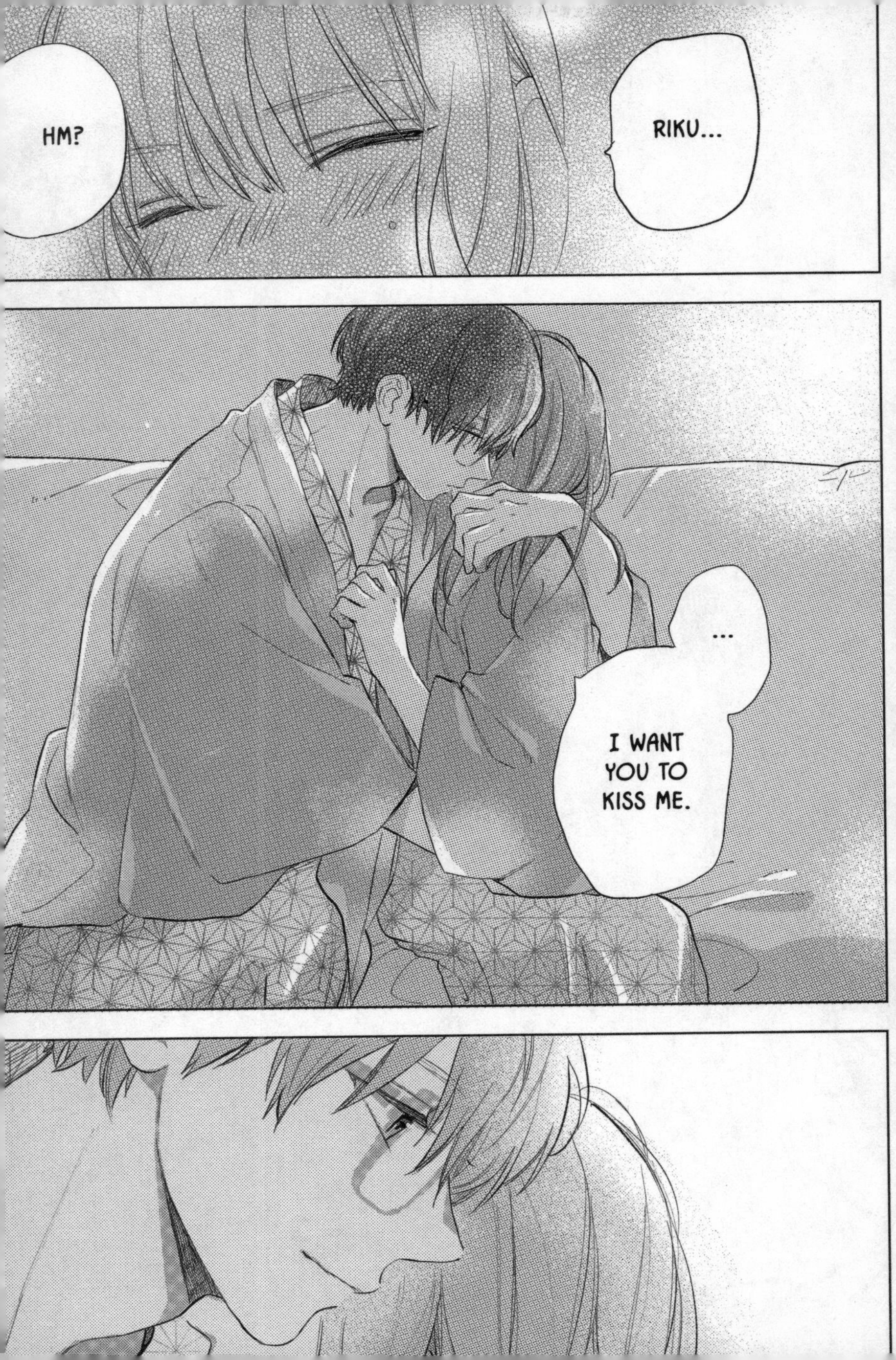
RIKU...
HM?
...
I WANT YOU TO KISS ME.

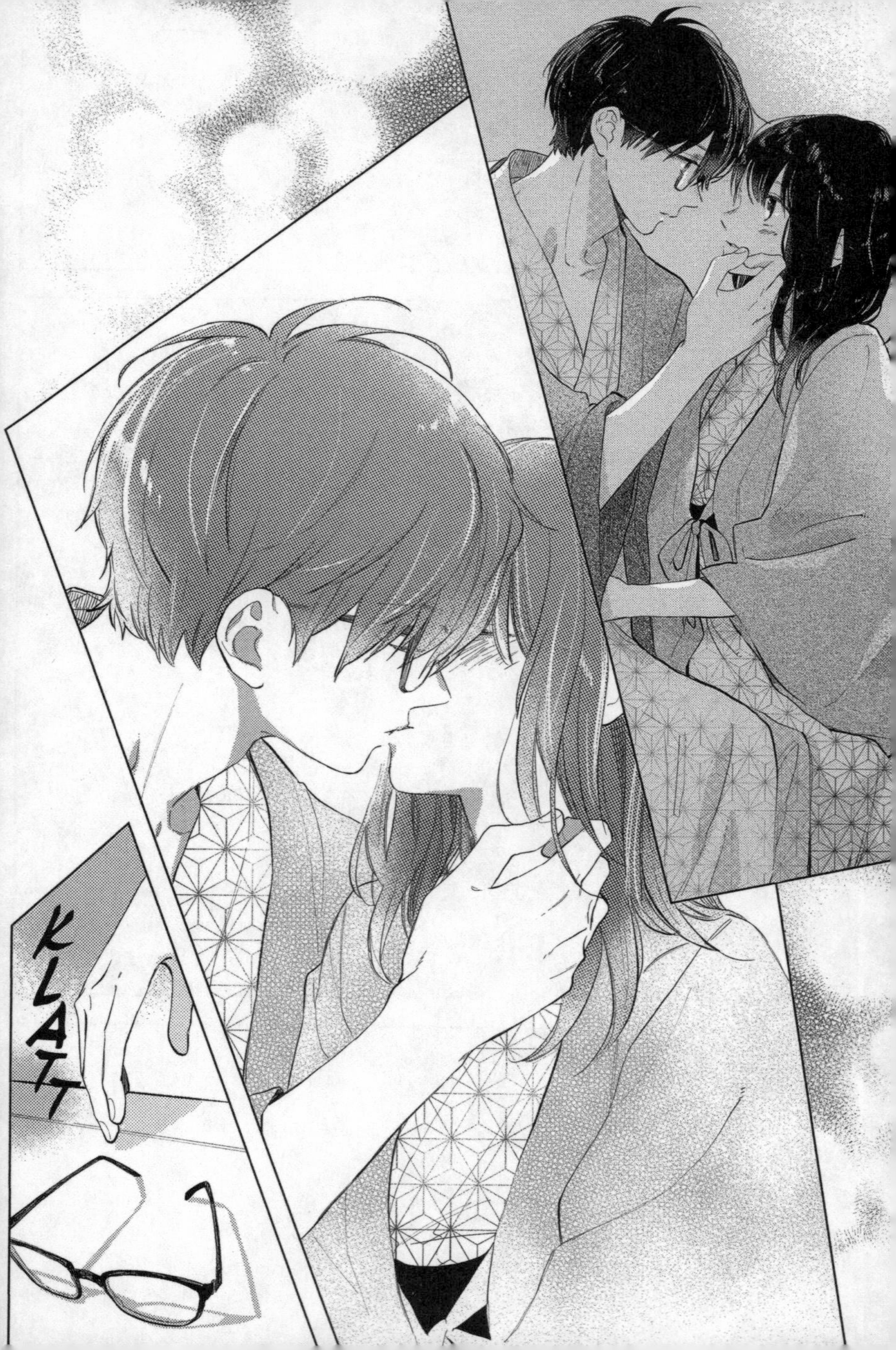
KLATT

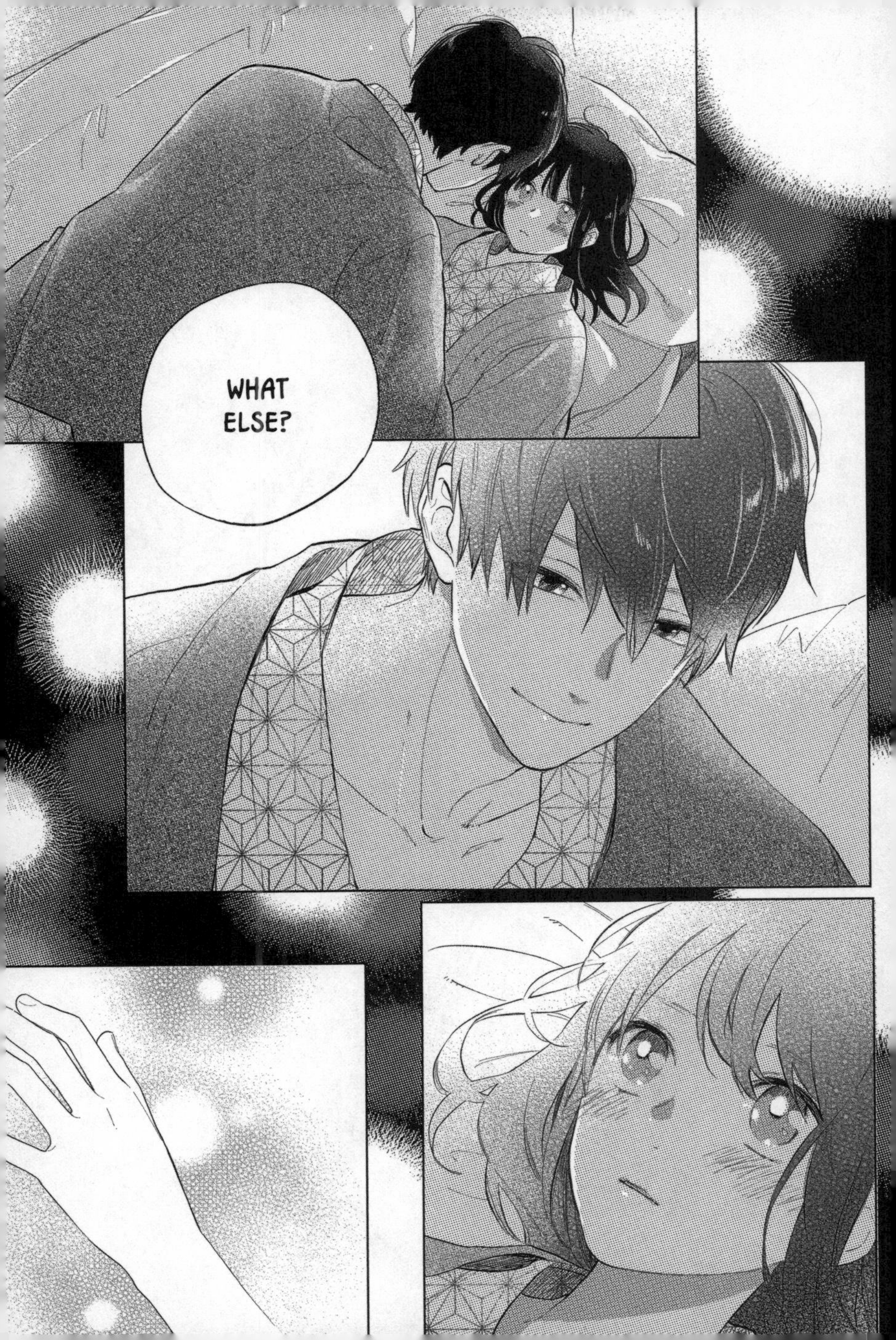
WHAT ELSE?

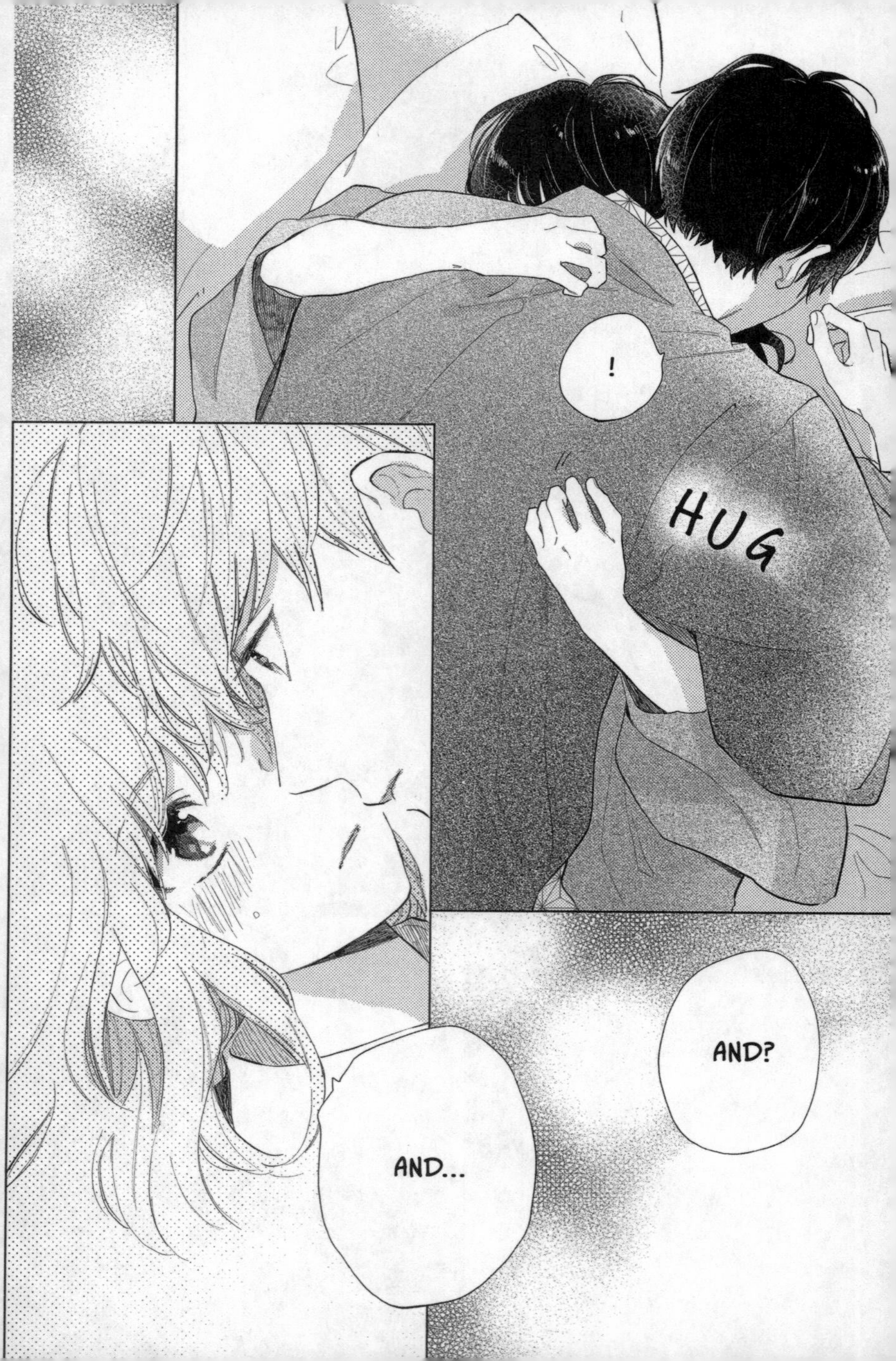
!
HUG
AND?
AND...

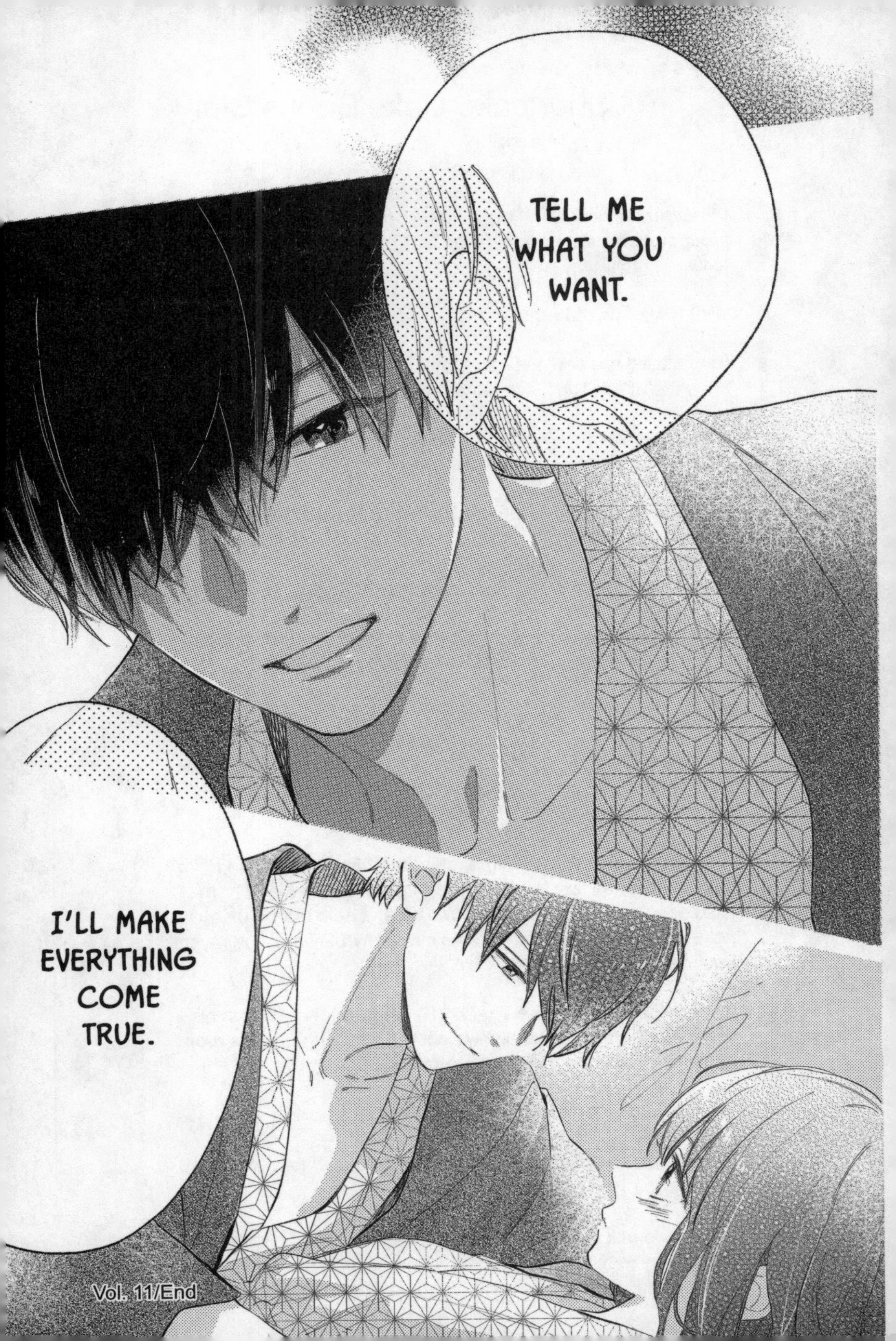
TELL ME WHAT YOU WANT.
I'LL MAKE EVERYTHING COME TRUE.
Vol. 11/End

Genre ▸ Other (spinoff)

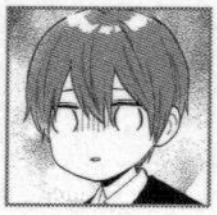

Shortcake Cake Bonus Story

suu Morishita

Last Updated on 2/25/2019

Three pages | 665 words

I heard footsteps travel the long hallway, growing closer. They stopped outside the room I was in. Then the door opened with force.

"Oh! Riku, you're home!"

Riku stared me down in that familiar way that's exactly the opposite of my 100% beaming face.

"Don't give me that. And quit hanging out in my room every day."

He somewhat roughly threw his school bag onto the futon where I was laying.

"We're having tempura for dinner tonight," I said.

Riku plopped down on the sofa and replied, "You're supposed to eat at the boardinghouse. Ran is cooking for you."

"Yeah, yeah."

I'd already planned to let Ran know I'd be eating dinner at the Mizuhara house and had discussed the matter with Hadano in the kitchen earlier.

I really think that Riku living back at the Mizuhara house is for the best. But having lived a mere three seconds away from Riku's room at the boardinghouse, I can't help but be disappointed now that he's so far away. It's why I always find myself back here.

"Ninomiya, are you here again?" Rei entered the room in his school uniform. I bet he always comes straight to Riku's room after school without bothering to change first.

"As you know, my name is Kasadera."

Rei ignored me and sat down next to Riku as if he belonged there.

Those two talk as if they're trying to make up for lost time. When they're together, their demeanor is different from what they normally show the world. I feel privileged to witness it.

As I stood up and walked towards the door, Riku raised his voice. "Are you finally leaving?"

"I'm going to take a bath before dinner."

That's right. I'm not taking a hint. If I didn't pretend to be obtuse, I wouldn't be able to be stay. And besides, I already have a bottle of shampoo stored here.

I took off my clothes and headed into the bath.

Huh?

My rubber ducky should've been tucked away in one corner of the large Mizuhara bath.

I hurried back down that long hallway in just my bath towel.

"Hey, you guys! Do you know where my duck is?"

"Huh?"

"Oh, you mean that yellow thing that looked like a dog?"

"A dog? It's a duck..."

"Well, I threw it out."

"What?!"

****

GYAAAH!

I finished my bath and sat down with my back to those two.

"Was it really that important to you?"

"Yes! I can't believe you threw it away without asking!"

"Well, maybe you shouldn't have left it here without asking."

Riku was right, but I hated that he was siding with his brother. I mean, I could easily buy another duck, but still...

I sat there weeping. I admit it was a bit overdramatic of a display. They ignored me for a while, but later Riku sat down behind me.

"Men don't cry like that!"

Hmph! That's what he thinks. I refused to look at him. It was the gamble of a lifetime. If I lost, a crack would be born within our friendship. Yes, I was constantly putting my life on the line for this friendship. And this time, I was afraid to see Riku's face.

Riku sighed. "Where do they sell that thing?"

Rikuuuuuu!!!

Honestly, I wanted to turn around and hug him. I love, love, love Riku so much.

I opened my mouth, still pretending to sulk. "I'll tell you later. Can I stay over tonight?"

With a look of exasperation, Riku replied, "Just make sure to tell Ran."

At that moment, I dove into his arms.

His brother rolled his eyes. But I know Rei doesn't have anything to hold over me, so I have no plans to stop what I'm doing.

And I know Riku (probably) doesn't mind spending his days like this with just the three of us.

Mr. Shiraoka popped in to tell us that dinner was ready.

"Yes, sir!" I gave my reply with a 200% beaming face.

My best friend is the one who brings out the best in me.
—Henry Ford

The End

Afterword

Thank you for reading volume 11!
The very long sibling feud is over. We wanted
to show strength and kindness through love,
friendship and brotherhood. We'd be happy if the
emotion in the story touched you.

The next volume is the final one, in which we'd like
to give some more insight into the overall setting.
We hope you'll join us through to the end. ☺

Special Thanks

- Editor J
- Designer Yasuhisa Kawatani
- Assistant Nao Hamaguchi
- Helper Kame-chan
- Assistant Helper Megumi Hazuki
- The many people who helped along the way

&  ♥

SHORTCAKE CAKE
Title Page Collection
Chapter 57

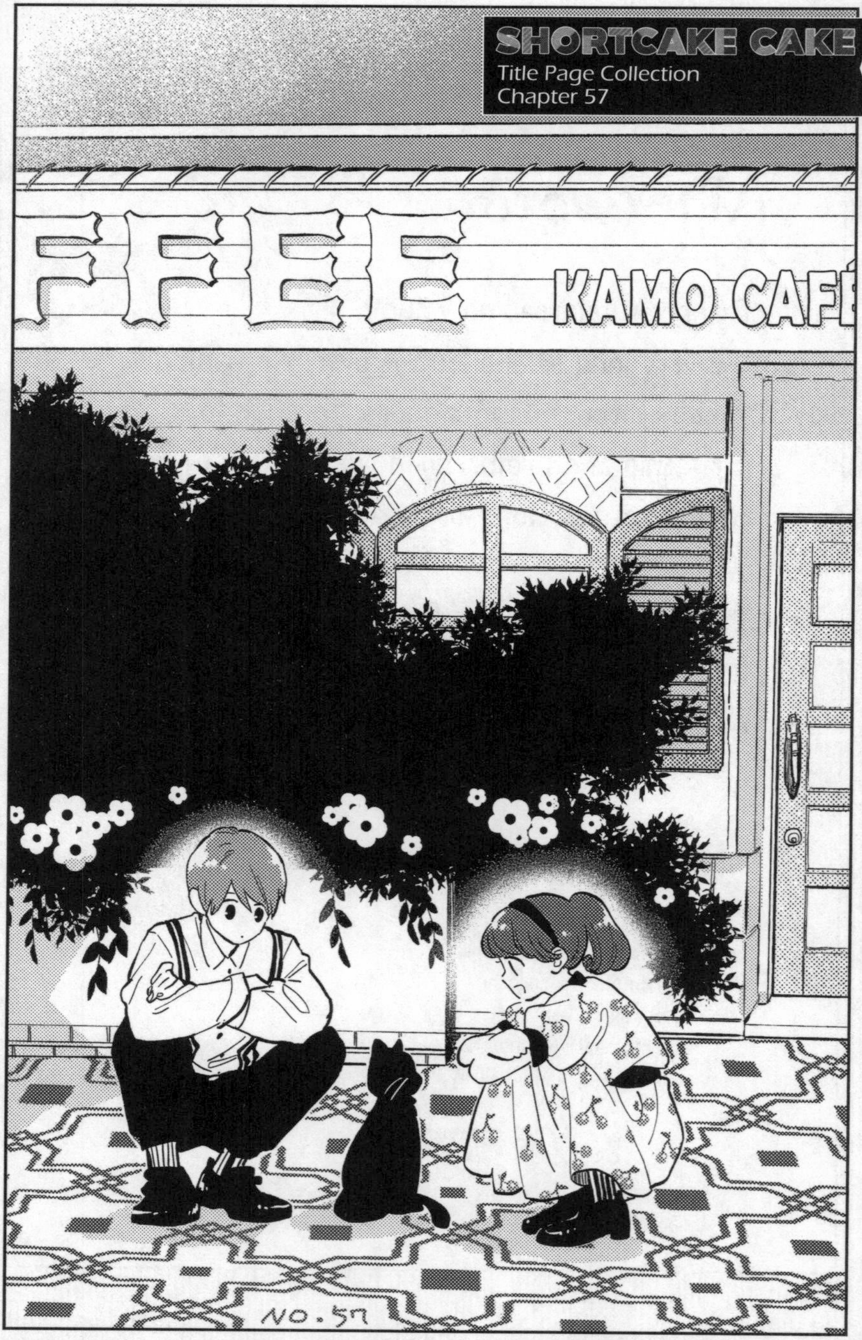
FFEE
KAMO CAFÉ
NO. 57

SHORTCAKE CAKE
Title Page Collection
Issue 23 Magazine Cover

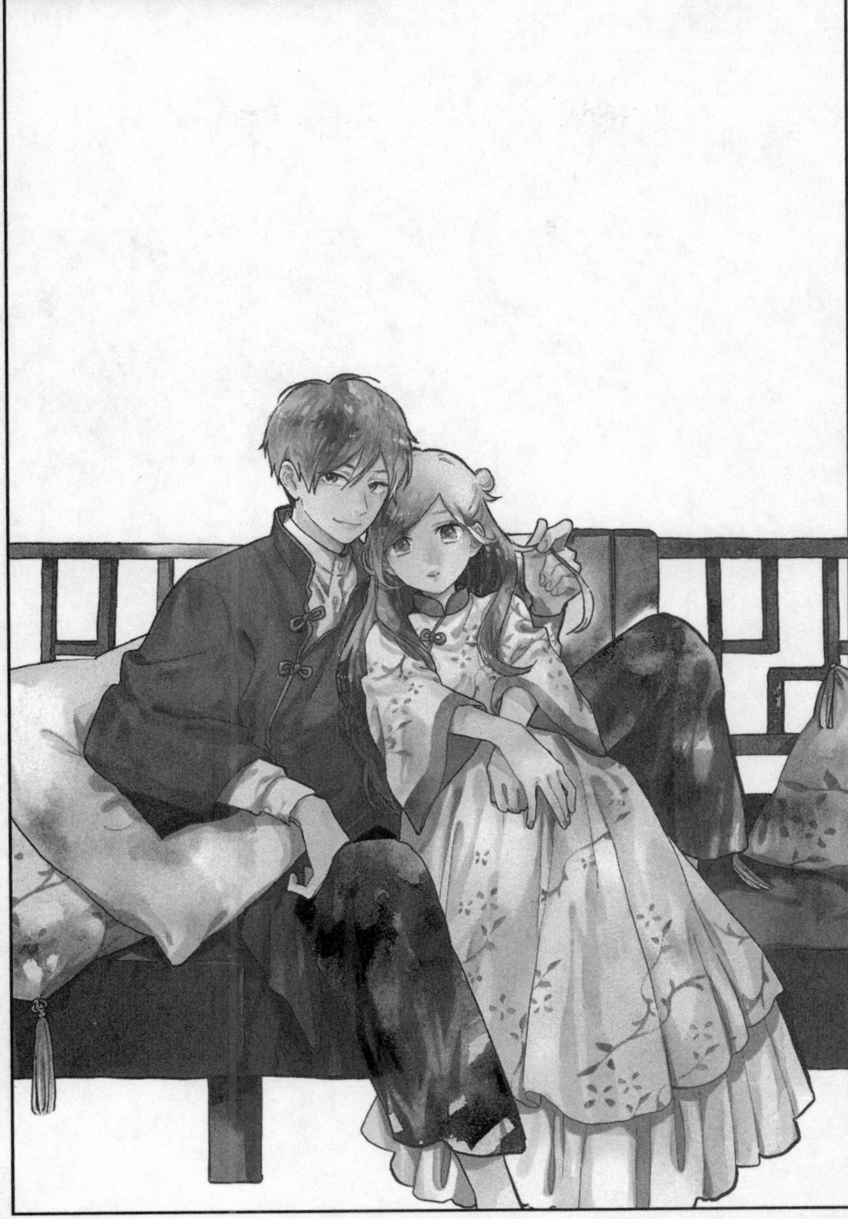

SHORTCAKE CAKE

Title Page Collection
Chapter 58

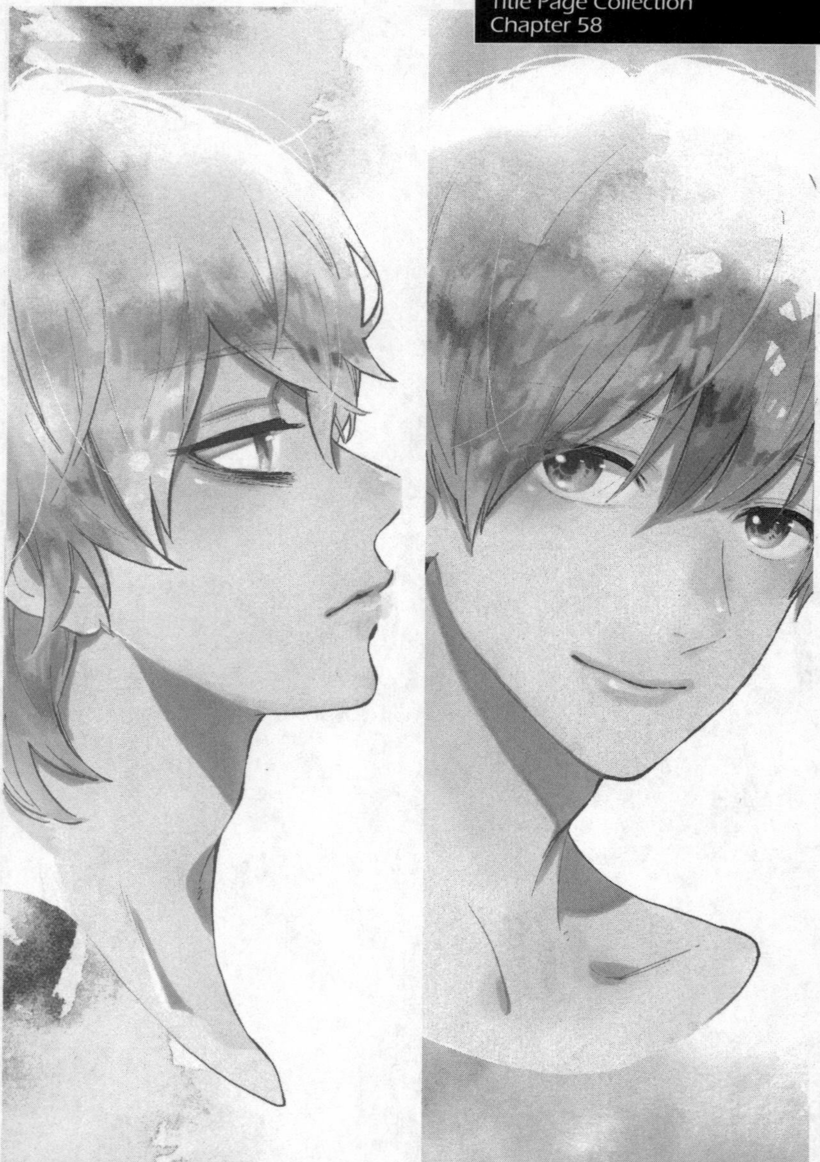

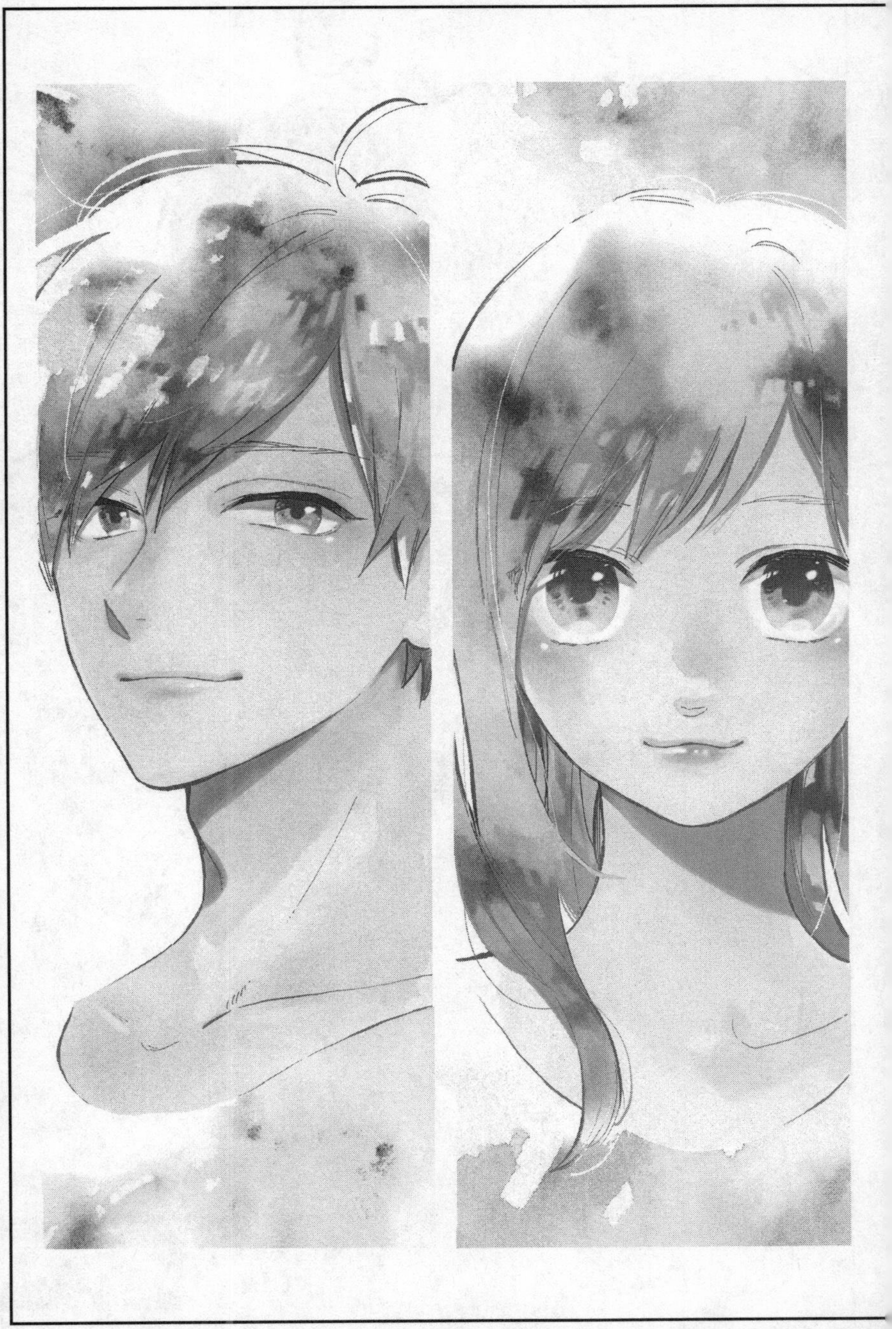

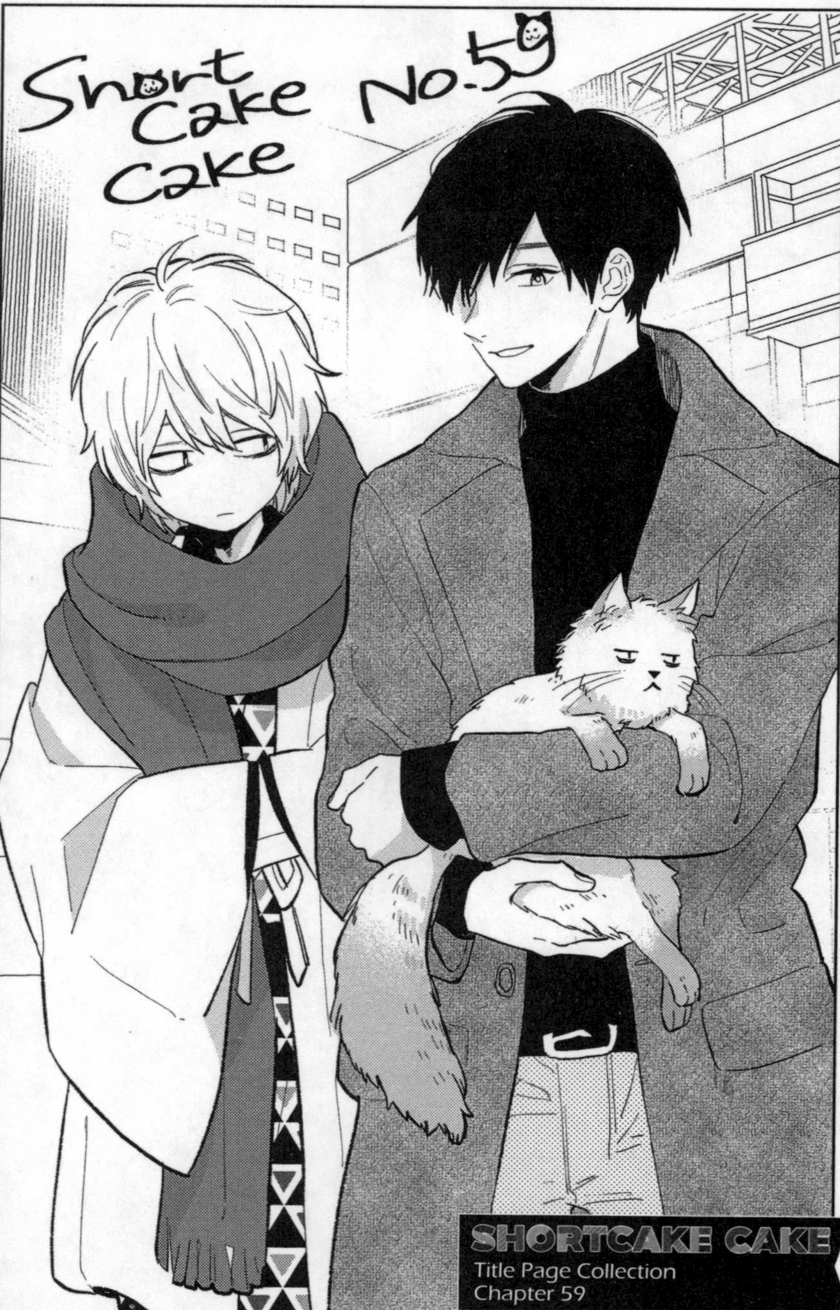
Short Cake Cake No.59
SHORTCAKE CAKE
Title Page Collection
Chapter 59

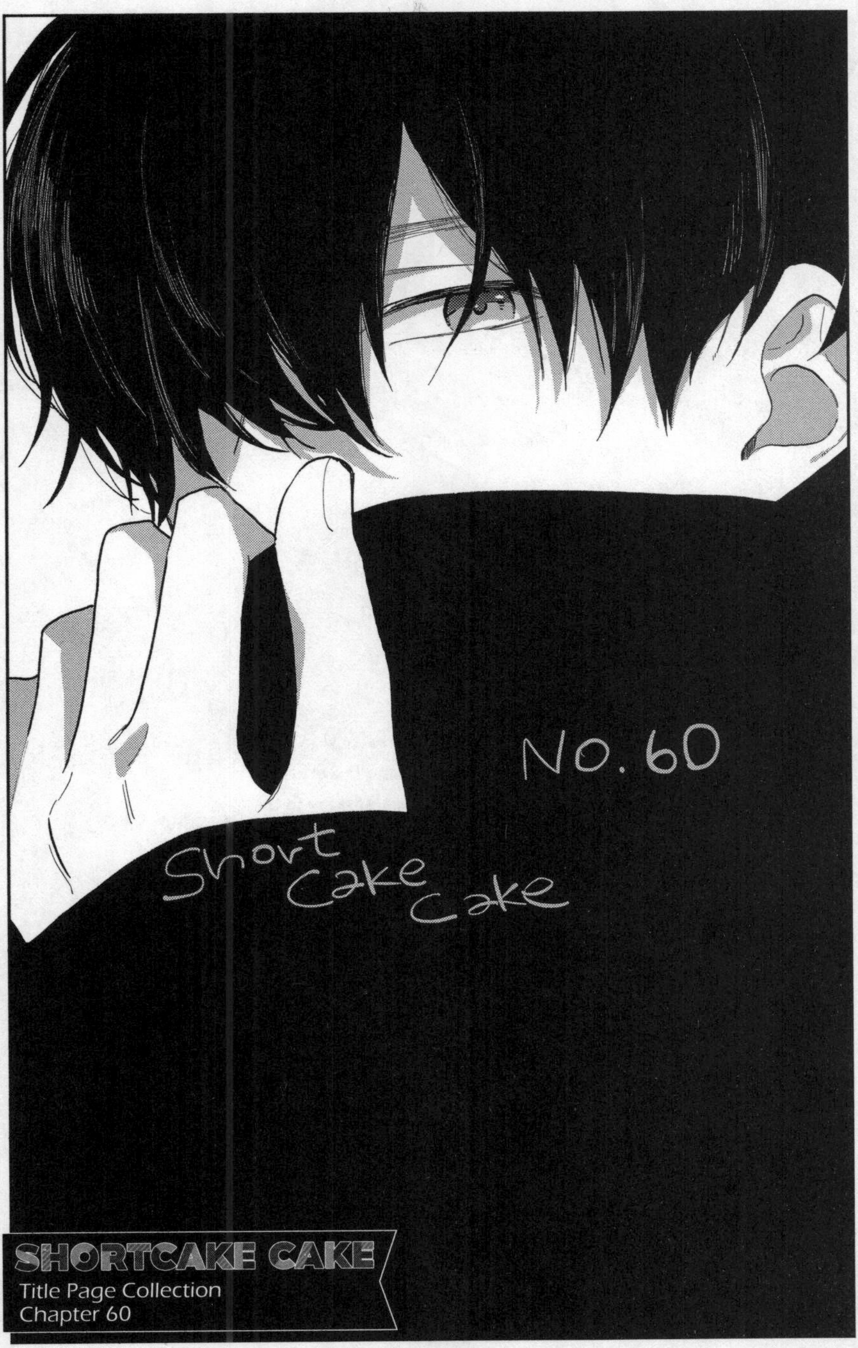
NO.60
Short Cake Cake

SHORTCAKE CAKE
Title Page Collection
Chapter 60

Cocoa survived.

—suu Morishita

suu Morishita is a creator duo.
The story is by Makiro, and the art is by
Nachiyan. In 2010 they debuted with the
one-shot "Anote Konote." Their works include
Hibi Chouchou and *Shortcake Cake*.

VOLUME 11
SHOJO BEAT EDITION

STORY + ART BY **suu Morishita**

TRANSLATION **Emi Louie-Nishikawa**
TOUCH-UP ART + LETTERING **Inori Fukuda Trant**
DESIGN **Joy Zhang**
EDITOR **Nancy Thistlethwaite**

SHORTCAKE CAKE © 2015 by Suu Morishita
All rights reserved.
First published in Japan in 2015 by SHUEISHA Inc., Tokyo.
English translation rights arranged by SHUEISHA Inc.

The stories, characters and incidents mentioned
in this publication are entirely fictional.

Printed in the U.S.A.

Published by VIZ Media, LLC
P.O. Box 77010
San Francisco, CA 94107

10 9 8 7 6 5 4 3 2 1
First printing, February 2021

PARENTAL ADVISORY
SHORTCAKE CAKE is rated T for Teen
and is recommended for ages 13 and up.

viz.com

shojobeat.com

Shojo Beat Romances by IO SAKISAKA

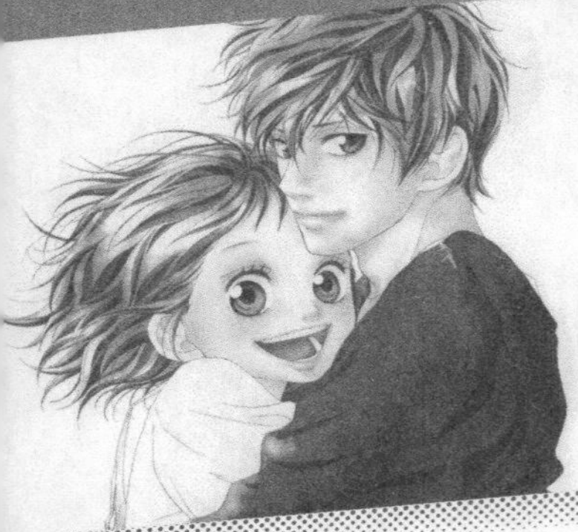

STROBE EDGE

When Ninako meets Ren, the handsome, enigmatic guy that all the girls worship, her life takes an unexpected turn. With just a few words and a smile, he changes her world...

Ao Haru Ride

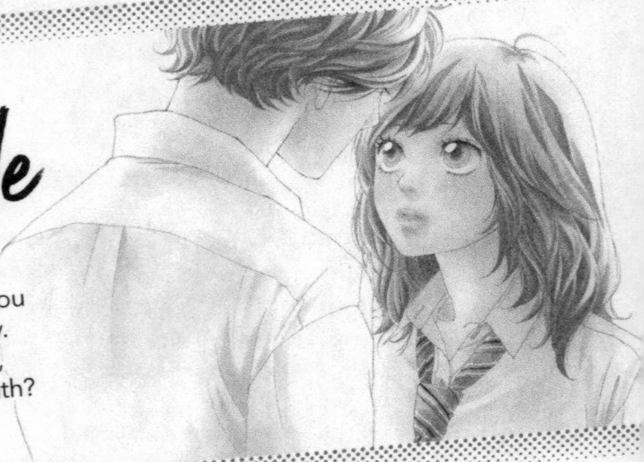

As soon as Futaba realized she really liked Kou in junior high, he had already moved away. Now, in high school, Kou has reappeared, but is he still the same boy she fell in love with?

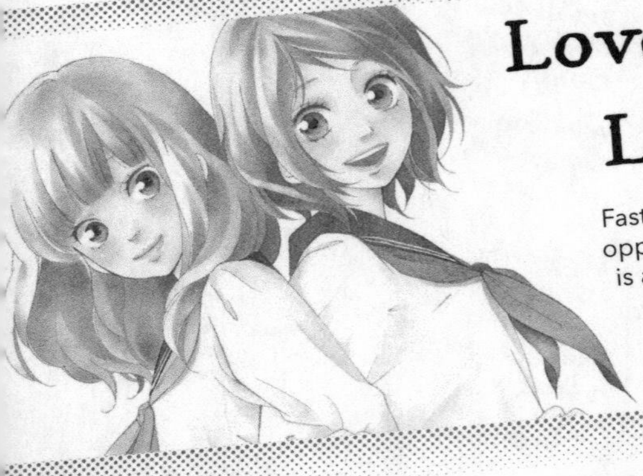

Love Me, Love Me Not

Fast friends Yuna and Akari are complete opposites—Yuna is an idealist, while Akari is a realist. When lady-killer Rio and the oblivious Kazuomi join their ranks, love and friendship become quite complicated!

RATED T TEEN

VIZ

DAYTIME SHOOTING STAR

Story & Art by
Mika Yamamori

Small town girl Suzume moves to Tokyo and finds her heart caught between two men!

After arriving in Tokyo to live with her uncle, Suzume collapses in a nearby park when she remembers once seeing a shooting star during the day. A handsome stranger brings her to her new home and tells her they'll meet again. Suzume starts her first day at her new high school sitting next to a boy who blushes furiously at her touch. And her homeroom teacher is none other than the handsome stranger!

 VIZ

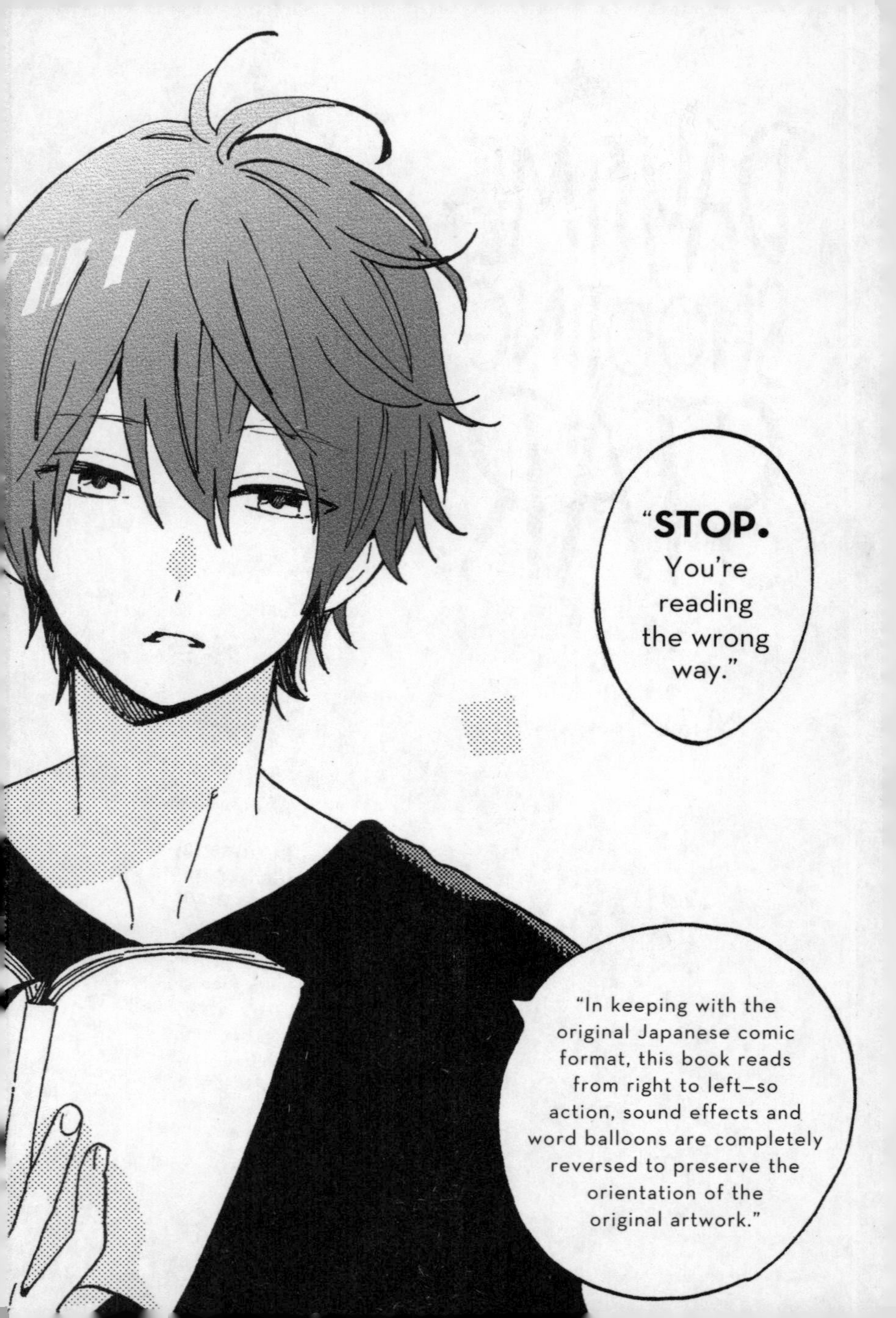
"STOP. You're reading the wrong way."
"In keeping with the original Japanese comic format, this book reads from right to left—so action, sound effects and word balloons are completely reversed to preserve the orientation of the original artwork."